# Legisprudence Library

Studies on the Theory and Practice of Legislation

Volume 7

The objective of the *Legisprudence Library* is to publish excellent research on legislation and related areas (such as regulation and policy-making) from the standpoint of legal theory. This series' title points to an emerging, comprehensive conception of lawmaking which focuses on the justification of laws and the overarching principles which should guide legislation and norm-giving altogether, with the rationality, the reasonableness and the quality of legislation being its major concerns. Taking on legal theory as its pivotal perspective, the series attempts to fill a significant gap in the field of legislative studies, where political science and sociological approaches remain dominant through date. Inasmuch as it fosters legal-theoretical research in lawmaking, it also contributes to widen the scope of standard jurisprudence, which has been up to recent times overwhelmingly centred on the judicial application and the interpretation of law, thereby underestimating the central role of lawmakers within the legal system.

Contributions preferably address topics connected to legislation theory, including (but not limited to) legislative rationality, legislative technique, legistics, legislative effectiveness and social compliance of laws, legislative efficiency and lawmaking economics, evaluation, legislative and regulative impact assessment, regulation management, legislative implementation, public access to legislation, democratic legitimacy of legislation, codification, legislative reasoning and argumentation, science and expertise within lawmaking, legislative language, symbolic legislation, legal policy analysis, lawmaking and adjudication, or judicial review of legislation and legislative process. Comparative and system transcending approaches are encouraged. Purely dogmatic descriptions of positive law or legislative proceedings are not taken into consideration though connections with legislative and legal practice are welcomed. The series welcomes monographs and edited volumes.

More information about this series at http://www.springer.com/series/11058

José Becerra
Editor

# Criminal Law-Making

## Theory and Practice

Springer

*Editor*
José Becerra
Criminal Law Department and Institute of
Criminology
University of Malaga
Malaga, Spain

ISSN 2213-2813 ISSN 2213-2856 (electronic)
Legisprudence Library
ISBN 978-3-030-71347-8 ISBN 978-3-030-71348-5 (eBook)
https://doi.org/10.1007/978-3-030-71348-5



This Springer imprint is published by the registered company Springer Nature Switzerland AG.
The registered company address is: Gewerbestrasse 11, 6330 Cham, Switzerland

# Foreword

The need to argue legal decisions barely needs any argument. The law, together with economy and culture, constitutes the backbone of every organized society. The difference between the law and the other two components lies in its larger scope for action, in the larger number of alternatives that it offers. While the structure of the economy and culture is highly conditioned by ever-scarce resources or previous collective experiences, respectively, the law has greater room for manoeuvre as far as its configuration goes. The construction of a social order that, within the framework of a pacific coexistence and social interaction, allows for the planning and development of individual and collective life projects under equal conditions very often forces legal decisions with major social impact and which are far from being apparent.

However, nowadays, when we discuss legal argumentation, the first thing that comes to mind is not the collective decision-making process that concludes in the passing of legal norms for a specific social activity, but rather the decision-making process carried out by individuals or small groups exercising jurisdictional activity. In other words, legal argumentation is usually linked to the exposition and review of the reasons argued by judges and by those who precede them in the line of reasoning, so they are related to specific cases and necessarily adjusted to the legal norms that they apply. Thus, the decision-making process carried out by the bodies in charge of legislative activity, and whose results will decisively organize social interactions and therefore determine the scope in which judicial argumentation may take place, is disregarded. It is thereby understood that this is a social activity immune to argumentative criteria or, at best, to a discursive process based on the review of the arguments put forward.

Still, claims for a good theory and practice of legislative argumentation have an immense significance. The objective is not only to demand collective decisions that have a considerable impact on society as a whole to be well-founded, but rather to take a closer look at the democratic nature of our societies. Moreover, to justify the relevance that collective deliberation and social majorities should have when it comes to making decisions about social transformation or stabilization through such a powerful tool as the law. Ultimately, this is a battle against citizen alienation resulting from the arrogant stance adopted by expert bodies, among them those of legislative or judicial nature.

This big democratic endeavour entails two considerable risks: On the one hand, populist democracy, which intends to put an end to careful social deliberation or, at least, distorts it in such a way that collective decisions are no more than a reflection of prejudice, commonplace, discredit, and preconceived attitudes on the part of those who should be safeguarding public debate. On the other hand, technocratic democracy, embodied by certain elites whose origin depends on the issue discussed, and who claim to have all the knowledge on the matter being collectively deliberated or, even worse, the exclusive power to make a decision about it. It is not hard to identify the strong presence of such trends in contemporary penal policy and, more precisely, in current legislative penal policy.

In order to get rid of both risks, there is no other option but to delve into two lines of thought which are actually interconnected. First, we must be able to reach an agreement on which should be the normative criteria that allow us to describe a law-making decision as rationale or well-founded. Second, we must work hard so that the social and legal process which leads to the adoption of those legislative decisions can be transformed in such a way that it can meet those normative requirements.

As far as the first of these resolutions is concerned, the convergence of existing theoretical constructs towards normative models that are comparable, or even unified, must be encouraged. This endeavour requires us to bring together proposals coming from different fields, from legal philosophy and political science to specific legal branches such as singularly, constitutional law, criminal law, or administrative law, among others. This aim is actually within reach if two things are taken into account. On the one hand, normative models do not need to focus on judging the legislative product, meaning the law, being said task as fruitful as it may. Rather, the idea is to create a normative tool that guides and assesses the development of the legislative argumentative process from beginning to end. On the other hand, simple and clear normative models need to be made so that they can be handled easily by the main agents involved in the different phases and stages of the social and legal process of law-making.

As for the second resolution, in order to change the socio-legal process through which legislative decisions are made so that it complies with normative requirements for argumentation, we first need to be familiar with its current features. Only when we are familiar with its restrictions, limitations, and scope for improvement, we will be able to propose improvements in a reliable way. The relevance and difficulty of this task should not be underestimated, as it entails remarkable changes in our political practices.

Among other things, we need to make it easier for driving forces and decision-makers to access the reality of the social phenomena that the legislative decision in question intends to impact. Additionally, we need to facilitate the free interaction and flow of social opinions based on this empirical and informed substratum. Public debate should also be encouraged to take place without serious miscommunication resulting from pressure by powerful groups or from ideological short-circuits that prevent the transmission of sound arguments. Besides, there should be a guarantee that all institutions involved restrict their contributions to their responsibilities and act both protective of their fields of action and cautious not to intervene in others. It is common knowledge that one of the most serious institutional problems related to legislative production is the blurring of the separation of powers, which results in the legislative bodies being progressively pushed aside in favour of the executive bodies. This serves as a yet another example of the precarious situation of legislative argumentation, besieged by the unfounded decisions made by the executive and the strong set of arguments of the jurisdiction. It goes without saying that accountability should be a part of the process, and therefore all agents involved in the legislative decision would be held accountable.

In order to keep pace with this second resolution, approaches from very diverse fields should be included, too. Sociology, political science and administration sciences, managerialism and organization management, as well as the set of political and empirical knowledge that base or illustrate law branches, such as criminal policy and criminology for criminal law, should get to work.

This is a considerable challenge. We need to work hard on building social majorities that are able to make collective decisions which are, in this case, legislative, founded, and rationale. The idea is not to flee from those social majorities, as overbearing experts often claim. Neither is it to manipulate them, as populisms intend, but to put them face to face with their own inconsistency.

This book deals with many of these issues reliably and through an excellent selection. It focuses to a large extent on the problem of legislative criminal decisions, which should not come as a surprise: because of different circumstances that we are not going to discuss here, legislative criminal policy has been and is especially subject to the tensions between elitism and populism that we mentioned earlier and that have led it to a particularly worrying degradation. This volume constitutes yet another step towards the rise of legisprudence to its rightful place. It does so as part of a collection, the Legisprudence Library, by Springer Publishing, which deserves the highest recognition for the contribution that it is making to disseminating this type of research.

Facultad de Derecho
Universidad de Málaga
Málaga, Spain
15 June 2020

José Luis Díez-Ripollés

# Contents

**Criminal Lawmaking Policy as a Field of Knowledge in Criminal Studies** . . . . . 1
José Becerra

**Part I Lawmaking Principles and International Lawmaking Policy**

**Legislative Policy in Spain. Analysis of the Current Situation and the Challenges for a Quality Legislative Technique** . . . . . 11
Elsa Marina Álvarez González

**Sword or Shield? The Influence of International Organisations in Counterterrorism Law and Policy Making** . . . . . 47
Claire Hamilton

**EU Law-Making Process in Criminal Matters After Lisbon. In Search of a *Better* EU Criminal Policy** . . . . . 63
Noelia Corral-Maraver

**From Lobbying to Corruption: The Strategies of Interest Groups to Influence the Law-Making Process** . . . . . 85
Patrícia Carraro Rossetto

**Part II Rationality Standards and the Legislative Phase**

**Does Public Opinion Matter for Criminal Law? Revisable Life Imprisonment in Spain and Its Relationship with Social Demands** . . . . . 109
Fernando Miró-Llinares and Ana B. Gómez-Bellvís

**The Influence of the Law-and-Order Model in the Spanish Juvenile Criminal Law-Making Policy** . . . . . 127
Deborah García-Magna

**Instrumental Rationality of the Legislator and Social Stereotypes About Crime: Models of Punitive Argumentation** . . . . . . . . . . . . . . . . . . 147
José Manuel Paredes

**Part III The Post-Legislative Stage: Implementation and Result Analysis**

**The Victim As a Client of the Penal System** . . . . . . . . . . . . . . . . . . . . . . 171
Claudio González

**Punitiveness and Criminal Law-Making Policy. Four Homogeneous Legislative Terms (1996–2011)** . . . . . . . . . . . . . . . . . . . . . . . . . . . . . . 189
José Luis Díez-Ripollés

**Brazilian Post-1988 Constitution Criminal Policies: Comparing Law-Making with Impacts on Incarceration** . . . . . . . . . . . . . . . . . . . . . . 203
Carolina Costa Ferreira, Clara Moura Masiero, and Érica Babini Lapa do Amaral Machado

# Criminal Lawmaking Policy as a Field of Knowledge in Criminal Studies

**José Becerra**

The study of the conditions under which legislation is made does not have a solid tradition in Civil Law or Continental Europe systems. Legal scholars have traditionally preferred to focus their attention on the interpretation of the law as an artefact created by a supposed rational actor: the legislator.[1] Therefore, attention to lawmaking in recent History has been, at most, deeply uneven.[2]

At the end of the twentieth Century, however, some efforts started to take shape in Legal Philosophy environments,[3] but it wasn't until 2003 that the first work addressed the topic from a Criminal Law perspective.[4]

Ever since then, this discipline has been growing in the number of researchers involved and topics studied. A poof of which is the emergence of two parallel working groups on the matter at national as well as international level: the Spanish Group on Criminal Lawmaking Policy and the European version built into the Working Groups section of the European Society of Criminology (ESC). From their formal foundation in 2013 both Groups have organized meetings and seminars, participated in several conferences and, of course, promoted research and publications.[5]

[1]Wintgens (2007), p. 3.

[2]For a brief but thorough review on Western legal scholar's concern about lawmaking from the eighteenth to twenty-first Century see Pineda Garfias (2009), pp. 137–156.

[3]Atienza Rodriguez (1984), p. 33.

[4]Diéz Ripollés (2013).

[5]See https://www.uma.es/grupo-espanol-politica-legislativa-penal/ and https://esc-eurocrim.org/index.php/activities/working-groups/54-criminal-lawmaking-policy, respectively for more information. I've been lucky enough to co-found and coordinate both groups together with their main impeller, professor José Luis Díez-Ripollés.

J. Becerra (✉)
Criminal Law Department and Institute of Criminology, University of Malaga, Malaga, Spain
e-mail: josebecerra@uma.es

 
J. Becerra (ed.), *Criminal Law-Making*, Legisprudence Library 7,
https://doi.org/10.1007/978-3-030-71348-5_1

But, what are Criminal Lawmaking Policy studies? This is indeed a fair question since the contents of this field of knowledge have not, I believe, been clearly defined yet. There are some constraints in the expression itself:

First, we must leave out of the field non-legal instruments at public administration disposal. Therefore, we will not deal with other instruments or public artifacts apart from Law in a narrow sense (which can be only made by the Legislative Power) such as Executive Power normative instruments or not normative possibilities like communication campaigns, for instance. These are very important tools of public policies but will only be of interest to Criminal Lawmaking Policy studies whenever they are able to touch criminal legislation somehow.

A second constraint comes from the word "criminal", which refers to a material definition of the problems that will be studied. These will be, however, flexible limits since the notion of criminal problems are themselves in constant evolution, most of the times expanding its frontiers to areas traditionally regulated by Administrative or Civil Law (road traffic, digital communication, etc.).

Despite such efforts in setting limits, I wouldn't argue that there is a clear notion of what Criminal Lawmaking Policy studies are. The field's lack of tradition and stability comes with a blurred image of it, with which we probably have to make ourselves comfortable for some time.

In recent times there have been different attempts to model the field around a specific concept or concepts: levels of rationality; legislation science vs. legislation technique; the legislative process stages (pre-legislative, legislative, post-legislative), the evaluation process (ex-ante, ex-post), but they just represent scientific approaches and none of them perform clearly better than the rest. My attempt to combine them into one holistic model has not been successful, probably because it requires the knowledge of all of them and it is not clear it comes with any advantage to those who should push for such a new view.[6]

None of such models have been able to impose over the rest and none of them have successfully been used in applied environments such as the technical services of the Parliament, for instance. This doesn't mean, however, that they have not been used by scholars or that they are not useful to enrich theoretical debate, it might be just a matter of youth of the discipline, but it is my believe that we are in the need of a common language which we still lack.

A sort of muddling-through decision took place in this regard when the Criminal Lawmaking Policy ESC Working Group was formed and the need to list our interests and aims was essential in order to be correctly identified and distinguished from other initiatives inside the Society. To assembly scholars from different disciplines around this issue, we needed to explain our matters of interest in a way that could be clearly understood by all of them, mainly social scientists and law

[6]See Chapter IV in Becerra Muñoz (2013).

experts. We probably didn't entirely succeed in our task but, nevertheless, the tentative list of topics to be addressed by the field at hand was the following:[7]

1. Transverse matters:
   a. The discussion on the concept of legislative rationality and its description in Criminal Law.
   b. The content of the principles that lead to and set limits to Criminal Law and Criminal Policy.
2. International lawmaking policy:
   a. Compared analysis of political and legal systems of lawmaking.
   b. Criminal lawmaking in international organizations.
   c. Role or influence of international organizations in national criminal reforms.
3. Pre-legislative, pre-parliamentary or governmental stage:
   a. Regulatory analysis (applicable rules, protocols or proceedings).
   b. Actors analysis:
      i. Government.
      ii. Political parties.
      iii. Lobbies.
      iv. Media.
      v. Public opinion.
      vi. Experts.
      vii. Other formal or informal actors that participate in the stage.
4. Legislative or parliamentary phase:
   a. Regulatory analysis (applicable rules, protocols or proceedings).
   b. Actors analysis
      i. Legislative chambers and their bodies.
      ii. Government.
      iii. Political parties.
      iv. Lobbies.
      v. Media.
      vi. Public opinion.
      vii. Experts.
      viii. Other formal or informal actors that participate in the stage.
5. Implementation stage:
   a. Resources issues (material or personal).
   b. Internal communication systems between actors.

---

[7]This is an updated version of the list published in Díez-Ripollés and Becerra Muñoz (2018). Such list of topis originally comes from my discussions with professor Díez-Ripollés on the matter.

c. Implementation control tools.
d. Partial, temporary or pilot implementation cases.

6. Evaluation stages:

a. Evaluation of design.
b. Implementation evaluation.
c. Results evaluation.
d. Impact evaluation.
e. Different perspectives in evaluation: economic, social, legal evaluation (or other).

As it can be seen in the latter list of issues, Criminal Lawmaking Studies interests go far beyond the Law itself. It is mandatory to take into account that a great amount of clues to understand Criminal Policy hide behind the complexity of political decision making in contemporary societies and it is precisely that which makes this field of knowledge socially useful and scientifically attractive.

We are dealing with an arena in which political, institutional, mass media and social debates are brought together around a decision to make. This forces every actor to negotiate and take positions. As in poker, the lawmaking process is the showdown, that is, the moment in which all players show and compare their cards to determine who wins the pot.

In such an environment, criminal matters have in the last decades become one of the big legislative trophies available during the four-years-term. Probably together with Education and Budget bills, Criminal Law reforms attract headlines, messages and minutes like no other field of political attention. Consequently, the pressure is high on all actors to show their power and benefit from the votes that come along with new measures that are allegedly able to face a social unrest and, of course, with which no one has dealt with properly before.

All controversies and debates that take place in newspapers, radio and tv shows as well as in Twitter or Facebook converge through lawmaking in Parliament. It is the step right before actual social change and everyone wants a piece of that cake. Ministers looking for their moment of glory; majority groups in the chambers wanting to show their power by imposing their view on the issue; minority leaders revealing a poor policy design and announcing the inability of the proposed legislation to solve real problems; lobbies seeking the opportunity to reform the law in their interest and media being able to focus viewers and readers on theatrical interventions full of dramatic overacting.

It is a multi-ring circus in which the centre is probably not expertise or knowledge on the material aspects of the issues at hand, but communication strategies and information management in its many forms. Science and technical expertise are secondary and most of the time found to be exasperating by the public because of the language used by experts, their inability to build simple messages and their internal disagreements in many fronts, just to give a few of the many reasons. Little wonder it has become a commonplace among Criminal Law experts to complain about the usual disregard of expert's knowledge in almost every phase of the lawmaking process.[8]

Thanks to recent Criminal Lawmaking Studies on topics that gather around a great deal of public attention, we have been able to describe how the political process is independent from scientific knowledge and how public debate usually lacks key information and focuses on only some parts of hot issues.[9] Together with that, a deficit in many countries on public policy evaluation makes it impossible to learn from previous mistakes.

Still, we are probably just scratching the surface of all there is to know about Criminal Lawmaking, which is why contributions like the ones presented in this book are essential to continue our knowledge gathering. Only by doing so we will be able to set the appropriate strategies to strengthen the process and its problem-solving capacities.

This is a book about Criminal Lawmaking, not about Criminal Law itself. Many of the themes dealt with in its pages can also be applied to other fields of Law, also to other topics outside the legal sphere. Our focus, therefore, is expandable to a broader audience.

The approach is, we could say, reversible, since we can also see it the other way around: Criminal Lawmaking studies in general, and this book in particular, welcomes approaches, frameworks, findings and tools coming from different fields of knowledge to help in developing a solid discipline. According to such view, the reader will find discussions from Administrative Law, Political Science, Management Sciences or Criminology perspectives.

First things first, the book is organized in three parts, in connection with the aforementioned distribution of themes, and starts with a **foreword by José Luis Díez-Ripollés**. He is the key reference in Spanish academic literature in Criminal Lawmaking Studies since his 2003 book on "The Rationality of Criminal Laws".[10] His research from that point on has brought to the first line the topic, bringing together a new field of knowledge concerned with themes and actors long forgotten since the Nineteenth Century.

**Part I** deals both with lawmaking principles as well as with international lawmaking policy. It starts with **Alvarez-González**'s contribution, which offers a general overview of the problems that legal production is facing in the last decades. The author states that the massive production of legislation takes place in an unclear scenario where the Rule of Law as well as the hierarchy principle are in permanent crisis. The author calls for a more developed theory of legislation that establishes minimum standards of quality and rationality that guarantee the effectiveness of the norms.

---

[8]See Becerra Muñoz for an analysis on Government and Parliament's role in several countries (2013, pp. 355 and 447, respectively); García Magna (2018), p. 119; Becerra Muñoz (2020, in press).

[9]Paredes Castañón (2018), pp. 92–115.

[10]Currently on a 2nd. Edition from 2013.

To shed some light on it she analyses the current situation in Spain, where recent law reforms have introduced some principles and criteria for good legislation. Nevertheless, according to the author, the description of principles (necessity, effectiveness, proportionality, legal certainty, transparency and efficiency) as well as the instructions to check whether the cost and burdens of a piece of legislation were justified and correctly quantified, are far away from actually building a viable model to improve lawmaking.

With a case-scenario methodology, **Hamilton** studies how human rights protection and punitivism are confronted as competing paradigms for lawmaking in international organizations. Counterterrorism measures are analyzed through the role of two crucial policy actors: the United Nations and the European Union. Both of them are depicted as complex organizations in which both perspectives are simultaneously promoted but also in which specific narratives dominate over others.

The author describes how both organizations use their power and rather unique organizational structure to pass new legislation in contradiction to their own provisions.

Continuing with the analysis of crucial and international policy making actors, **Corral-Maraver** unravels the details of the European Union lawmaking process in all its stages. With a specific focus on criminal matters, the author describes the EU as a more rational actor when compared to national legislators and points out its virtues to defend itself from populist policies due to its technocratization.

There are, despite such statement, several shortcomings through which such alleged rationality could be objected, which are of crucial importance in a lawmaking actor with key duties connected to Criminal Policy.

As some kind of conceptual bridge between the international world and national realities, **Carraro Rossetto** analyses one of the key actors in political processes in modern democracies: lobbies, and she does it by revealing how international organization's decisions in regulating lobbies' activities influence national lawmaking processes.

She discussed the regulation of such activities and the principles of good governance through which lobbying should be monitored as developed by the Organisation for Economic Co-operation and Development (OECD). She pays also attention to the threat to the legislative branch that comes from a grand corruption (known as "State capture") that takes place when political elites and interests groups manipulate democratic decision making in their favour. Control and regulation, therefore, to confront the two faces of lobbying: participation and reinforcement of political legitimacy in making policy decisions or abuse of power when private interests gain privileged access to the process.

In **Part II**, changing the focus to national perspectives, more specifically to the legislative phases of lawmaking, that is, the work done in Parliament, **Miró-Llinares and Gómez-Bellvís** focus on public opinion's impact in the recent incorporation of life imprisonment to the list of penalties available in the Spanish Criminal Code. The authors discuss the scientific value of legislator's data on public support to such penalty in the light of some criminological experiments conducted on the matter. They also reveal numerous undemonstrated assumptions defended by legislators when they attach such new legislation to a greater legitimacy allegedly perceived by the public as well as to a more effective crime prevention strategy.

Still in the legislative phase (though looking also at some pre-legislative materials), **García Magna** studies a set of consecutive legislation reforms related to juvenile justice to understand whether their rationality is driven or not by the need to respond to alleged social claims for harsher responses in this area.

Placing her analysis in the ethical and teleological rationality arena, she scrutinizes legislator's discourse and decisions by studying the pieces of legislation passed as well as their corresponding projects, reports, special committee opinions and session's records from the lawmaking process.

Also in connection with rationality standards and its potential as a theoretical model for lawmaking, the work of **Paredes** is intended to deeply scrutinize the instrumental rationality put into practice by the criminal legislator. In order to try this analytic framework in real lawmaking scenarios, he studies how instrumental rationality is revealed in a set Criminal Law reforms carried out in the early 2000s by the Spanish legislator regarding four topics: terrorism, road safety, gender violence and theft.

Once again in this set of contributions that analyse the legislative phase, this empirical approach allows the author to underline the biases and prejudices in which the law-maker arguments rest. Due to such results the author emphasises the need of empirical analyses of, among other, the preventive capabilities of criminal legislation as well as the effects of penalties.

In **Part III** and moving on to the next phases in the lawmaking cycle: implementation and results analysis, **González**'s work uses a public administration theoretical framework, more specifically the client-user paradigm, to analyse the implementation of criminal legislation. His work is an interesting example of how institutional environments have the capacity to interfere the law implementation process by creating their own policies.

His case-study focuses on the Chilean public prosecution experience with ambivalent results. According to the author's view, this new approach to users of the criminal justice system offers true improvements in justice services but also hides more controvertible effects of „user satisfaction" managing models, dangerously connected to marketing techniques and far from core values of the system.

Concentrating on results evaluation, **Díez-Ripollés**' work offers an empirical analysis of criminal lawmaking decisions during a period of 16 years. This study participates from an evidence-based perspective in the discussion about whether or not the punitive turn described in other European countries constitutes a plausible explanation to the Spanish recent legislative history. It also discusses the differences in the consecutive periods in connection to the political party responsible for every criminal reform.

The period analysed constitutes the four last stable legislatures in which the two main political parties in Spain have been able to develop their Criminal Policy program through two consecutive terms each (in both cases with one absolute majority term). That same period also covers the implementation years of the so called "Criminal Code of Democracy", passed in 1995, which has been, as claimed by the author, frenetically changed through that period.

Lastly, with a similar longitudinal approach, **Costa Ferreira, Moura Masiero and Lapa do Amaral Machado** study Brazilian criminal legislation's evolution since the Constitution of 1988 came into force.

Authors specifically focus on criminal legislation intended to tackle race and gender motivated crimes to find a very interesting effect on incarceration that questions the most extended argument that causally connects the rise of both phenomena. Opposed to such idea, they defend the ambiguity of Brazilian criminal legislation, which combines penal populism and left realism responses to such issues.

The book offers, therefore, a very complete image of the perspectives, methodologies, interests and international connections of Criminal Lawmaking Studies. It shows the field's ability to tackle very complex issues thanks to its wide set of technical tools and resources as well as how the uncertainty provided by unclear discipline boundaries are necessary to develop a relevant scientific approach.

## References

Atienza Rodriguez M (1984) Problemas abiertos en la Filosofia del Derecho. Doxa. Cuadernos de Filosofía del Derecho 1

Becerra Muñoz J (2013) La toma de decisiones en política criminal. Bases para un análisis multidisciplinar. Tirant lo Blanch

Becerra Muñoz J (2020) Una nueva estrategia de comunicación para una nueva política criminal basada en información relevante. Política criminal basada en datos: de la utopía a la realidad. Tirant lo Blanch. In press

Diéz Ripollés J (2013) La racionalidad de las leyes penales: práctica y teoriá (2a ed. amp.). Trotta

Díez-Ripollés JL, Becerra Muñoz J (2018) La política legislativa penal como campo de estudio: algunas ideas para seguir avanzando. Revista Brasileira de Ciencias Criminais (147) Sep. Thomson Reuters-Revista dos Tribunais, Brasil

García Magna D (2018) La lógica de la seguridad en la gestión de la delincuencia. Marcial Pons

Paredes Castañón JM (2018) La interacción entre los medios de comunicación social y la política criminal en las democracias de masas. Teoría y derecho: revista de pensamiento jurídico (Ejemplar dedicado a: Garantías constitucionales, prensa y Derecho penal) 24:92–115

Pineda Garfias R (2009) Teoría de la Legislación. Algunos planteamientos generales. Revista Nomos 3:137–156. Universidad de Viña del Mar, Chile

Wintgens LJ (2007) Legitimacy and Legislation from the Legisprudential Perspective. In: Wintgens LJ, Thion P (eds) Legislation in context: essays in legisprudence. Aldershot, England, pp 4–42

# Part I
# Lawmaking Principles and International Lawmaking Policy

# Legislative Policy in Spain. Analysis of the Current Situation and the Challenges for a Quality Legislative Technique

**Elsa Marina Álvarez González**

**Abstract** This paper addresses the current problems of the Spanish regulatory system, which have arisen as a consequence of the crisis of the principle of legality and the alteration of the hierarchy of norms principle. This highlights some important distortions both in legislative and regulatory powers, which ultimately translate into a reduction in the minimum guarantees that citizens must have in the face of legislative activity and administrative action. Moreover, this is closely linked to a broader issue: the proliferation of regulations and the lack of quality and rationality that prevails in our norms. We believe this is due to the absence of a "legislative theory" that establishes the guidelines for an effective and efficient legislative technique. It is necessary to reflect carefully on what legislative policy is needed, as only then can we provide some clarity to the current confusing regulatory system and guarantee citizens the legal certainty they need. We aim to analyse these issues and propose several initiatives to improve the quality and rationality of our legislative technique.

**Keywords** Legislative policy · Legislative technique · Theory of legislation · Normative rationality

E. M. Álvarez González (✉)
Faculty of Law, Department of Public Law, Universidad de Málaga, Malaga, Spain
e-mail: emalvarez@uma.es

 
J. Becerra (ed.), *Criminal Law-Making*, Legisprudence Library 7,
https://doi.org/10.1007/978-3-030-71348-5_2

# 1 Introduction

If we stop and look around, the upheavals going on in all areas, whether social, political or economic, are patently apparent. It is also felt also in the field of law, which is evolving extremely rapidly. One thing which characterises the law field at present is, without doubt, its radical evolution and transformation.[1]

As is to be expected, this frenetic pace of change in the rule of Law is directly affecting legislative policy. This has led to the serious problem of having an excess of regulations. Indeed, the proliferation of norms in recent times is one of the main causes behind the decline of the legal resources system. In 1932, Carl Schmitt[2] was already speaking of "motorised legislation", which, together with the current design of normative production, the absence of clear instructions regarding the procedures by which new norms are issued or existing ones are modified, etc., is leading us to "legal disorder" as described by Baño León.[3] This is the opposite of "legal order", as coined by Santi Romano, to evoke the idea of a systematic or rational order regarding norms.[4]

There are different reasons for this problem, but the most serious, in our opinion, is the crisis of the rule of law, and the breaking of a hierarchy of norms principle. This has torn apart the Spanish regulatory system.

Moreover, with regards to legal and regulatory norms, we believe that the lack of quality and rationality that prevails in our legislative technique and which creates a violation of the principle of legal certainty justifies citizens' current distrust of the policies of the legislative system.

The increasing use being made of decree law as the common mechanism with which to legislate is symbolic of distortion in legislative policy. Thus, a normative instrument with force of law reserved for extraordinary situations and moments of urgency is now used as a common technique in order to circumvent parliamentary law-making. Another very striking example is the regulation and organisation of specific situations through unique laws, thus losing their general and abstract nature which characterises the rule of law. Worse still, this incurs the violation of the right to effective judicial protection of the individuals who have been affected by a particular norm.

It is true that with the implementation of Law 39/2015, of 1st October, of the Common Administrative Procedure of Public Administrations (hereinafter LPAC), some measures have been taken to improve the quality of our norms. However, we must go further. The main problem is the absence of a legislative theory that establishes minimum standards of quality and rationality that guarantee the

---

[1]Gamero Casado (2015, p. 2) uses the word 'disruption' to define these abrupt changes in administrative law, thus justifying the title of his work *Desafíos del Derecho Administrativo ante un mundo en disrupción*.

[2]Schmitt (1998).

[3]See Baño León (2006, p. 20).

[4]Romano (1918).

effectiveness of the norms. We need a legislative theory which has been clearly and systematically established, based on the principle of legal certainty and legitimate expectations. It is impossible not to reflect on how legislation has affected legislative conditions and the quality and actual effectiveness of laws, something that has not been done in the field of legal theory with the depth and systematisation required.[5]

Not only should we consider what legislative policy we want, but also collect postulates in a legal norm that establish obligations and legal consequences for parliaments and public administrations when they exercise their legislative and regulatory powers. Without a regulation which designs the theoretical and practical framework of the legislative theory, it is not possible to solve the problems we have identified.

It is clear that the isolated, partial and unsystematic nature of the regulation of some aspects of legislative technique carried out to date is insufficient to improve the quality of our norms. Only quality norms can guarantee the freedom and security of citizens.

We will concentrate on the analysis of these questions and the creation of some *de lege ferenda* proposals, working towards the development of a legislative theory in Spain in order to improve the quality and rationality of our legislative technique.

# 2 The Causes of the Fragility of the Spanish Regulatory System

## *2.1 The Crisis of the Principle of Legality*

It is well known that the legal resource system is embedded in legal positivism, a philosophy of law that studies positive law and the general theory of law.[6] As GARCIA DE ENTERRÍA states, the establishment of the State legislator, created by the French Revolution, aimed to reduce the right to a systematic and closed set of positive norms and the exclusion of any reference to the material value of justice, which only the legislator, not the applicator of the law, were entitled to address.[7] Therefore, the legal resources theory includes the State law, that is, the set of valid legal norms of the State, namely the Constitution and the laws.

However, it must be highlighted that during the first beginnings of legal positivism, which also saw the beginnings of modern States, the main source of State justice was the law and not the Constitution, which does not appear until the twentieth century. Therefore, there is talk of a new judicial culture born after the Second World War, based on the understanding of constitutionalism as a legal theory.[8] Indeed, state

[5]On a similar line, see Pineda Garfias (2009), p. 138.

[6]Bobbio (1993).

[7]García De Enterría (1963), p. 191.

[8]Prieto Sanchís (2001), pp. 201–228.

constitutional justice seems to demand a new theory of justice, a new explanation that largely deviates from the schemes of so-called theoretical positivism.[9] This is fundamentally due to what we can call the crisis of the law, a crisis that responds not only to the existence of a higher norm, but also to other phenomena more or less connected to constitutionalism, such as the emergence of the State of Autonomous Regions and integration into the European Union.[10] Undoubtedly, these two phenomena were catalysts in the system of legal resources regulated by the Civil Code.

## *2.2 The Breaking of the Hierarchy of Norms Principle After the CE: The State of Autonomies and Integration into the European Union*

With the establishment of the *Constitución Española* (Spanish Constitution), hereinafter CE, in 1978, important innovations were introduced into the system of legal resources. Firstly, the following were enshrined as general principles; the principle of legality, the hierarchy of norms, the publication of norms, the non-retroactivity of the non-favourable or restrictive sanctioning provisions of individual rights, legal certainty and responsibility, and the interdiction of the arbitrariness of public powers. In addition, it regulates different types of laws: organic, ordinary, framework, harmonisation and transfer laws. One whole chapter is dedicated to regulating international treaties and their incorporation into internal organisations. It also establishes several legal reservations: i.e. matters whose regulation must necessarily be made by legal norms.

In short, significant changes were made to the established resource system, since the CE became the resource of the highest laws in the legal system and in some sense the basis of all others.[11] Thus, Art. 9 of the Constitution states that: "*Citizens and public authorities are bound by the Constitution and all other legal provisions*." The Constitution is the primary source of law, due to its superiority and recognition that it regulates laws from law-making bodies. Its principles shape the interpretation of other legal resources, and some of its norms have a direct application in both vertical relationships between citizens and public authorities, and horizontal relationships among citizens.

---

[9]On the same line, Huanca Ayaviri (2016).

[10]As causes for the crisis of the law, Prieto Sanchís (1998), pp. 17 *et seq.*, had already added the revitalisation of the social legal resources and the loss or deterioration of the own conditions of legislative rationality, such as generality and abstraction.

[11]Its nature as supreme law of the judicial order is affirmed in Art. 5 of the Organic Law of the Judiciary, where Section 1 provides: "The Constitution is the supreme norm of the legal system, and links all Judges and Courts, who shall interpret and apply laws and regulations according to the constitutional precepts and principles, in accordance with their interpretation resulting from the decisions handed down by the Constitutional Court in all types of proceedings".

However, the most significant changes introduced in the resource system in the constitutional provisions are those derived from the new territorial organisation of the Spanish State and the integration of Spain into the European Union. In fact, on the one hand, the Spanish State was constituted in autonomous communities with freedom to govern their own interests, the power to dictate legal norms was no longer limited to the State, and autonomies then had equal power through its legislative bodies in matters that fell within its competence and within its respective territory. However, on the other hand, with the entry of Spain into the European Union, we became part of a supranational organisation that has the power to enact legal norms effectively within Spain. This is permitted under Art. 93 CE, which provides for the possibility of vesting powers derived from the Constitution itself into an international organisation or institution. In this regard, the impact of EC law on our resource system is expressed in one basic principle: Community Law takes precedence over internal justice, which is displaced, preventing the adoption of internal norms that conflict with it or which would modify it.

Both the new territorial state organisation and the integration into the European Union had one important consequence in the resource system: the crisis of the hierarchy of norms principle. As is well known, under this principle, legal resources are applied according to precedence.[12] However, the appearance of new types of norms, in some cases a consequence of the new territorial order (basic laws, harmonisation laws, transfer or delegation laws, Autonomy Statutes) or the result of part of the constitutional process (organic law), are elements that have shaken the empire of the hierarchy of norms principle. This, combined with the emergence of the so-called principle of competence-competence to coordinate the system of autonomies, and relationships between Community law and domestic law, marked the end of it.[13]

Undoubtedly, the principle of competence-competence has responded to the plurality and regulatory complexity that arises with the new territorial structure to coordinate the relationship between the various ordinances that have emerged from that territorial structure, such as the constitutional organisation (the CE and the constitutional corpus), and general and regional systems. However, it should also be noted the principle of pre-eminence and complementarity of State law (Art. 149.3 CE) where, in case of conflict, State legislation prevails over that of the Autonomous

[12]This follows from Art. 1 CC, which states that: "*Any provisions which contradict another of a higher ranking are invalid. Custom only applies in the absence of any applicable law*". It is also included in the EC itself which enshrines the principle of normative hierarchy, and where Art. 9.1 states that citizens and public authorities are subject to the EC and the rest of the legal system. Art. 6 LOPJ also orders Judges and Courts not to apply the Regulations or any other provision which is contrary to the EC, law or principle of normative hierarchy.

[13]In this regard, the work by Requena López (2004) is interesting. The author states that "hierarchy is no longer the main mechanism configuring the structure of the legal system" and proposes to revalue the principle of normative hierarchy to place it in its proper place in the resource system. This, moreover, is considering that it is the most important regulatory structural principle, because its violation causes invalidity, so that it is this which confers virtuality to the principle of competition, thus constituting the immediate basis of the latter.

Communities and the supplementary application of State law in the absence of autonomous legislation.

With regards to Community law, the principles of primacy and competence must also be highlighted, which together address the integration of Community law into domestic law. Effectively, the principle of primacy explains the relationship between the two systems, and with due regard to the fact that within Community law there is a clear hierarchy of norms between Community treaties and secondary legislation. Thus, the principle of competence-competence serves to provide coherence between the CE and its legal system and international treaties, excluding primacy relations.

However, the CE has expressly provided for its relations with international treaties, but does not rule on the position of the law produced or derived from treaties signed under Art. 93 CE, or on relations between said secondary legislation and internal law. Therefore, there are no clear norms which define the position of secondary legislation from the European Union in the Spanish legal system. This explains the position of the Constitutional Court to reject a constitutional conflict when confrontation occurs between internal justice and secondary legislation, framing it as an infra-constitutional conflict,[14] although this conflict should be described as an extra-constitutional conflict, since the CE is not in a position of supremacy with regards to treaties, nor vice versa, so that a conflict between the two legal orders would be extra-constitutional.[15] Thus, the parameter to determine the rule applicable in a controversial case, in case of conflict between the orders, is not provided for by the CE, assuming that the CC's competence would arise. This is because competence to resolve conflicts between Community law and internal law has been transferred to the Court of the European Union as a last resort. Therefore, the resolution of conflicts between CE secondary legislation and treaties and secondary legislation, are made in accordance with the treaties and not with the CE.

## 2.3 *The Normative Hierarchy in Community Law*

While, as we have seen, the autonomous state and integration into the European Union came to alter our legal resource system, the evolution undergone by Community law in recent times has complicated the resource system even more, and, in particular, the hierarchy of norms principle, as we will see.

The Treaty on the Functioning of the Union (hereinafter, TFEU) regulates a series of principles that determine the proper functioning of the European Union (hereinafter EU) and, more specifically, decision-making when competent. Thus, it regulates the principles of conferral, subsidiarity and proportionality (Art. 5). The principle of conferral determines the powers that treaties grant to the EU. The subsidiarity principle, meanwhile, aims to determine the most relevant level of

[14]SSTC 28/1991, 14th February; 58/2004, April 19; 173/2005, June 23.

[15]According to Professor Linde Paniagua (2014), p. 230.

intervention in the areas of shared competences between the EU and EU countries, taking into account that the EU can only intervene when its performance is more effective than that of the EU countries at national or local level. Under the principle of proportionality, the means applied by the EU to achieve the objectives set by the treaties cannot go beyond what is necessary. In this way, the EU can only act in a political sphere if: (a) this action is part of the powers that the treaties have attributed to the EU (principle of conferral); (b) in the framework of the competences shared with the EU countries, the EU scale is the most appropriate to achieve the objectives set by the treaties (principle of subsidiarity); and (c) the content and form of the action does not exceed what is necessary to meet the objectives established by the treaties (principle of proportionality).

In this sense, and the principle of subsidiarity and the principle of proportionality govern the EU's exercise of powers. In areas that are not the exclusive competence of the Union, the principle of subsidiarity seeks to protect the Member States' capacity for decision-making and action, and legitimises the intervention of the Union when '*the objectives of the proposed action cannot be sufficiently achieved by the Member States, either at central level or at regional and local level, but can rather, by reason of the scale or effects of the proposed action, be better achieved at Union level*'

In addition, among the functions national parliaments have in the European Community system, the Treaty of Lisbon has incorporated a set of functions through which national parliaments actively contribute to the proper functioning of the Union. Among these is to ensure respect for subsidiarity "... *the principle of subsidiarity is respected in accordance with the procedures established in the Protocol on the application of the principles of subsidiarity and proportionality*" (Art. 12). Through this control, direct participation of national parliaments in the European Union's legislative procedures has been established. National parliaments electronically receive the legislative proposals drawn up by the European Commission (and eventually by the other institutions if they have been attributed power of initiative), at the same time they are sent to the Community legislator—the European Parliament and Council. They then have eight weeks to exercise control of suitability to the principle of subsidiarity. This principle aims to safeguard state powers against a hypothetical excess in the exercise of the powers attributed to the Union, given the open and flexible nature with which those powers have been conferred. The articulation of the procedure, denominated in community jargon as an 'early warning' mechanism, has created a balance between the wariest of community institutions and those that saw in this mechanism the risk that community action could be blocked.[16]

---

[16]The General Courts have been fully incorporated into this system since the passing of Law 24/2009, an amendment of Law 8/1994, regulator of the Joint Commission for the European Union, and of the Resolution of the Bureau of Congress, of Members of Parliament and the Senate, of 27th May 2010, which produced its regulatory development. In this regulation, power of control is attributed to the Joint Commission of the European Union, providing the possibility of a call-back at a plenary session of both Chambers. In weekly or biweekly meetings, the Bureau and the speakers of the Joint Commission of the European Union carry out a follow-up of all European legislative

The competences conferred on the Union have been more precisely demarcated through the principle of conferral. The competences of the Union are divided in three categories: exclusive competences (Art. 3), shared competences (Art. 4) and supporting competencies (Art. 6), which allow the Union adopt measures to support or supplement the Member States' policies. Art. 288 of the TFEU lists the Union's legal instruments: regulations, directives, decisions, recommendations and opinions. Union institutions can only take such actions if a treaty provision gives them the authority to do so. There is also a whole series of modalities of action, such as recommendations and communications, as well as acts related to the organisation and operation of institutions (including inter-institutional agreements), whose denomination, structure and legal effects derive from different provisions of the treaties or from the norms adopted in their application.

A hierarchy of secondary legislation is established by Articles 289, 290 and 291 TFEU between legislative acts, delegated acts and implementing acts. Legislative acts are legal acts which are adopted through an ordinary or special legislative procedure. Delegated acts, for their part, are non-legislative acts of general application to supplement or amend certain non-essential elements of a legislative act. The power to adopt these acts may be delegated to the Commission by the legislator (Parliament and Council). The objectives, content, scope and duration of the delegation of power are defined in the legislative acts, as are any urgent procedures, where applicable. In addition, the legislator lays down the conditions to which the delegation is subject, which may be the authority to revoke the delegation or the right to express an objection. Implementing acts are generally adopted by the Commission, which is competent to do so in cases in which uniform conditions for implementing legally binding acts are needed. Implementing acts are a matter for the Council only in specific cases which are duly justified and in areas of common foreign and security policy.

It should be remembered that as legislative acts, which legal instruments are, they have different legal effects. Thus, regulations are of general application, binding in their entirety and directly applicable. They must be complied with fully by those to whom they apply (private persons, Member States, Union institutions). Regulations are directly applicable in all Member States as soon as they enter into force (on the date stipulated or, failing this, on the twentieth day following their publication in the Official Journal of the European Union) and do not need to be transposed into national law. They are designed to ensure the uniform application of the Union's law in all Member States. In turn, regulations supersede national laws incompatible with their substantive provisions.

initiatives sent—on the basis of an electronic indicator prepared by the Secretariat of the Joint Commission—and decide which of them will be subject to a report, appointing a rapporteur, requesting an urgent report from the Government and setting a date for the session in which the said report will be discussed. The rapporteur will be handed the reports that Autonomous Parliaments have been able to create, to whom all the initiatives received in the General Courts are automatically sent. The report is subject to debate by the Joint Commission for the European Union, being approved in most cases by unanimity.

Directives are binding as to the result to be achieved, upon any or all of the Member States to whom they are addressed, but leave to the national authorities the choice of form and methods. National legislators must adopt a transposing act or 'national implementing measure' to transpose directives and bring national law into line with their objectives. It is this act of transposition that essentially confers rights and imposes obligations on citizens. Member States are given some discretion in transposing directives to take account of specific national circumstances. Transposition must be carried out within the period set forth in the directive. In transposing directives, Member States guarantee the effectiveness of EU law, in accordance with the principle of sincere cooperation established in Article 4(3) TEU. In principle, directives are not directly applicable. The Court of Justice of the European Union, however, has ruled that certain provisions of a directive may, exceptionally, have direct effects in a Member State even if the latter has not yet adopted a transposing act.[17]

Decisions are binding in their entirety. Where those to whom they are addressed are stipulated (Member States, natural or legal persons), they are binding only on them, and address situations specific to those Member States or persons. An individual may invoke the rights conferred by a decision addressed to a Member State only if that Member State has adopted a transposing act. Decisions may be directly applicable on the same basis as directives. Finally, recommendations and opinions do not confer any rights or obligations on those to whom they are addressed, but may provide guidance as to the interpretation and content of the Union's law.

Therefore, whatever the principles governing and organising these legislative instruments in hierarchical supremacy with regards to delegated and implementing acts making up secondary EU legislation, they help us to understand the resource system not only of Community law, but also the relationship between secondary EU legislation and domestic law itself. However, Art. 296.1 of the TFEU states that

---

[17]For this reason, it is essential that: (a) the directive has not been transposed or transposed incorrectly; (b) the provisions of the directive are unconditional and sufficiently clear and precise; and (c) the provisions of the directive confer rights to individuals. If these conditions are met, an individual can enforce the provisions of the directive before any public authority. Even if the provision does not confer any rights on the individual and, consequently, only the first two conditions are met, the authorities of the Member States have an obligation to take into account the directive which has not been transposed. The jurisprudence in this regard is fundamentally justified in the principles of effectiveness, sanction of conduct contrary to the Treaty and judicial protection. On the other hand, an individual cannot invoke against another directive the direct effect of a directive not directly transposed (the so-called "horizontal effect"; Faccini Dori case, C-91/92, Rec. 1994, p. I-3325, paragraph 25). In this sense, according to the jurisprudence of the Court of Justice of the European Union (Joined Cases C-6/90 and C-9/90 Francovich), a private individual has the right to claim compensation for a damage suffered to a Member State that does not respect the Union's law. In the case of a directive not transposed or poorly transposed, such recourse is possible on the condition that: (a) the directive implies the attribution of rights in favour of individuals; (b) the content of the rights can be determined on the basis of the provisions of the directive; and (c) there is a causal relationship between the breach of the obligation to transpose and the damage suffered by the affected persons. The Member State incurs responsibility without having to prove the existence of a breach attributable to it.

*"institutions shall select it on a case-by-case basis, in compliance with the applicable procedures and with the principle of proportionality."* It must be added that, neither in the aforementioned Art. 288 of the TFEU, nor in Community jurisprudence can we see the hierarchy of norms principle.[18] This implies, therefore, that these legislative acts can be adopted by Community institutions with the same legal effects, so an act adopted by the Commission may have a direct effect and equal primacy as acts adopted by the Council. This interpretation was corroborated by the Court of Justice in the 1980s, when, in the judgment of 6th July 1982, before the challenge of a community directive by France, Italy and the United Kingdom which questioned the legislative competence of the Commission to adopt it, the Community Court rejected the arguments of the United Kingdom, who claimed that by adopting the contested directive, the Commission had violated the principle governing the distribution of powers and responsibilities between the Community institutions. According to the Court, *"It follows that the limits of the powers conferred on the commission by a specific provision of the treaty are to be inferred not from a general principle, but from an interpretation of the particular wording of the provision in question, analysed in the light of its purpose and its place in the scheme of the treaty"*.

However, it is interesting to note that regarding the Supreme Court's judgment 6834/2011, of the 13th October, in an appeal against the judgment of the National High Court against the alleged resolution of the Ministry of Economy applying for state liability regarding pensions, it was argued that the damage caused by, among other reasons, the delay in the transposition of an EU directive, and takes advantage of being in Court to discuss the distinct rank the Community's legal instruments have (Court Consideration 15). Thus, it states that only the regulations *"are of general application, binding in their entirety and directly applicable. They must be complied with fully by those to whom they apply (private persons, Member States, Union institutions"*.[19] The directives, on the other hand, are, in principle, not directly

[18]As Millán Moro (2010), p. 414, points out: *"In Art. 288 TFEU, which defines and enumerates the legal instruments of the community pillar, among which are those considered "legislative acts" (regulations, directives and in some cases, decisions), there is no indication of a principle of separation of powers, where there is a hierarchy among the different acts, making some superior to the others, according to the authority that adopts them"*.

[19]Concerning this, the TS states that: *"As the norm is considered complete, initially, it does not need further regulatory development after its entry into force, from the moment it is published in the Official Journal of the European Union. The foregoing guarantees the uniformity pursued by the aforementioned community instrument and facilitates the work of implementation undertaken by national judges and courts. It prevails in its application against any type of internal regulations, whatever its rank. Moreover, it is not necessary to previously declare national regulations incompatible or repeal those that contradict it. At an earlier stage, it was possible for a regulation to expressly enable the Member States to adopt development measures, also, the Court of Justice has been adopting a restrictive interpretation of the authorization (Lahaille judgment September 30, Case 10-14/75). The reproduction of community regulations has not been specifically prohibited by reiteration in internal regulations. However, the Court understands that "Consequently, all methods of implementation are contrary to the Treaty which would have the result of creating an obstacle to the direct effect of Union Regulations and of jeopardizing their*

applicable, and that: "*Directives are binding, as to the result to be achieved, upon any or all of the Member States to whom they are addressed, but leave to the national authorities the choice of form and methods. National legislators must adopt a transposing act or 'national implementing measure' to transpose directives and bring national law into line with their objectives". The Court of Justice of the European Union, however, has ruled that certain provisions of a directive may, exceptionally, have direct effects in a Member State even if the latter has not yet adopted a transposing act in cases where: (a) the directive has not been transposed into national law or has been transposed incorrectly; (b) the provisions of the directive are imperative and sufficiently clear and precise; and (c) the provisions of the directive confer rights on individuals.*". This is the so-called useful effect that prevents a State from objecting to an individual's breach of obligations a directive entails.[20] Moreover, in a significant development, a citizen's right to claim compensation for damages from the State due to lack of transposition or poor transposition of the directive has been recognised.[21]

It is therefore unquestionable that, according to the Court, in the Community Legal resource system, the content of a Regulation prevails over a Directive, and where States must limit themselves to applying it without proceeding to reproduce it in internal regulations. It seems, therefore, that the Supreme Court does not only apply a precedence principle on the directive, but also a supremacy principle. Indeed, perhaps due to its effects and direct applicability, the fact is that regulation is the preferred instrument for institutions (in quantitative terms).

However, in practice, the reality is very different. Firstly, despite a regulation being directly applicable without a transposition act to internal law and binding in its entirety, it can sometimes allow, and even force, internal developments.[22] The directives, which do require internal developments in establishing obligations of result and are directed, in principle, to Member States, can also establish clear and precise obligations directly invoked by the interested parties, as if it were a regulation.

On the other hand, regulations and directives share supremacy and the vertical direct effect, and only regulations, the horizontal direct effect. However, following

*simultaneous and uniform application in the whole of the Union" (paragraph 17 judgment of 7th February, 1973. Commission v Italy, Case 39/1972). A similar matter is in the Fratelli Variola judgment, 10th October 1973, Case 34/73, paragraph 10".*

[20]On the same line, the Van Duyn judgments, 4th December 1974, Case 41/1974; Ratti, 5th April, 1979, Case 148/1978 and Becker, January 19, 1982, Case 8/1981.

[21]Brasserie du Pêcheur/Factortame, judgement, 5th March 1996, Cases 46/1993 and 48/19 93.

[22]This is stated in the Judgment of 25th October 2012, Case c-592/11, paragraph. 37, on allowing that "*although due to the nature of the Regulations and their role in the system of sources of Union law, their provisions have an immediate effect on national legal systems, some provisions of the Regulations may require, for its implementation, the adoption of implementing measures by the Member States. It is therefore necessary to refer to the specific provisions of each Regulation to verify whether they, interpreted with the objectives thereof, prohibit, require or allow Member States to adopt certain implementing measures and, in particular, in the latter case, if the measure in question is within the margin of discretion acknowledged for all Member States*".

the primacy principle, a national judge must interpret the internal law according to the directive in a lawsuit between two individuals, which is in fact attributing to it effects similar to the horizontal direct effect.

The decision, defined as having limited recipients, may have a general application, and a regulation, which is defined as having a general application, can be addressed to individuals. It also enjoys primacy and direct effectiveness, that is, it can be invoked directly by individuals. Like the directive, it has no horizontal direct effect, but it is a benchmark for interpretation in a dispute between individuals.

One particular case is that of recommendations which are not binding for anyone except a judge (national judges are required to take recommendations into account) whose sentence obliges both administrations and individuals.

There is no doubt, then, that all these issues highlight the absence of an order or hierarchy in the application of the rules of law derived from the Union. This is further aggravated when regulations are used by community institutions to modify, apply and repeal directives and decisions,[23] replacing directives while changing other regulations and directives,[24] or, in the end, to regulate on the same material and on

---

[23]Commission Regulation (EC) No. 1430/2007, 5th December 2007, among others, which amends Annexes II and III of Directive 2005/36/EC of the European Parliament and of the Council on the recognition of professional qualifications, OJ L 320, 6.12.2007, p. 3; Regulation (EC) No 717/2007 of the European Parliament and of the Council, of 27th June 2007 on roaming in public mobile telephone networks in the Community and amending Directive 2002/21 / CE, OJ L 171, 06.29.2007, p. 32; Commission Regulation (EU) No. 371/2010, of 16th April 2010, replacing Annexes V, X, XV and XVI to Directive 2007/46/EC of the European Parliament and of the Council establishing a framework for the approval of motor vehicles and their trailers, and of systems, components and separate technical units intended for such vehicles (Framework Directive), OJ L 110, 05/01/2010, p. 1.

As an example of repeal of Directives, among others, Regulation (EC) No 21 6/2008 of the European Parliament and of the Council, of 20th February 2008, on common rules in the field of civil aviation and establishing a European Aviation Safety Agency, and repealing Council Directive 91/670/EEC, Regulation (EC) No 1592/2002 and Directive 2004/36/EC, OJ L 79, 19.03.2008, p. 1. Additionally, as an example of the repeal of Decisions, Commission Regulation (EC) No 657/2006, of 10th April 2006, amending Regulation (EC) No 999/2001 of the European Parliament and of the Council as regards the United Kingdom and repealing Council Decision 98/256/EC and Decisions 98/351/EC and 1999/514/EC, OJ L 116, 04.29.2006, p. 1.

As an example of the use of the Regulation for the application of Directives, among many others, Commission Regulation (EC) No 706/2007, of 21st June 2007, laying down, pursuant to Directive 2006/40/EC of the European Parliament and of the Council, administrative provisions for the EC type-approval of vehicles, and a harmonised test for measuring leakages from certain air conditioning systems OJ L 161, 22.06.2007, p. 33; Commission Regulation (EU) No. 175/2010, of 2nd March 2010, implementing Council Directive 2006/88/EC as regards measures to control increased mortality in oysters of the species Crassostrea gigas in connection with the detection of Ostreid herpesvirus 1 μvar (OsHV-1 μvar), OJ L 52, 3.03.2010, p. 1.

[24]Among many others, Regulation (EC) No. 1394/2007 of the European Parliament and of the Council, of 13th November 2007, on advanced therapy medicinal products and amending Directive 2001/83/EC and Regulation (EC) No 726/2004, OJ L 324, 10.12.2007, p. 121; Commission Regulation (EC) No 213/2008, of 28th November 2007, amending Regulation (EC) No 2195/ 2002 of the European Parliament and of the Council on the Common Procurement Vocabulary

the same date as a regulation and directive;[25] when decisions have also modified directives,[26] directives and other decisions together,[27] and even when directives are repealed,[28] or when, less frequently, directives have been used to modify other acts.[29]

In addition, there is a variety of European Union legal instruments that could fit perfectly into the category of administrative acts rather than in that of legal norms. Among these, we can highlight, for example, preparatory instruments of legislative acts or acts in general (adopted by the Directorate General or the Secretary-General of the European Commission), instructions, internal regulations, opinions, communications, and some decisions. Of course, in these cases it would be necessary to differentiate between with effects on third parties and acts with merely internal effects in the organisation. The ECJ itself has recognised the current confusion, stating that the alleged difference between a legislative measure and administrative

(CPV) and Directives 2004/17/EC and 2004/18/EC of the European Parliament and of the Council on public procurement procedures, as regards the revision of the CPV; OJ L 74, 03.15.2008, p. 1.

[25]Regulation (EC) No 1907/2006 of the European Parliament and of the Council, of 18th December 2006 concerning the Registration, Evaluation, Authorisation and Restriction of Chemicals (REACH), establishing a European Chemicals Agency, amending Directive 1999/45/EC and repealing Council Regulation (EEC) No 793/93 and Commission Regulation (EC) No 1488/94 as well as Council Directive 76/769/EEC and Commission Directives 91/155/EEC, 93/67/EEC, 93/105/EC and 2000/21/EC, OJ L 396, 30.12. 2006, p. 1; Directive 2006/121/EC of the European Parliament and of the Council, of 18th December 2006, amending Council Directive 67/548/EEC on the approximation of laws, regulations and administrative provisions relating to the classification, packaging and labelling of dangerous substances in order to adapt it to Regulation (EC) No 1907/2006 concerning the Registration, Evaluation, Authorisation and Restriction of Chemicals (REACH) and establishing a European Chemicals Agency, OJ L 396, 30.12.2006, p. 853.

[26]Among many others, Commission Decision 2007/699/EC, of 29th October 2007, amending Council Directive 92/33/EEC to extend the derogation relating to import conditions for vegetable propagating and planting material from third countries (notified under document number, OJ L 284, 30.10.2007, p. 33; Commission Decision 2007/394 / EC, of 7th June 2007, amending Council Directive 90/377/EEC with regards to the methodology to be applied for the collection of gas and electricity prices charged to industrial end-users, OJ L 148, 9.06.2007, p. 11.

[27]2006/128/EC: Commission Decision, of 3rd February 2006, amending Directive 2001/109/EC of the European Parliament and of the Council and Commission Decision 2002/38/EC concerning the statistical surveys carried out on plantations of certain species of fruit trees OJ L 51, 02.22.2006, p. 21.

[28]Decision No 714/2007/EC of the European Parliament and of the Council, of 20th June 2007, repealing Council Directive 68/89/EEC on the approximation of the laws of the Member States concerning the classification of wood in the rough, OJ L 163, 06.23.2007, p. 16.

[29]Directive 2004/38/EC of the European Parliament and of the Council, of 29th April 2004, on the right of citizens of the Union and their family members to move and reside freely within the territory of the Member States amending Regulation (EEC) No 1612/68 and repealing Directives 64/221/EEC, 68/360/EEC, 72/194/EEC, 73/148/EEC, 75/34/EEC, 75/35/EEC, 90/364/EEC, 90/365/EEC and 93/96/EEC, OJ No. L 158, of 30.4.2004. p. 77.

act is not relevant in community law and the specific content of each legal instrument must always be analysed to determine its effects.[30]

In short, it seems that the community system has developed as a differentiated whole, where appropriate, from the national systems, for which we have a series of principles and rules of application, but the same does not happen between the different instruments of secondary law. Hence, the substantial amount of litigation that has questioned the purpose and nature of each source of European law, both between institutions and between these and States, economic operators, etc. Without a doubt, we believe that it is a chaotic resource system which, as one author has described it,[31] is in need of reorganisation and the establishment of basic principles to order the different regulatory instruments of community law.

# 3 Current Situation of Legislative and Regulatory Power in Spain

Considering legislative power as the ability to dictate norms with the rank of law and, within executive power, considering regulatory power as the capacity of Public Administrations to also dictate legal norms, we are going to focus not on analysing both powers, as these have already received a lot of attention in the doctrine, but rather on establishing some basic ideas for the analysis we will undertake of the legislative technique in general, as a technique applied both in the development of norms (whether laws or regulations) and in their evaluation, and to which we dedicate Section IV of this paper.

## *3.1 Constitutional Basis and Legal System*

Both legislative and regulatory powers have their foundation in the CE itself. Therefore, legislative power corresponds primarily to Parliament (Art. 66.2 CE), but the Government also takes part in it by submitting bills (Art. 87), legislative delegation (Arts. 82 to 85 CE) and urgent legislation (Art. 86 CE). These last two mechanisms lead, as is known, to regulations that carry the force of law.

Autonomous parliaments also have legislative power in the scope of the respective Autonomous Community as provided for in Art. 152.3 EC and in the different Autonomy Statutes. These include mostly delegated legislation, that is, the power of the autonomous government to issue legislative decrees (only the Canary Islands, Murcia and the Basque Country have no express provision in their Statutes), while urgent legislation through the adoption of Decree-Laws has been incorporated into

[30] See in this regard the CJEU Judgment of 10th December 1998, case C-221/1997.

[31] Gil Ibánez and Ordóñez Solis (2011), pp. 111–174.

the second generation Autonomy Statutes (the autonomous communities of Valencia, Catalonia, Andalusia, the Balearic Islands, Extremadura, Castilla y Leon, Navarra and Aragon),[32] although, in practice, all autonomous executives use these normative instruments and adopt norms carrying the force of law.

Therefore, legislative authority is attributed to the legislative power and, to a lesser extent, to the power of the court. While it is true that both the CE and the Autonomy Statutes take on the role of government legislator de minimis, and is mainly for legislating in situations of extraordinary and urgent need, we must not forget that at present the initial situation is quite different, not only because of the abuse that is made of the law as a legal instrument, but also because the absence of majorities in Parliament has made the procedure for passing laws in a strict sense difficult in recent legislatures. Hence, the current situation is that Decree-Law has become the usual instrument with which to legislate.

This is, in any case, the legislative authority of an authority linked only to the CE, since the law is not subject to judicial control, only to judicial review exercised by the Constitutional Court, which precisely represents its subordination to the Constitution only.

Regulatory authority, meanwhile, is also recognised in the CE., specifically in Art. 97, which expressly attributes regulatory power to the Government (primary attribution). However, it is also implicitly deduced from Art. 137 CE which recognises the autonomy of territorial public entities (State, Autonomous Communities and local authorities). The autonomous governments find the specific attribution in their respective Autonomy Statutes, and local authorities through the law—Law 7/1985, of 2nd April, governing the *Bases del Régimen Local* (hereinafter, LBRL)-(legal attribution).

The administrative authority to dictate legal norms under the law and judicial control is characterised by being a legislative function subordinate to law. It is precisely this formal subordination of regulation to the law, together with the constitutional legal reserve in certain matters, which legitimises the existence of the regulatory power in the constitutional system and, together with the judicial control of the regulatory power, allows the distinguishing of both legal products: law and regulation.[33]

Concerning the legal system, we must highlight the regulation contained in the *Ley Procedimiento Administrativo Común de las Administraciones Públicas* (LPAC), (Legal System of Public Administrations and Common Administrative Procedures) which in Art. 1.1 established, within its purpose, regulation of the principles to which legislative initiative and regulatory power must adhere. In fact, as we will see later, Title VI of said law regulates the principles to which the Administrations must comply to enforce constitutional rights on this matter. As for the legislative initiative, few developments are contemplated, since Art. 127 is limited to a reminder that the preparation and approval of preliminary bills

---

[32]See Donaire Villa (2012).

[33]Similarly, Gamero Casado (2015), p. 37.

corresponds to the national government in accordance with the provisions of the EC, and the governing bodies of the autonomous communities in accordance with the provisions of the Constitution and in their respective Autonomy Statutes. Likewise, the third section refers to the constitutionally recognised power of national governments to approve norms with the rank of law, law-decrees and legislative decrees; and that respective governing bodies of the autonomous communities can approve regulations equivalent to those in their territorial scope, in accordance with the provisions of the CE and its Autonomy Statutes. Therefore, it must be noted that the LPAC only regulates the legislative initiative that corresponds to the Government, whether central or autonomous, not the one that corresponds to the legislative bodies.

As for regulatory powers, Art. 128 establishes that this corresponds to the national government ex Article 97 of the EC, to the governing bodies of autonomous communities in accordance with their respective Autonomy Statutes, and to local governing bodies in accordance with the *Ley de Bases de Régimen Local* (LBRL) (Law Regulating the Bases of the Local Government.). Therefore, it refers to the exercise of regulatory power in a broad sense, including both the initiative and instruction or processing of its content or final result, as well as the regulatory power of local entities.[34]

## 3.2 *Procedure for the Development of Legal Norms*

The EC devotes a whole chapter to the procedure of drafting laws,[35] although its content deals more with the delimitation of the kinds of laws (organic laws; delegated legislation; law of bases and decree-laws—Arts. 81 to 86-) and only in Art. 87 do we find the procedure regarding their preparation. Thus, legislative initiative is attributed to the Government, Congress and the Senate, in accordance with the CE and by-laws.[36] However, Autonomous Community assemblies can also request that the Government adopts a bill, or presents a legislative proposal to the bureau of Congress, delegating up to three members of the assembly who are

[34]Prieto Romero (2016), p. 341, specifies that local ordinances and regulations are not the result of regulatory power, that is, they are not norms produced by the executive, but by the Plenary, which represents popular sovereignty. Therefore, local regulations have a different legal nature from executive regulations, their relations with the law are determined by the principle of negative linkage and their development procedure is also different from that of an executive regulation, for example, for this consultation procedure with the Council of State or the advisory body of the respective autonomous community, it is considered an essential procedure. However, in the case of municipal norms, such a procedure does not exist, even in cases where said norms directly develop a norm with rank of law.

[35]Arts. 81–92 of the EC.

[36]Regulations of the Congress of Deputies, of 10th February 1982, and Regulations of the Senate of 3rd May 1994.

responsible for their defence to stand before said chamber. In addition, even the people's legislative initiative is recognised by virtue of being able to submit bills.[37]

Government bills are passed by the Council of Ministers, which refers them to Congress, accompanied by a statement setting forth the necessary grounds and facts in order for them to reach a decision thereon (Art. 88 CE). Moreover "*the passage of non-governmental bills shall be regulated by the Standing Orders of the Houses*" (Art. 89 CE).

Once an ordinary or organic governmental bill has been passed by the Congress of Deputies, the Speaker of Congress immediately reports it to the Speaker of the Senate, who submits it to the latter for consideration.

Within 2 months of receiving the text, the Senate may, by means of a considered opinion, veto it or introduce amendments. The veto must be passed by absolute majority. The bill may not be submitted to the King for his approval unless, in the event of veto, Congress has ratified the initial text by absolute majority (or by simple majority if two months have elapsed since its introduction), or has reached a decision relative to the amendments, accepting them or not by simple majority. The period of two months allocated to the Senate for vetoing or amending a bill shall be reduced to twenty calendar days for bills declared urgent by the Government or the Congress of Deputies.

Finally, within a period of fifteen days, the King approves the laws passed by the Cortes Generales, who promulgates them and orders their immediate publication. (Art. 91 CE).

Therefore, three phases can be differentiated in the development procedure of laws. An initial (initiative) phase, which constitutes the necessary impetus for subsequent actions; a central (constitutive) phase in which the content of the future law is specified and developed in parliamentary headquarters, and a final phase (integrative of effectiveness), in which the necessary material actions are carried out so that the law can acquire full effectiveness.[38]

It should be noted that in other constitutional precepts some rules on the development of laws are also found. Thus, special legislative procedures such as budgetary[39] and the delegate in omission,[40] or the legislative procedure of certain types of laws, such as those provided for in Art. 150 and the Autonomies Statutes.

In Spain, unlike in the Anglo-Saxon system,[41] there is no professional body responsible for drafting the bills, but the different ministries are the ones that prepare the preliminary drafts in the areas of their competence. The beginning of the process of drafting laws occurs once the political decision has been adopted by the

---

[37] According to Art. 87.3 CE, legislative proposals presented by the popular initiative require no less than 500,000 accredited signatures. Moreover, this initiative will not proceed in matters of organic, tax or international law, or in relation to the prerogative of grace.

[38] See in this regard García-Escudero Márquez (2000), pp. 61 *et seq.*

[39] See Art. 134 CE.

[40] See Art. 75 CE.

[41] See Tur Ausina (2009), pp. 103–131.

competent ministries. They commission the respective technical general secretaries with the drafting of the bill, or an administrative unit specifically created for this purpose, or also—especially in the case of very technical matters—to a group of experts so that, according to previous guidelines, the draft can be prepared.

The bills, as we have seen, must be accompanied by a statement setting forth the necessary grounds and facts in order for them to reach a decision thereon. This requirement imposed by Art. 88 CE obliges the government to provide the bill with all the necessary grounds and facts so that Congress can decide on the matter to be regulated with full knowledge of the situation of the sector.[42] In addition, the bills must be accompanied by a report which analyses the impact of the norm, as provided for in the first additional provision of Royal Decree 931/2017, of 27th October 2017, governing the Regulatory Impact Analysis Report.[43] The purpose of this Report is to regulate the content of reports and studies on the need and timeliness of the projected norms, as well as the economic review and the report on gender impact, which must accompany the preliminary draft law and draft regulations.[44]

The ultimate aim of this Report is to ensure that when drawing up and approving a project, all the necessary information is included in order to estimate the impact the norm will have on recipients and agents. In order to do this, it is essential to provide a motive for the need and timeliness of the projected norm, assess the different alternatives available for the achievement of the desired objectives and analyse in detail the legal and economic consequences, especially regarding competence, which will be derived for the affected agents, as well as its effect from a budgetary point of view, its impact on gender, and in the constitutional order of distribution of competences.

It is therefore understood that the expression "necessary grounds" referred to in Art. 88 C E refers precisely to this regulatory impact analysis report.[45] Moreover, with regards to the explanatory statement, it is simply highlighted that it has no normative value,[46] as affirmed by the Constitutional Court.

---

[42]In this regard, Santamaría Pastor (2001), pp. 1397–1404.

[43]This repeals the previous norm on this matter, Royal Decree 1083/2009, of 3rd July, regulating the normative impact analysis report.

[44]According to Articles 22 and 24 of Law 50/1997, of 27th November, which were modified by Law 30/2003, of 13th October, on measures to incorporate assessment of gender impact in the normative dispositions the Government elaborates, a valuation reiterated by the Organic Law 3/2007, of 22nd March, for the effective equality of women and men.

[45]On the same line, Sebastían Lorente (1992), says the term "background" must be related to studies and previous reports, and include all technical documents ranging from reports—supporting and economical—to feasibility studies and objectives and, of course, reports and issued rulings, especially those of a prescriptive nature.

[46]Among others, in SSTC 36/1981, (FJ 7. 2); 54/1982, (FJ 2); 35/1984; 150/1990, (FJ 2); 212/1996, (FJ 15); 173/1998, (FJ 4); 116/1999 (FJ2). In particular, in STC 31/2010, of 28th June, on Organic Law 6/2006, on the reform of the Statute of Autonomy of Catalonia, the TC, reiterating its doctrine, states that: (FJ 7) "*The legal value of preambles to laws is therefore exhausted in their qualified condition as a hermeneutic criterion*"... and, after previously stating that: "*..lack of normative value does not amount to lack of legal value, in the same way as the impossibility of becoming the*

With regards to the procedure for the elaboration of regulations, at state level this is governed by Law 50/1997, of 27th November, and at government level (Arts. 23 and 24), and in the autonomous sphere, in the corresponding laws of the government of the respective Autonomous Community, although it should be noted that these have not been very innovative in the elaboration procedure and practically all the municipalities have regulated a procedure identical to that of the state.

This procedure is characterised by its simplicity, which has been highlighted as a cause of the excessive proliferation of regulatory norms; hasty approval; the lack of maturation of normative texts; and the non-weighting of the different public interests affected by the new norm.[47]

In any case, the most relevant stage of this procedure is the hearing procedure that, unlike the others,[48] is considered legally binding. This has been established by the TS on numerous occasions, having also highlighted the transcendental purposes fulfilled by said procedure, which is aimed at "*contributing to the correctness and legality of the text that is approved, allowing all points of consideration to be taken into account, whereby the matter regarding the regulation can be analysed, enriching, therefore, the general provision with the observations of the sectors, persons or entities consulted*".[49]

## 4 The Legislative Technique in Spain

As mentioned in the Introduction, legislative power is experiencing difficulties as a result of the proliferation of norms that we are witnessing, in which the norms are approved without respecting the minimum standards of quality and rationality. This problem is already unleashing a fatal consequence: the inefficiency of laws, and, therefore, legislative power, thus leading to the implementation of a chaotic regulatory system with strong dose of legal uncertainty. This justifies the need to reflect on our legislative technique and make some proposals that allow the introduction of rationality and quality into the legislative functions.

---

*direct subject matter of an action of appeal of unconstitutionality does not imply that preambles are inaccessible for any pronouncement by our jurisdiction insofar as a possible accessory in proceedings referring mainly to a normative provision*"..., in the first point of the ruling declares the following: *"The references in the preamble to the Statute of Autonomy of Catalonia to "Catalonia as a nation" and "the national reality of Catalonia", have no interpretative legal effect.*

[47] In this respect, Lavilla Rubira (2009), p. 19.

[48] In fact, the TS has pointed out that: "...a functional and teleological interpretation of the procedural guarantees established for the elaboration of general provisions, are justified not by the pure formalism of their production, but by their purpose", so that when we are faced with "a transcendent non-observance of fulfilment of purpose, which is a requirement of the omitted procedure, a declaration of invalidity of the norm will proceed. (STS 13th May 2009).

[49] STC May 8, 2009.

## 4.1 Concept and Link to the Principle of Legal Certainty

Legislative technique has been defined as "*the art of legislating clearly and effectively*"[50] and has as its objective "*not only the good drafting of laws, but also more general and important issues, such as the unity and coherence of the legal system and the quality, publicity and viability of the rules*".[51] However, despite its doctrinal definition,[52] legislative technique is not regulated in the CE or in the law. As such, we have no norm or precept that defines its meaning and how to respect it.

Even so, legislative technique has been linked to the principle of legal certainty in order to understand the constitutional value it represents.[53] Since 1990, the TC itself has been doing this, because it understands that "*the requirement of article 9.3 regarding the principle of legal certainty implies that the legislator must pursue clarity and not regulatory confusion, It must be ensured that the legal operators and citizens know what to do about the subject matter, and must avoid objectively confusing situations, as the one that is undoubtedly generated in this case given the very complicated set of references between norms that have occurred here. We must promote and seek certainty as to what is Law and not, as could be the case, cause groupings and relations between norms, as a result of which perplexities are introduced that are hardly salvageable with respect to the predictability of what the applicable Law is, what the consequences derived from the norms in force are, even what they are. The violation of legal certainty is clear and unconstitutionality must also be declared for this reason*".[54]

It seems obvious, then, the importance of clarity in the norms, in such a way that the lack of clarity, certainty and the existence of norms that do not meet minimum quality criteria violate the principle of legal certainty. In addition, this violation can lead to a declaration of unconstitutionality. In fact, the TC itself has indicated on occasions that "*the mere possibility of a misuse of the norms can never be in itself reason enough to declare its unconstitutionality, because, although the rule of law tends to replacement of government by men to government by laws, there is no legislator, wise as they may be, capable of producing laws that a ruler cannot misuse.*".[55]

In any case, despite the absence of a tradition in Spain in the field of legislative theory, we have recently seen concern regarding the need to establish norms on legislative technique. Thus, the approval by the Council of Ministers of several Guidelines in this area must be highlighted. Specifically, the Agreement of the Council of Ministers, of 18th October 1991, approves the Guidelines on the form

[50]García-Escudero Márquez (2005), pp. 121–164.

[51]Sainz Moreno (1995), pp. 6485–6489.

[52]See Corona Ferrero (1994), pp. 49–56; Gómez Orfanel (1991), pp. 11–18; Muñoz Machado (1986). p. 217; Ruiz Sanz (1996–1997), pp. 637–650.

[53]See also Segovia Marco (2015).

[54]STC 46/1990 on water legislation in the Canary Islands.

[55]Also, in SSTC 58/1982; 132/1989; 204/1994; 235/2000; 134/2006; and 238/2012.

and structure of draft bills[56] and the Agreement of the Council of Ministers, of 22nd July 2005, approving the Guidelines on normative technique.[57] Both are guidelines and technical references on how to prepare and, in particular, draft legal provisions. They do not give rise to rights and obligations for third parties, nor can they be invoked before the courts as a system resource, as they are not legislative. They are approved in order to facilitate the understanding and application of the norms. The Guidelines of 2005 replaced those of 1991, since the increase in normative production required an extension to the aims of the Guidelines and their scope of application.[58] According to its preamble, this was to approach more closely the constitutional principle of legal certainty by improving the technical and linguistic quality of all the norms of governmental origin with the homogenising and standardisation of the texts of the provisions.[59]

Perhaps the most innovative of the Guidelines approved in 2005 is that referring to the language used in norms. They refer to the need to use clear, precise and accessible language, given that the legal norms are intended for the "average citizen". More specifically, we can find recommendations such as the following: use common lexicon, provide explanatory descriptions of technical terms (if the use of such terms is necessary), avoid the use of foreign words if there is an equivalent in Spanish, and the use of uncommon words and constructions.

There is no doubt that establishing linguistic criteria in the development of norms is an important step on the way to achieving higher regulatory quality. However, as the doctrine has pointed out, in practice we cannot affirm that norms are approved in clear, precise and accessible language.[60]

To these Guidelines on legislative techniques, we must add some aspects linked directly or indirectly to the legislative techniques that have, somewhat unsystematically, regulated several laws. Thus, for example, the obligation, when exercising regulatory initiative, to respect the principles of necessity, proportionality, legal certainty, transparency, accessibility, simplicity and effectiveness, the *ex ante* and *ex post* analysis of the norms and the guarantee of a public hearing in the development phase of the norms, pursuant to Law 2/20 11, of 4th March, on Sustainable Economy. Law 19/2013, of 9th December, on Transparency, Access to Public Information and Good Government can also be cited, which aims to increase and strengthen transparency in public activity through active publication

[56]Published in the Official State Gazette, of 18th November 1991.

[57]Published in the Official State Gazette, of 29th July 2005.

[58]Indeed, the 1991 Guidelines were limited to the draft laws and only contained technical quality guidelines, while those of 2005 address both technical and linguistic issues and apply to any bills, including draft laws, royal legislative decree proposals, royal decree-law, royal decree, Council of Ministers agreement proposals and, as far as possible, to the provisions and administrative acts of State Administration Bodies published in the Official State Gazette.

[59]See also Santaolalla López (2006), pp. 41–92.

[60]In this regard, see Centenera Sánchez-Seco (2012), pp. 15–34. Here, the author presents an interesting proposal from the Anglo-Saxon doctrinal field, offering higher levels of functionality for the drafting of norms.

obligations for all Public Administrations and public entities regarding institutional, organisational and planning information; and Law 20/2013, of 9th December, on the Guarantee of the Market Unit, which promotes an efficient regulatory framework for economic activities, that simplifies existing legislation, eliminates unnecessary regulations, establishes more agile procedures and minimises administrative burdens. In order to do this, it is essential to adopt criteria of good regulation, some of which are provided for in the LPAC[61] and which are analysed in the following section.

## 4.2 Some Criteria of Regulatory Quality in the Light of Law 39/2015, of 1st October, on the Common Administrative Procedure of Public Administrations

In this unsystematic regulation that deals with some aspects of the legislative technique, special attention must be paid to the innovations introduced by the LPAC in 2015. It contains some principles and criteria of good legislation. Thus, Title VI is dedicated to the legislative initiative and normative power of public administrations. In it, together with some improvements in the current regulation hierarchy, publication rules and principles of good regulation, several new features are meant to increase the participation of citizens in the process of developing norms, including, among others: the need to seek, prior to the development of the norm, the opinion of citizens and entities regarding the problems that are intended to be solved with the initiative; the need and opportunity for approval; the objectives of the norm and possible regulatory and non-regulatory alternative solutions.[62]

Likewise, for the sake of greater legal certainty and the predictability of the system, it is committed to improving the *ex ante* regulatory planning. To do this, all Administrations will publish an annual plan in which all proposals with the rank of law or regulation to be submitted for approval the following year will be collected. At the same time, *ex post* evaluation is strengthened, since together with the duty to continuously review the adaptation of the norms to the principles of good regulation,

[61] Note that Articles 4–7 of the Sustainable Economy Act have been expressly repealed by the sole repealing provision of the Common Administrative Procedure of Public Administrations Law, integrating its contents into Title VI of this Law, and those corresponding to the Law on the Guarantee of Market Unity remain valid in the economic activities field.

[62] In anticipation, the Council of Ministers Agreement, of 30th September 2016, has been approved, in which instructions are given to enable public participation in the process of regulatory development through the departments' internet portals. Its purpose is to obtain the opinion of citizens, organisations and associations before the development of a State Administration draft bill. Thus, the instruction, in the case of opting for prior public consultation, contains a list of the initiatives for which the procedure is open. In relation to each draft, information will be provided on: (a) the background of the norm, with brief reference to the regulatory background; (b) problems that are intended to be solved with the new norm; (c) need and opportunity for approval; (d) objectives of the norm; and, (e) possible alternative, regulatory and non-regulatory solutions.

the obligation to periodically evaluate the application of the regulations in force is imposed, in order to verify they have fulfilled the objectives pursued, and if the cost and charges derived from them were justified and adequately assessed.[63]

These measures take care of both the development of norms phase and the results achieved by the approved norms, that is, they focus on both technique-form quality and material, by carrying out an *ex ante* and *ex post* evaluation of the norms. Both are part of the legislative technique. Indeed, the legislative technique should not only deal with the formal aspects of the laws (language, structure and system), but they must also meet the objectives pursued with their approval, that is, that they are materially adequate.[64] To this end, the *ex post* evaluation of norms arises. A norm will be considered of quality when it conforms with the following principles of good regulation: proportionality, consistency, transparency, responsibility and effectiveness.[65]

In this sense, the first principles Art. 129 of the LPAC introduces are the principles of good regulation. Thus, "*in the exercise of legislative initiative and regulatory power, Public Administrations will act in accordance with the principles of necessity, effectiveness, proportionality, legal certainty, transparency, and efficiency*". In the explanatory memorandum or in the preamble of bills or draft regulations, respectively, their adjustment to these principles must be sufficiently substantiated. In addition, the legislative initiative must be justified to be of general interest, based on a clear identification of the aims pursued and being the most appropriate instrument to guarantee its achievement. Remember the obligation introduced by the legislator in this article ("must be"), therefore, its violation may now be grounds for appeal.

Under the principle of proportionality, the proposed initiative must contain the essential regulation to meet the need which is to be covered by the norm, after finding that there are no other measures less restrictive on rights, or that impose less obligations on the recipients. Moreover, in order to guarantee the principle of legal certainty, the legal initiative will be exercised in a manner consistent with the rest of the legal system, both of the European Union and national, to generate a stable, predictable, integrated, clear and secure regulatory framework, which facilitates knowledge and understanding and, consequently, the action and decision-making facilities of people and entities.

In applying the transparency principle, Public Administrations will allow simple, universal and up-to-date access to the regulations in force and the documents regarding their elaboration process; they will clearly define the objectives of the legislative initiatives and their justification in the explanatory memorandum; and they will enable potential recipients to actively participate in the development of the norm.

---

[63]See the Explanatory Memorandum in Common Administrative Procedure of Public Administrations Law.

[64]García-Escudero Márquez (2011), p. 73.

[65]Ponce Solé (2009), pp. 485 *et seq*.

In applying the principle of efficiency, on the other hand, the legislative initiative must avoid unnecessary or accessory administrative burdens and rationalise, in its application, the management of public resources; and, when the normative initiative affects current or future public expenses or revenues, its repercussions and effects must be quantified and assessed, and subject to compliance with the principles of budgetary stability and financial sustainability.

In short, a series of principles of good regulation that, without doubt, constitute a mandate to the Public Administrations in the exercise of their normative powers. Principles, on the other hand, well known, since those that do not derive from the EC itself, proportionality, necessity or transparency (the principles of legal certainty; effectiveness and efficiency are reflected in the constitutional text), had already been regulated by the Law on Sustainable Economy or the Law on Guarantee of the Market Unit as principles of good economic regulation.[66] Even so, they are now considered as a set of principles of general application to any matter which is subject to regulation and that will undoubtedly improve regulatory quality.

The need to annually plan the regulatory initiatives (whether laws or regulations) that are intended to be approved[67] is particularly novel. Said regulatory plan, set forth in Art. 132, shall be published on the transparency portal of the corresponding Public Administration. This instrument has been developed by Royal Decree 286/2017, of 24th March, which regulates the Annual Regulatory Plan and the Annual Regulatory Evaluation Report of the General State Administration and creates the Planning and Regulatory Evaluation Board. Undoubtedly, this measure introduces criteria of rationality in the approval of norms.

The *ex post* evaluation of norms is introduced in Art. 130 LPAC, which requires that Public Administrations periodically check their current regulations for the extent to which the norms have achieved the intended objectives and whether the cost and burdens imposed on them were justified and correctly quantified. The result of this evaluation will be reflected in a report that will be made public and will be detailed, periodical and produced by the body that determines the legislative regulations of the corresponding Administration. It is important to note that the *ex post* evaluation only applies to the norms approved by Public Administrations, therefore without covering laws and it is a minimum regulation requiring a regulatory development that has not yet been carried out.[68]

---

[66] See also Fernández Farreres (2016), pp. 55–74.

[67] Art. 28 of the LRJSP also states that the annual evaluation report should reflect the degree of compliance with the annual plan for the previous year, adding that when such plan has identified norms that will be subject to an analysis on the results of its application, the Report will include an *ex post* analysis of the effectiveness, efficiency and sustainability of the norm, identifying administrative burdens that may not have been necessary. Regarding the effects of this *ex post* evaluation, the only thing included in this Article is that the aforementioned report may contain specific recommendations for the modification, and, where appropriate, repeal of the norms evaluated.

[68] Currently, we can only highlight Royal Decree 931/2017, of 27th October, which regulates the memorandum of the normative impact analysis, in which, although it regulates the *ex ante*

The obligation also includes the publication of norms with the force of law, regulations and administrative provisions (Art. 131 LPAC).

Finally, the obligation to publish norms is regulated,[69] as well as the participation of citizens in the process of developing norms with the force of law and regulations (Art. 133 of LPAC). These provisions derive from Art. 105.a) of the CE that contemplates, as is known, the principle of citizen participation, and which are specified here in the process of public hearing and public information.[70] Different forms of citizen participation are characterised: public consultation, which takes place prior to the elaboration and drafting of the bill or draft law or draft regulation[71] and the public hearing that takes place when the rule affects the legitimate rights and interests of individuals.[72] It is important to ensure that the potential recipients of the norms and those who contribute to it are able to express their opinion. In order to do so, they must make available the necessary documents, which will be clear, concise and contain all the necessary information to be able to pronounce on the matter. With the process of public consultation, the norm to be published is guaranteed to be necessary and timely, and there is no other non-regulatory solution to the problem the projected norm aims to solve. A public hearing, meanwhile, is a procedure that guarantees the defence of the rights and interests of the people affected by the regulation subject. Given that the LPAC, on regulating the process of public hearing, provides for the public information process to gather as many additional contributions as they can from other persons or entities, some authors consider the process of public consultation a duplication of procedures, as its purpose can be achieved by later procedures such as, for example, through the participation of the subjects and

normative impact analysis and their evaluation, it includes minimum provisions for *ex post* evaluation.

[69]Art. 131 of the LPAC states that these must be published in the corresponding Official State Gazette in order for them to enter into force and produce legal effects. However, additionally, and optionally, Public Administrations may establish other complementary means of publicity. Thus, the publication of the official newspapers or gazettes in the electronic headquarters of the Administration, Body, Public Organisation or competent Entity will have, under the conditions and with the guarantees that each Public Administration determines, the same effects as those attributed to its print edition. For its part, the publication of the Official State Gazette in the electronic headquarters of the competent Agency shall be official and authentic in the conditions, and with the guarantees determined by regulation deriving from said publication, the effects, as provided for in the preliminary title of the Civil Code and in the remaining applicable norms.

[70]See also Alonso Timón (2016), pp. 76–102.

[71]Public consultation is carried out through the portal of the competent Administration, and contain the opinion of the most representative subjects and organizations potentially affected by the future rule regarding: (a) The problems that are they try to solve with the initiative; (b) The need and opportunity for approval; (c) The objectives of the normative; (d) Possible alternative regulatory and non-regulatory solutions.

[72]In this case, the competent management center will publish the text on the corresponding portal to collect as many additional contributions as may be made by other persons or entities. Likewise, the opinion of organizations or associations recognized by law, that group or represent people whose legitimate rights or interests are affected by the rule, and whose purposes are directly targeted at, may also be directly sought.

the most representative of the organisations potentially affected in the hearing process or public informing, where they will rule on the need and the timeliness of the particular bill, or of the existence or not of non-regulatory alternatives, etc.[73] In our opinion, if used properly, prior consultation can be a very positive procedure because it will help the Administrations to become aware of the perceptions and contributions of citizens before creating a first draft of the norm. For this, the purpose of the consultation must be well defined and objective, so as not to influence the opinions of citizens. However, it can be stated that the use that has been made of it since its entry into force has not fulfilled our expectations. The Administration limits itself to complying with the procedure using expressions such as "*for greater legal certainty, it is necessary to undertake regulatory development*"; "*It is more advisable for greater legal certainty, draw up a newly planned royal decree*", etc., without further motivation or justification.[74]

In short, there is no doubt that this regulation has made progress, as the legislature was absolutely necessary to improve regulatory quality, however it is also true that it seems insufficient to fill gaps in our legislative technique, since it is not clear in these precepts what is required and desirable for the purpose of regulatory quality improvement.[75]

In addition, it must also be highlighted that the TC currently does not consider the legislative technique subject to supervision in its judgements. In this regard, it was stated: "*As we have said, "the constitutionality trial is not of legislative technique" (SSTC 10 9/1987, of June 29, FJ 3 c) and 195/1996, of November 28, FJ 4), which is why it does not "correspond to the constitutional jurisdiction to pronounce on the technical perfection of the laws" (SSTC 226/1993, of July 8, FJ 4), given that "the jurisdictional control of the law has nothing to do with its technical debugging" (SSTC 226/1993, of July 8, FJ 5; and 195/1996, of November 28, FJ 3), nor can it be accepted that the Constitution imposes unique and exclusive solutions "completely abolishing the freedom of configuration of the legislator" (STC 226/1993, of July 8, FJ 4; and in the same sense, STC 225/1998, of 25th November, FJ 2 A).*".[76] Moreover, he has reiterated that his judgement "*is strictly a judgment on the rules of law based on the superior norm of the Ordinance and according to strictly legal criteria of interpretation*".[77] It is possible that this position should be modulated by regulating some criteria of legislative technique in the LPAC itself, since it would no longer be a matter of assessing the violation of constitutional principles, but also violation of a law.

---

[73]Prieto Romero (2016), p. 360.

[74]Araguas Galcera (2016), p. 106.

[75]As Montoro Chiner (2017) states, in these precepts, it is difficult to find where the rules are, the binding mandate of the phases of the procedure, the steps required to draft a valid norm; where the essential nucleus of the elaboration procedure is the formally essential part of the procedure, which allows the addressee and the Judge to come to the conclusion that, including its material content, the norm will not be wrongful.

[76]STC 176/2011.

[77]STC 191/2016.

Finally, it should be noted that despite the absence of a uniform regulation on legislative technique, the advisory councils have been working to control the quality of norms by virtue of their competence, to assess aspects of timeliness and suitability, as well as the greater effectiveness of the Administrations in the fulfilment of its purposes.[78] Thus, the prior intervention of the advisory councils, even if the content of their opinions is not binding, implies a global control and especially with the capacity to assess, among others, relevant aspects of the timeliness of the norm in question.[79] In this way, the advisory function is in the transition phase, from legal control of the exercise of administrative and governmental powers, towards the collaboration and assistance of said powers within legality.[80] This is because it functions considering that the norms comply with certain principles, and searches for elements of rigor in legislative technique and compliance with the principle of proportionality of regulation, i.e. the norm is suitable, necessary and guarantees transparency, among other things. There is no doubt that this preventive control function must be carried out carefully in order to find the necessary balance between the requirement of the formal elements of compliance, with the phases of the procedure and the requirements of simplification, expediting procedures and facilitating administrative action.[81]

## 5 Some *de Lege Ferenda* Proposals

The analysis carried out over the previous pages highlights the urgent need to formulate a legislative theory. It has been demonstrated that the regulation carried out to date, in an isolated, partial and unsystematic nature, of some aspects of the legislative technique, is insufficient to improve regulatory quality. Even the European Union, with its recommendations and the objectives that the European Commission establishes with the "better law-making" initiative, has not been able to transfer the concerns about these issues[82] to public authorities.

---

[78]Thus, for example, in its annual reports, the State Council has reiterated various observations and suggestions on the legislative technique used by the Government, seeking as its purpose that the norms that are finally approved as being as clear and perfect as possible. The 2011 report must be highlighted, in which the State Council notes that sometimes the impact analysis reports used to "*justify the need and opportunity of the draft regulation, are not sufficiently expressive of its purpose, content and scope*" or, that, "on *certain occasions, reports are omitted or incomplete hearings are held*".

[79]Álvarez Vélez (2017), p. 53.

[80]Font I Llovet (1995), p. 48.

[81]See also Font I Llovet (2009), p. 146.

[82]Indeed, on this matter, the momentum given by the European Union to the need to improve legislation is significant. Thus, since the Recommendation of the Council of the Organisation on Economic Cooperation and Development (OECD) for the improvement of the quality of government regulations (1995), several documents and recommendations have been approved by the EU. Among these, it is important to highlight the "Interinstitutional Agreement on Better

Therefore, as follows some ideas will be proposed that we consider fundamental to start that path towards the development of a Spanish legislative theory that allows improvement regarding the quality and rationality of our legislative technique.

## *5.1 The Principle of Legal Certainty: Its Necessary Reconstruction*

It seems clear that the main consequence of the absence of rules of legislative technique is the breaking of the principle of legal certainty. Indeed, regulatory proliferation,[83] the antinomies and redundancies of the content of the norms, the lack of minimal regulatory coordination,[84] ineffectiveness, etc., brings not only the lack of legal certainty but even the distrust of citizens in the legislative system.[85]

---

Law-making" adopted by the European Parliament, the Council and the European Commission in December 2003, and the "*Better Law-making to Enhance Growth and Employment in the European Union*", action plan, March 2005, which updates and completes the "*Simplify and improve the regulatory framework*", action plan, 2002. Moreover, in "Guiding Principles for Regulatory Quality and Performance." (2005), it states that normative quality is crucial for the effectiveness of government action, and through Regulatory Impact Analysis, both the need to evaluate, structure and support the adoption of political decisions, and the obligation of the Commission to submit an annual report to the European Council and the European Parliament on the application of the principles of subsidiarity and proportionality, as well as of activities aimed at improving the quality and accessibility of legislation, was implemented in the European Union.

The "*Better Law-making* 2006" report, expressly reflects the objectives of the European Union in this area: "*A regulatory measure which is well-designed, clear, understandable and as simple as possible, is essential for the protection of the well-being of citizens, public health and the environment. At the same time, it guarantees an equitable market, in which European companies can compete effectively and with innovative products. The "Better law-making" program aims to achieve this, both in the EU and at national level, in a concerted effort by the EU institutions and the Member States, and in a way that maximizes the benefits of public policies, while at the same time minimizing the costs that regulations impose on the EU economy*".

Finally, in the 2010 Communication on "Smart Regulation in the EU", in addition to completing and reformulating some of the principles of regulatory quality included in the "Better Law-making" initiative, it adds some principles such as *ex post* evaluation of legislation and the improvement of electronic access to all EU legislation. All the measures adopted by the European Commission dedicated to legislation improvement are easily accessible on the websites Better lawmaking (http://ec.europa.eu/governance/better_regulation/index_es.htm) and Impact Assessment (http://ec.europa.eu/governance/impact/index_en.htm).

[83]For Rubio Llorente (2006), p. 26, "*one of the causes of the current legal uncertainty and of the opacity of our regulations is the degradation, rather than the technique, of the rigor with which the general provisions must be elaborated, a defect that is an almost inevitable sequel to excess production*".

[84]As Oelckers (1998, p. 2.) highlights.

[85]As Pérez Luño (2011) states, "*the marked deficit in the degrees of effectiveness of the rules entails a weakening and distrust of the legislation as a framework for the solution of social conflicts*".

In light of this, the importance, in the first place, of a framework of general legal principles capable of inserting and linking the chaotic aggregate of norms into a fluid and functioning system seems clear, because otherwise, neither the law in general, nor in specific administrative, criminal or any other law, can be understood. We consider it essential to revitalise the principles of proportionality, necessity, efficacy and legal certainty in order to achieve essential legislative regulations, free from superfluous norms, clear and secure, understandable, appropriate to the recipients without impairing accuracy; drafted according to a stable regulatory framework, providing coherence to the legal system from the elaborated and approved norm.

However, of these principles, without doubt the main principle in terms of legislative policy is the principle of legal certainty. This is because it is the principle which serves clarity or certainty of the law, i.e., norms and technical or legal instruments that it contains, so the direction and forms of interpretation and application is known in advance.[86] The TC itself has linked the principle of legal certainty to the prohibition on acting arbitrarily, in the sense that public authorities cannot remain passive in the face of the concurrence of a procedural flaw that affects a rule whose application may favour achieving public interest objectives.[87] Therefore, it is the public authorities producing the legal norms that must observe the essential procedures for their development.

In addition, by virtue of this principle, the content of the norms or their omissions cannot cause confusion or doubt in their recipients which generates a reasonably insurmountable uncertainty about the behaviour required for compliance, or about the predictability of its effects.[88] Therefore, normative clarity in the face of the confusion generated by uncertainty is an indispensable condition for legal certainty. The legislator must ensure that from that clarity and certainty, the meaning of the norm is deduced for all legal operators.

Consequently, the elaboration methods of legal norms within a system are highly conditioned by the principle of legal certainty. This principle must operate not only as a recognised value, but also as a parameter or rule of law at the highest possible level. There can be no uncertainty in this area, since legal certainty, in its most elementary dimension of certainty and predictability, of clarity and precision, constitutes a genuine constitutional mandate directed especially at the bodies authorised for the production of norms.[89]

Indeed, this implies that lack of clarity, certainty, precision and predictability of the norms violates the principle of legal certainty and as a parameter or rule of law it must be appealable before the courts.

---

[86] On the same line, Bermejo Vera (2010), p. 75.

[87] STC 273/2000, of 15th November.

[88] As stated by the TC in its SSTC 150/1990, of 4th October, and 142/1993, of 22nd April.

[89] This is established by Bermejo Vera (2010), p. 86.

## 5.2 Criteria of Normative Rationality

Another consequence of the lack of legislative technique is the production of poor-quality norms that damage not only legal certainty but also legal rationality. Therefore, we must not only reformulate the most basic simple principles and develop them around a legislative theory that provides order and clarity to the legal system, but we must also develop some fundamental criteria or elements to take into account in the process of developing norms and the process of evaluating their results, because only then can we have an effective, efficient and quality legislative technique in our legal system. In our opinion, it is about introducing different doses of normative rationality, there being several criteria that must be present in any specification or delimitation of the legislative technique in Spain.[90] Namely:

(a) Linguistic rationality. If a norm does not have the quality that allows it to be clear and understandable, it can hardly be implemented. The norm must contain clear, precise, simple language, so that the principal recipient of the norms—the citizen—can understand the content of the same. This requires that when the regulation regulates more technical or complex issues, descriptive articles or definitions are introduced. Moreover, we must go further and assess the importance of language, in short, of words, using a common but precise and rigorous lexicon, avoiding ambiguities and redundancies. For this, perhaps the officials or technicians in charge of elaborating the norms should be trained. We must remember that our legislative is no longer, as in other times, composed of specialists.[91]
(b) Logical rationality. The norm should be consistent with current laws and avoid the reiteration or repetition of other norms. It is common to find systematic reiterations of higher norms in the higher rank. We must go to references and referrals, as this will avoid the unnecessary increase of legal norms.
(c) Formal or technical rationality. The procedure established for development and approval must be respected, and, in order to have legal effects, it must be published in the corresponding Official State Gazette. Within the procedure, the report analysing regulatory impact that justifies the need and proportionality of the norm, as well as the economic report that guarantees the budgetary availability to execute it, is essential.
(d) Systematic rationality. The norm must have a logical and systematic order that makes sense of its content. To this end, the Guidelines currently in force establish a basic structure. The norms must have a title, expository part

[90] A few years ago, the authors Atienza (1997), pp. 27–28 and Calsamiglia (1996) suggested providing norms with higher quality norms in the following areas: (1) communicative or linguistic; (2) formal jurisdiction; (3) pragmatic; (4) teleological, and (5) ethical.

[91] As during the time of the Enlightenment, in which the Legislative Assemblies were composed of "*educated and eloquent men who confer among themselves, who discuss the most sublime matters, who dispute with heated interest or offended self-esteem , and in those who do not decide the plurality of votes, but after long examination and great debates…*". Bentham (1981), p. 536.

(preamble or explanatory statement), proposals (structured), final part (transitory and final measures, exceptions etc.) and, where appropriate, annexes. In addition, everything must have a systematic order so that the content of the norm is distributed among the different titles or chapters of the norm with a certain sense of logic.

(e) Teleological rationality. The quality of the norm should not only address formal or technical quality, but also material quality. An *ex post* evaluation of the norm should be carried out to ensure the pursued objectives have been met and that the cost and burdens derived from it were justified and adequately assessed.[92] An approved norm must be evaluated to ensure it meets basic levels of rationality and, therefore, if it reaches acceptable levels of communicability, systematicity, efficacy, effectiveness, axiological adequacy and efficiency, criteria that, correctly applied, allow a distinction to be made between good and bad laws.

Indeed, we believe the content of the norm is as important as its effectiveness. In other words, "*it is not enough just to examine the norms in the abstract, it is also necessary to see them in the light of actual performance*".[93]

The criteria of normative rationality allows the guarantee of the principle of legitimate trust, essential in a legislative theory in order to protect citizens' rights against unpredictable changes in regulation, which include not only the protection of citizens' legitimate expectations, who adapt their economic behaviour to existing legislation against regulatory changes not reasonably foreseeable, as has been established in jurisprudence,[94] but also, more importantly, provide protection against

[92]Concerning the *ex post* evaluation of the norms, we could consider the questions that ATIENZA considers we should ask ourselves. Firstly, the objectives. What are they? Are there any objectives or results not declared (required or not by the "legislator")? Are they justified according to socially dominant values, constitutional principles or those of a particular conception of ethics? But also in relation to matters of a more technical nature: are the contents of the law (the obligations, prohibitions and permissions it contains) as well as the institutions that it considers, appropriate to achieve those objectives?; Are there incentives (positive or negative sanctions) and resources (for example, financial) that can ensure the effectiveness of the law?; Do you leave the law empty or create contradictions or, on the contrary, regulate everything you intend to regulate and do so harmoniously, taking into account all the articles and the rest of the legal system?; In short, is it written in such a way that the message of its rules is reasonably accurate and understood by its recipients—direct and indirect—so that it does not give rise to interpretive problems that could have been avoided?, in "Sobre la nueva Ley de Reproducción Humana Asistida", Curso de Argumentación Jurídica, Universidad de Alicante, 2007.

[93]Nieto (2016), p. 28.

[94]For clarification, we can highlight, for example, the STS of 23rd June 2014, which states that: "The principle that requires the protection of legitimate expectations is neither new nor strange in our jurisprudence. There are several sentences that have given it operability in different areas to protect the administrators that have acted under its coverage. Take the judgments of 23rd November 1984 (law reports 1984/5956), 30th June 2001 (appeal 8016/95), 26th April 2010 (appeal 1887/05), 28th November 2012 (cassation 5300/09) and 22nd January 2013 (cassation 470/11), the two penultimate passes on taxation, adopt the criteria already laid down in the Court of Justice of the European Union, according to which the principle in question is binding on all public authorities: (i) if the belief of the administration which supports it, is based on external signs and not in mere

unnecessary regulations that disrupt the current law, confuse it or make its application more difficult.[95] Only then would the mandate of Art. 3.1. E) of the LRJSP be fulfilled, where it establishes that Public Administrations must respect the principles of good faith and legitimate trust in their actions.

It is true that this principle, despite its expansion and use by jurisprudence for the control of very varied administrative proceedings, has not yet managed to consolidate itself in our jurisprudence. Indeed, in the doctrine of both the Constitutional Court and the Supreme Court, a comparison is seen between legitimate trust and the legitimacy of the regulatory modification, so that if the regulatory change is reasonable and responds to the general interest, there is no violation of legitimate trust. We understand that legislative changes cannot be questioned from the perspective of the legitimate trust principle, because this principle does not absolutely protect regulatory stability, or the immutability of the preceding norms. As established by the STC, of 17th December 2015 "*The principles of legal certainty and their corollary, that of legitimate trust, do not imply the right of economic actors to the permanence of the existing regulation at a given time in a particular sector of activity. Said regulatory stability is compatible with legislative changes, when they are foreseeable and derived from clear requirements of the general interest*". However, this does not prevent being able to assess whether the legislative change is proportional and necessary; if there is another less harmful solution, and if the change, however justified it is, frustrates a legitimate right. This must be the concept of the legitimate trust principle.

The normative rationality test should check each norm development process in its initial phase, by a body created ad hoc in each Public Administration with regulatory competence, since both legislative initiative and regulatory power are attributed to the government (whether state or autonomous, and even locally in the case of local authorities' regulatory power). Thus, when the norm reaches the parliamentary debate phase (in the case of laws), the text of the norm already meets all the linguistic, technical and formal criteria.

In short, it must be remembered that norms must provide areas of certainty for people, to enable proper individual and social development, and, in order to do this, the Law must be re-conceived as a "certainty dispenser", or as one author said "a marble column and bronze table".[96] Only in this way can we truly talk about the art of legislating, that it is nothing other than being able to elaborate a law that is understood by everyone, from the most educated to those without any education whatsoever. As Jovellanos said "*laws must speak precisely and clearly to those*

subjective appreciations or psychological convictions and, (ii) evaluating the interests at stake, the situation of those who have legitimately relied on the Administration is worthy of protection [Judgments of 26th April 1988, Krüechen (316/96); April 1, 1993, Lageder and others (cumulative cases C-31/91 through C-44/91); 5th October 1993, Driessen et al. (joined cases C-13/92 to C-16/92); 17th July, 1997, Affish (C-183/95); 3rd December 1998, Belgocodex (C-381/97); and 11th July 2002, Marks & Spencer (C-62/00)].

[95]Similarly, Muñoz Machado (2016), p. 160.

[96]Martinez Corral (2009), p. 36.

*around the throne and to those hidden in huts; laws must be understood by the one who has devoted their entire life to the search for wisdom, to the one who knows only that they are alive; laws which should be a guide to the traveller in the remotest parts of the earth, and as a light for the farmer in the quiet of his farmhouse.*" these laws that, according to our wise legislator "*must explain things as they are, and the true understanding of them*"; that must contain "*teachings and written punishment so that they bind and encourage a man's life*"; they must speak "in plain and strong words, so all can understand and retain them; they must be inclusive and to the point, because one cannot use the excuse of misuse through misunderstanding, nor show a lie by a truth, nor the truth by a lie...".[97] Although a long time has passed since this fragment was penned, it continues to be of great relevance, as the highest value of the law is that it is the means to govern everyone in complete freedom, and, to this day, this value remains intact.

## References


Álvarez Vélez, M.I., (2017) La potestad legislativa gubernamental: calidad de las normas y evaluación ex ante. *Revista Parlamentaria de la Asamblea* de Madrid 36:39–62

Alonso Timón, A.J., (2016) La participación ciudadana, transparencia y técnica normativa en las Leyes 39 y 40 de 2015. Los principios de buena regulación. *Revista Parlamentaria de la Asamblea de Madrid* 34:77–102

Araguas Galcera, I., (2016) La participación ciudadana en la elaboración de disposiciones generales: estado de la cuestión y perspectivas de futuro tras la aprobación de la Ley 39/2015, de 1 de octubre, de procedimiento administrativo común de las administraciones públicas. *Revista Andaluza de Administración pública* 96:85–126

Atienza, M. (1997) *Contribución a una Teoría de la Legislación.* Cuadernos Civitas, Civitas, Madrid

Baño León, J.M., (2006) Prólogo a la monografía de Doménech Pascual, G.: *Derechos fundamentales y riesgos tecnológicos.* CEPC, Madrid

Bentham, J .,(1981) *Tratados de Legislación Civil y Penal.* Editora Nacional, Madrid

Bermejo Vera, J., (2010) El principio de seguridad jurídica. *Los principios jurídicos del Derecho administrativo,* La Ley:73–109

Bobbio, N., (1993) *El positivismo jurídico* (trad. de Rafael de Asís y Andrea Greppi). Debate, Madrid

Calsamiglia, A., (1996) Ciencia Jurídica. El Derecho y la Justicia. Enciclopedia Iberoamericana de Filosofía 11

Centenera Sánchez-Seco, F., (2012) Los criterios lingüísticos de las directrices de técnica normativa: una propuesta para la solución de enfrentamientos entre principios. *Revista de Llengua i Dret* 58:15–34

Corona Ferrero, J.M., (1994) En torno al concepto de técnica legislativa. In: Corona Ferrero JM, Tudela J, Pau i Vall F (eds) *La técnica legislativa a debate.* Asociación Española de Letrados de Parlamentos. Tecnos, Madrid, pp 49–56

De Jovellanos, G.M., (1858) Discurso leído en su entrada a la Real Academia Española, sobre la necesidad del estudio de la lengua para comprender el espíritu de la legislación. In: Cándido


[97]De Jovellanos (1858), p. 299.

Nocedal (1858) Obras publicadas e inéditas de Don Gaspar Melchor de Jovellanos. Biblioteca de Autores Españoles. M. Rivadebeyra, Madrid, p 46
Fernández Farreres, G., (2016) Las nuevas leyes de Régimen Jurídico del Sector Público y del Procedimiento Administrativo Común: entre la cosmética y el enredo. *Revista Parlamentaria de la Asamblea de Madrid* 34:57–75
Font i Llovet, T. (1995) Función consultiva y Estado autonómico. *Revista de Administración Pública* 138:37–68
Font i Llovet, T., (2009) Los órganos consultivos y la calidad normativa. *Revista Española de la Función Consultiva* 11:133–150
Gamero Casado, E. (2015) *Desafíos del Derecho Administrativo ante un mundo en disrupción*. Granada, Comares
García De Enterría, E., (1963) Reflexiones sobre la Ley y los principios generales del Derecho. *Revista de Administración Pública* 40:189–224
García-Escudero Márquez, P., (2000) La iniciativa legislativa en la Constitución Española de 1978. *Revista Española de Derecho Constitucional* 59:57–91
García-Escudero Márquez, P., (2005) Nociones de técnica legislativa para uso parlamentario. Asamblea. *Revista Parlamentaria de la Asamblea de Madrid* 13:121–164
García-Escudero Márquez, P., (2011) *Manual de Técnica legislativa*. Thomson Reuters-Civitas
Gil Ibánez A.J., Ordóñez Solis, D., (2011) Introducción al sistema de fuentes del Derecho de la Unión europea: Especial referencia a los tipos de actos y su orden jerárquico. In: Beneyto Pérez JM (ed) *Tratado de Derecho y Políticas de la Unión europea*. Thomson Reuters Aranzadi, pp 111–174
Gómez Orfanel, G., (1991) Significado y alcance de la técnica normativa. Técnica normativa de las Comunidades Autónomas Jornadas celebradas por la Comunidad de Madrid en colaboración con el Centro de Estudios Constitucionales 13–18, Madrid, 16–26 April 1990
Huanca Ayaviri, F., (2016) Reflexiones sobre fuentes del derecho en el positivismo jurídico y neoconstitucionalismo. *Revista de Derecho Privado* de la UNAM, 5
Lavilla Rubira, J.J., (2009) El procedimiento de elaboración de los reglamentos en la Ley del Gobierno doce años después. Revista Española de la Función Consultiva 11:17–30
Linde Paniagua, E., (2014) Fundamentos de Derecho Administrativo. Del derecho del poder al derecho de los ciudadanos. Colex, Madrid
Martinez Corral, J.A., (2009) Los errores en la redacción y la publicación de las leyes: formas de corregirlos y su incidencia sobre la entrada en vigor de aquellas. *Revista Española de Función Consultiva* 11:31–76
Millán Moro, L., (2010) El ordenamiento jurídico comunitario: Del Tratado Constitucional al Tratado de Lisboa. *Revista de Derecho Comunitario Europeo* 36:401–438
Montoro Chiner, M.J., (2017) La sociedad requiere normas útiles. El esfuerzo por mejorar la legislación tras la Ley 39/2015, de 1 de octubre, del Procedimiento Administrativo Común de las Administraciones Públicas. ¿Principios, reglas y directrices de técnica legislativa o núcleo esencial del procedimiento de elaboración de normas? *Revista Española de Derecho Administrativo* 182:27–57
Muñoz machado, S., (1986) *Cinco estudios sobre el poder y la técnica de legislar*. Civitas, Madrid
Muñoz machado, S., (2016) Regulación y confianza legítima. *Revista de Administración Pública* 200:141–172
Nieto, A., (2016) El Derecho comunitario europeo como derecho común vulgar. *Revista de Administración Pública* 200:25–44
Oelckers, O., (1998) El contenido esencial de la Técnica Legislativa. Técnica Legislativa ante la elaboración de la Ley. Centro de Estudios y Asistencia Legislativa de la Universidad Católica de Valparaíso
Pérez Luño, A.E., (2011) *El desbordamiento de las fuentes del Derecho*. La Ley, Madrid
Pineda Garfias, R., (2009) Teoría de la Legislación. Algunos planteamientos generales. *Revista de Derechos Fundamentales* 3:137–156

Ponce Solé, J., (2009) ¿Mejores normas?: Directiva 2006/123/CE, relativa a los servicios en el mercado interior, calidad reglamentaria y control judicial. *Revista de Administración Pública* 180:201–243
Prieto Romero, C., (2016) El nuevo procedimiento para la iniciativa legislativa y el ejercicio de la potestad reglamentaria. *Revista de Administración Pública* 201:335–372
Prieto Sanchís, L., (1998) *Del mito a la decadencia de la ley. La ley en el Estado constitucional. Ley, principios, derechos*. Dykinson, España
Prieto Sanchís, L. (2001) *Neoconstitucionalismo y ponderación judicial*. AFDUAM 5:201–228
Requena López, T., (2004) *El principio de jerarquía normativa*. Thomson Civitas, Madrid
Romano, S., (1918) *L'Ordinamento giuridico*. Florencia
Rubio Llorente, F., (2006) El papel del Consejo de Estado en el control de la calidad técnica de las normas. *Revista Española de la Función Consultiva* 6:27–40
Ruiz Sanz, M., (1996) De la ciencia de la legislación hacia la técnica normativa. *Anuario de Filosofía del Derecho* 13:637–650
Sainz Moreno, F., (1995) *Técnica normativa*. Enciclopedia Jurídica, Civitas, Madrid
Santamaría Pastor, J.A., (2001) Articulo 88. Comentarios a la Constitución, dirigidos por F. Garrido Falla. Civitas, Madrid
Schmitt, C., (1998) *Legalität und Legitimität*. Duncker & Humblot, Berlin
Sebastían Lorente, J.J., (1992) La información y documentación administrativas de los proyectos normativos. *Actualidad Administrativa* 24:255–266
Segovia Marco, A., (2015) La técnica legislativa en la elaboración de los anteproyectos de leyes. *Revista Gabilex* 1:5–44
Tur Ausina, R., (2009) Técnica normativa, formas de gobierno y sistemas jurídicos. *Revista Española de la Función Consultiva* 11:103–132

# Sword or Shield? The Influence of International Organisations in Counterterrorism Law and Policy Making

Claire Hamilton

**Abstract** The protections afforded citizens in human rights treaties drafted by international organisations such as the United Nations may frequently be seen as a way of protecting unpopular minorities such as offenders or prisoners from the 'tyranny of the majority'. Yet, criminal justice policies promulgated by these same bodies can often cut, swordlike, deep into citizens' freedoms. This tension—between drives towards human rights, on the one hand, and towards criminalisation and punitive measures on the other—is particularly acute in the field of counterterrorism, where bodies such as the UN Security Council have been active since the events of 9/11. Taking the field of counterterrorism as an exemplar, it is the aim of this paper to explore the tension between the 'shield' and 'sword' functions of international organisations, drawing on two case studies. The first concerns the United Nations where the security of the state has secured a major advantage over the ethic of human rights, within rather than in conflict with the UN framework of international oversight. The second examines the European Union, where the enactment of a significant body of counterterrorism legislation since 9/11 has driven radical and permanent change in at least some areas of mainstream criminal law and procedure, with significant implications for human rights.

## 1 Introduction: Twenty-First Century Challenges: Globalisation, Counterterrorism and Criminology

One of the biggest contemporary challenges to the field of criminal law making, as in other policy arenas, is perhaps the challenge which is increasingly presented to the authority of the state itself. Within criminology, much has been written about the

C. Hamilton (✉)
Department of Law, Maynooth University, Maynooth, Ireland
e-mail: claire.hamilton@mu.ie

 
J. Becerra (ed.), *Criminal Law-Making*, Legisprudence Library 7,
https://doi.org/10.1007/978-3-030-71348-5_3

'hollowing out' of the state as a result of globalising (and localising) forces, mirroring developments in the field of capital and business (for an overview, see: Coleman and Sim 2005; Loader and Sparks 2007). While the challenges are many and varied, incorporating international courts, multinational private security enterprises, cross-border policing, policy networks, and flows and technologies of global surveillance, this paper chooses to focus on the challenges to national sovereignty posed by international organisations. United Nations (UN) agencies such as the United Nations Office of Drug Control and European agencies such as EUROPOL, circulate reports and make policy recommendations to governments and international civil society, constituting core components of the global justice policy discourse. Equally, however, other agencies affiliated with these same international organisations (UN and the European Union) promulgate and enforce human rights standards with important implications for a range of domestic criminal justice issues. Alongside the 'push' towards criminalisation and punishment of 'global crimes' such as terrorism, organised crime and various forms of trafficking, we may therefore identify the 'pull' of human rights compliance following ratification of human rights treaties. As Muncie (2005) has observed in the youth justice field, global processes of convergence may not be as one-dimensional as they may first appear, accommodating both punitive (neoliberal) and more 'progressive' impulses towards normative convergence (e.g. the UN Convention on the Rights of the Child). One area where this tension is particularly acute is the field of counterterrorism where various policy flows have led to the post 9/11 convergence of antiterrorist policies worldwide, arguably at the expense of respect for fundamental human rights standards (Human Rights Watch 2017). While these trends have been the subject of penetrating analysis from legal scholars (see, for example, Roach 2015), they have been relatively neglected by criminologists to date (Banks and Baker 2016, p. 10), reflecting perhaps a disciplinary tendency towards domestic crime or crimes of the 'inside' (Loader and Percy 2012). It is the consequent aim of this article to examine the capacity of international organisations to construct dominant narratives in the counterterrorism sphere that can marginalise alternative discourses for nation states and indeed promote policies that are in conflict with the human rights standards they themselves espouse. In exploring these tensions and their criminological implications the article draws on the 'sword vs. shield' dichotomy advanced by Dumortier et al. (2012) in their discussion of human rights in Europe. In that analysis European institutions such as the European Court of Human Rights were scrutinised for the restraint they exerted over the rise of the 'penal state' in Europe and, contrariwise, their role 'as a machine that encourages penal inflation' (De Hert and Gutwirth 2005, p. 752). In the instant case, counterterrorism measures adopted in the post 9/11 period are examined for the lessons they hold about the role of international organisations as a 'shield' against punitiveness or indeed their ability to cut, sword-like, deep into citizens' freedoms (Hamilton 2017).

The analysis proceeds by drawing on two case studies. The first concerns the United Nations where the security of the state has secured a major advantage over the ethic of human rights, within rather than in conflict with the UN framework of international oversight (Gearty 2017). The second examines the European Union, where the enactment of a significant body of counterterrorism legislation since 9/11 has driven radical and permanent change in at least some areas of mainstream criminal law and procedure, with significant implications for human rights (Hamilton 2017). It is important to note at the outset that the discussion is not intended as a comparison between these two bodies, one a supranational organisation and another an international body existing to promote cooperation between autonomous states, but rather an exploration of the global Realpolitik which has all too often subordinated human rights to the perceived imperative of security.

## 2 United Nations

### *2.1 Human Rights*

While human rights law represents only a small proportion of the international treaties negotiated through UN processes, we should not forget that human rights remain significant today largely because they have been translated into a body of international law underpinned by UN institutions (Weber et al. 2014). Moreover, moves such as the creation of the Office of the High Commissioner for Human Rights (OHCHR) in 1993 and the establishment of the International Criminal Court in 2002, have been significant in raising the profile of human rights within the UN. The wide range of human rights issues in respect of which UN treaties are now seized should also be acknowledged. Beyond the foundational treaties such as the International Covenant on Economic, Social and Cultural Rights (ICESCR) and the Internation Covenant on Civil and Political Rights (ICCPR), (which entered into force in 1976), literally hundreds of treaties and declarations have been agreed on topics ranging from racial discrimination to the prevention of torture, women's rights, children's rights, minority rights and, most recently, indigenous rights.

Against this picture of steady progress we may place the more cynical view that the ratification of UN treaties is largely 'symbolic' and most states have no intention of complying with their provisions. Certainly, it barely needs stating that the intricate web of monitoring systems that has been constructed around major treaties does not translate seamlessly into human rights compliance. Problems with enforceability of rights and the deference shown to Member State sovereignty, has meant that the effectiveness of international human rights varies considerably depending on the level of commitment and determination shown by individual governments (Lepard 2012). In similar vein, Haas's (2008) research has found positive effects on human rights compliance following the ratification of human rights treaties, but with significant variation according to mode of governance (democratic or autocratic nature, stability of the regime, etc). Indeed, a contemporary example of local agendas dominating the international one is the proposed bill in Brazil to raise the maximum time of internment for children from 3 to 10 years which, together with a constitutional amendment to allow 16 and 17 year olds accused of serious crimes to be tried and punished as adults, constitutes a clear violation of international norms (Human Rights Watch 2018).

## 2.2 Security

To these longstanding concerns about enforcement we may now add claims by governments to limit human rights in the interests of state security or combatting terrorism. The tragic events of 9/11 form an important watershed in this regard, spurring not only domestic governments into action, but also marking a major shift in the capacity of international organisations such as the UN Security Council to both make and enforce the laws for the international community (Lazarus and Goold 2007). Indeed, Gearty (2017) identifies 9/11 as a serious 'hammer blow' to the fate of human rights in the contemporary era, one which tipped the UN balance away from human rights and towards security, and, further one which, together with the economic crisis of 2008, exposed systemic faults in the architecture of the post-war global order.

On 28 September 2001, with hardly any recorded debate, the Security Council passed Resolution 1373, which required all states to ensure that terrorism and terrorism financing were treated as serious crimes without offering any guidance on how to define terrorism. One of the most controversial of these measures included travel bans and the freezing of an individual's assets based on executive listing of known terrorists. Subsequent measures have included Resolution 1624 which 'calls on' states to criminalise the incitement to terrorism and, most recently, Resolution 2178 which requires all states to ensure that travel to plan, prepare, provide or receive terrorist training, or participate in or perpetuate terrorist acts be treated as serious criminal offences. These actions have been accompanied by a bureaucracy in the form of a Counter-Terrorism Committee (CTC) which, in addition to monitoring and evaluating compliance with the range of obligations set out in counterterrorism resolutions, provides a list of best practices and models for domestic anti-terrorism legislation (Powell 2007).

The critiques that have come hot on the heels of these measures can be classed as both substantive and procedural. In a substantive sense, the practice of 'blacklisting' on the basis of names suggested to the UN Sanctions Committee by Member States can be criticised for the absence of any intervening judicial process that could check either whether a suspected terrorist really is the person they are believed to be (Sheppele 2011). Given that the person concerned will not be able to work, travel, drive or support their families, (Statewatch have described it as a 'financial Guantanamo' (Hayes 2008)), this is clearly a retreat from the procedural guarantees that ensure constitutionalist norms apply to the limitation of rights. Indeed, there is little doubt that the anti-terrorism programme pursued by the Security Council threatens a range of internationally recognised human rights such as the right to property and the right to due process (Powell 2007). The absence of a definition of terrorism is another point of contention given that it falls to Member States to define it by default. The clear latitude this affords states to criminalise those who simply dissent from authoritarian regimes or to carry out their own oppressive security programme under the cover of what Gearty (2017) describes as 'western-pleasing counterterrorism clothes' is obvious (Roach 2015). Despite these concerns, the most recent Resolution (2178), passed in response to the challenges of foreign terrorist fighters, confirms the Security Council's commitment to the practice of listing and travel and financing bans as a means to combat terror. The resolution places travel with intent to join a terrorist group on the same plane as terrorism financing, namely, as a global threat requiring strong national laws and robust international cooperation. Moreover, it compounds the problems discussed above in relation to the definition of terrorism in two ways. First, by linking it to 'violent extremism' and 'radicalization' and second, by imposing new legal obligations against terrorism 'in all forms and manifestations'—not just *international* terrorism or specific forms of it (Scheinin 2014; Roach 2015).

Procedural criticism of Security Council action in this field is equally concerning, if not more so, given suggestions that the actions of the Security Council were in fact anti-constitutional or *ultra vires*. For various commentators, Resolution 1373 marked an important break with previous practice given that it involved the Security Council arrogating to itself the power to legislate (Szasz 2002; Powell 2007; Sheppele 2011; Scheinin 2014). While the Security Council had used its mandatory Chapter VII powers in the past against specific states or entities to force compliance with international law, Resolution 1373 constituted a mandatory order with no time limit aimed at an undefined threat, namely, global terrorism. As argued by commentators such as Szasz (2002) this constitutes a far-reaching and essentially legislative resolution that, for the first time in the Security Council's history, used binding authority under Chapter VII of the UN Charter to establish new rules of international law.

In terms of impact, virtually all member states of the United Nations have changed their laws since 9/11 to comply with Resolution 1373 and subsequent Security Council edicts. Perhaps concerningly, the Security Council's legislative acts in this area, unlike its executive and administrative decisions, have largely met with Member State acquiescence or approval (Talmon 2005). In this regard, Sheppele (2011) observes striking similarities across counterterrorism laws in North America, China, India, Argentina and Europe:

> [V]irtually all of the laws criminalize terrorism, ease restrictions on surveillance on domestic publics, increase monitoring of financial transactions, beef up the security services, make it easier to monitor and prosecute those who may be associated, however loosely, with suspicious persons and groups, and use immigration law to crack down on non-citizens. Given that this is what Resolution 1373 ordered states to do, the similarities are not coincidental.

Human Rights Watch (2018) similarly observes that the need to comply with the most recent Resolution on foreign terrorist fighters (2178) has resulted in at least 47 countries passing foreign terrorist fighter laws since 2013—the largest wave of counterterrorism measures since the immediate aftermath of the Twin Tower attacks.

The push to criminalise terrorism and associated activities relating to financing and travel has probably had the greatest impact in countries with no history of terrorism. Brazil is an interesting example of one such country where violent urban criminality, rather than terrorism, forms the main focus of public concern about crime (de Souza Costa 2015). Given this focus, and the existence of very real social concerns about the use of terrorist laws against protestors and freedom fighters, for many years the substantive criminal law lacked a specific definition of the crime of terrorism (despite specific reference to terrorism in the Brazilian Constitution). Previous attempts by the government to establish terrorism as a separate crime had failed in the face of strong opposition from organised civil society (Oliveira de Sousa 2014). In the end, it was pressure imposed by a US-led anti-terrorism body known as the Financial Action Task Force (FATF) that forced the government's hand on this issue. In 2010 FATF drafted a report urging the Brazilian government to create a counterterrorism criminal law framework in anticipation of the 2016 Olympics in Rio. That report, in turn, based its recommendations on the need for Brazil to honour its international commitments including implementation of Security Council Resolutions (1267 and 1373). From the instant perspective, the role of FATF in 'enforcing' compliance with these resolutions is particularly interesting given its power to impose economic sanctions on governments that do not comply with its directives. Leading up to the congressional vote in 2016, government minister Ricardo Berzoini issued a strong appeal to law makers, warning them that if Brazil did not approve the measure it would face sanctions from the FATF for failing to comply with its recommendations (Telesur 2016). In the event, the counterterrorism bill passed (Law No. 13.260 of 2016) incorporates a sweeping definition of terrorism as behaviour which 'infringes upon persons, through violence or serious threat, and is motivated by political extremism, religious intolerance or racial, ethnic, gender or xenophobic prejudice, in order to cause widespread panic', sparking fears that it could criminalise acts of social protest. Prior to the March 2016 law, Brazil also enacted legislation to combat the threat from terrorist financing. In October 2015, Brazilian President Dilma Rousseff signed Law No. 13.170, allowing Brazil to meet international standards for the practice of countering terrorist financing, including by freezing assets related to UN Security Council Resolutions.

The Brazilian example discussed above in many ways epitomizes the tensions which exist between UN human rights bodies, on the one hand, and UN Security Council moves to criminalise conduct related to terrorism on the other. Thus, the 2016 counterterrorism bill was criticised by Amerigo Incalcaterra, the OHCHR Representative in South America, for its vaguely worded definition of terrorism which in his view was probably incompatible with international human rights standards (Telesur 2016). In an attempt to square this circle, the Security Council has increasingly incorporated in its Resolutions so-called 'human rights clauses', with both Security Council Resolution 1822 (2008) and General Assembly resolution 62/272 recognising United Nations action to counter terrorism must fully comply with international law, including human rights law. While the creation of a Special Rapporteur on the promotion and protection of human rights and fundamental freedoms while countering terrorism in 2005 marks an important step in this regard, significant difficulties remain with the translation of these human rights commitments into the practice of the Counter-Terrorism Committee, and it is no coincidence that the new Special Rapporteur, Fionnuala Ní Aoláin, has identified as one of her priorities the need for greater clarity in the legal relationship between human rights and international security regimes regulating terrorism (UN 2010; Ní Aoláin 2017).

The recent Resolution (2178) on foreign terrorist fighters does not give much cause for optimism in this regard with the first UN Special Rapporteur on human rights and counterterrorism, Martin Scheinin (2014), describing it as 'panic' legislation which 'wipes out the piecemeal progress made over 13 long years in introducing protections of human rights and the rule of law into the highly problematic manner in which the Security Council exercises its supranational powers.' As with Resolution 1373 (2001) the Resolution contains no reference to human rights and there is a noticeable failure to maintain and further develop the idea first adopted in 2008 in SCR 1822 that the UN itself must comply with human rights when combatting terrorism. In respect of at least this most recent manifestation of UN Security Council law-making, it is difficult to disagree with Gearty's (2017) portrayal of human rights defenders as 'supplicants', knocking on the door of a global counterterrorist bureaucracy that is largely indifferent to human rights. As the same author contends, it is precisely in this fashion that 9/11 and the subsequent attacks have afforded the security of the state a major advantage over the ethic of human rights, within rather than in conflict with the UN framework of international oversight (ibid).

## 3 European Union

### *3.1 Human Rights*

Much has been written recently on the significance of European values and human rights standards in the field of punishment, particularly the opportunities they provide for 'resistance' to American-style punitive policies (Snacken and Dumortier 2012). Snacken (2010), for example, has pointed to policies such as the rejection of the death penalty, the steady evolution of the European Court of Human Rights (ECtHR) case law on prison conditions, and the limits placed by the Court on states' ability to criminalise certain behaviours in support of her argument that 'penal moderation is in accordance with some of those fundamental values cherished by many Europeans' (ibid, p. 287). Taking up the mantle, Daems (2013) makes the case for a 'European Penology', while emphasising the common values that unite Europeans such as a liberal and cosmopolitan tradition. In the same volume Snacken and van Zyl Smit (2013) argue that an understanding of European penology is better reached by focussing on the specific European institutional context, namely, the Council of Europe but also the European Union (EU), an actor which since the creation of the area for Security, Freedom and Justice (ASFJ) in 1999 has become increasingly active in the penal field. Here too we are witnessing a deepening commitment to human rights in its activities, with the role of human rights now formally reflected in the form of the European Charter on Fundamental Rights, now in force and legally binding on Member States when implementing EU law.

## *3.2 Security*

Despite these strong human rights credentials, the 9/11 attacks had important ramifications for criminal justice law making in the European Union, marking a significant break with previous practice. Partly, this was due to timing: the 9/11 terrorism emergency occurred precisely at the moment when the EU was beginning to assert itself in the criminal justice field (the EU had created an 'area of security, justice and freedom' in 1999.) resulting in counterterrorism becoming the focal point for the development of the EU's role in this area (Murphy 2011). The sheer volume of counterterrorism measures adopted by the EU bears testament to this with a recent report by SECILE identifying 239 such measures for the period 2001–2013 (SECILE 2013). While implementation of some of these measures has been patchy (den Boer 2006; European Commission 2007), many of the most significant (and controversial) instruments in terms of their impact on domestic criminal justice, for example, the European Arrest Warrant[1] have now been successfully transposed and implemented by Member States (Coolaset 2016; European Commission 2014).

Following the attacks the European Council hastily arranged an extraordinary (emergency) meeting of the *chefs de cabinet* in Brussels on 20th-21st September. The meeting sought to address perceived deficiencies in EU action in this area, namely, the lack of a common legal definition of terrorism, the absence of a harmonised system of penalties and a basis for accelerated extradition, and set itself the deadline of December 2001 to reach agreement on several legal acts (Monar 2005). While the European Commission had been working on proposals in these areas for many months it is difficult to overstate the transformative effect of the 9/11 attacks in this area: as den Boer (2006, p. 90) has written, 'All of a sudden decisions were possible on dormant dossiers'. By 27th December 2001, the EU had constructed the two main pillars of its counterterrorism strategy: a common definition of terrorism (the first such definition by an international body)[2] and a Framework Decision overhauling the law on extradition between Member States.[3]

As the trigger for a wide range of coercive powers (Amnesty International 2005; Murphy 2012a) the definition of terrorism is obviously critical, however, in an EU

[1]Council of the European Union (2002) Council Framework Decision of 13 June 2002 on the European Arrest Warrant and the Surrender Procedures between Member States. 2002/584/JHA.

[2]Council of the European Union (2002) Council Framework Decision of 13 June 2002 on Combating Terrorism. 2002/475/JHA.

[3]Council of the European Union (2002/584/JHA).

context this issue assumed particular importance as so few Member States had any specific legislation criminalising terrorism prior to the adoption of the Framework Decision in 2002 (Argomaniz 2009; Amnesty International 2005). Indeed, the number of Member States with legislation which criminalised terrorist acts autonomously went from six prior to 9/11 to 22 by 2007 (Chaves 2015). Roach (2013, p. 29) describes this as 'an explosive growth' or 'viral propagation of anti-terrorism laws in Europe' whose impact should not be underestimated.

In terms of reforms at Member State level, the definition of terrorist offences inevitably led to the adoption of new criminal offences in those states without anti-terrorism legislation (Chaves 2015). Legislation was also required in those states which already had counterterrorism legislation in place given that they all had definitions of terrorism that were narrower than the EU's (ibid). In the 2002 Framework Decision on Combating Terrorism (FDCT)[4] these new offences took the form of directing, creating, supporting or participating in a terrorist group and this was extended in 2008 to include offences of public provocation to commit a terrorist offence, recruitment, and training for terrorism (including via the internet). These offences have been criticised for the threat they pose to fundamental legal principles as well as the preventative or pre-emptive direction in which they take the criminal law (Murphy 2012a). Indeed, such was the concern of the European Parliament about the 2008 amendments that it sought to introduce human rights safeguards into the legislation, amendments which were rejected by the Council, save for a declaratory (and arguably superfluous) statement regarding the general requirement to respect fundamental rights (European Parliament 2008). It is worth noting that all of these offences are subject to enhanced sentencing as the Decision also provided for minimum maximum sentences (15 years for directing and eight for participatory or preparatory acts). This is the case even if group offences are not applicable to an individual given the requirement for Member States to enact 'effective, proportionate and dissuasive' criminal penalties for all offences linked to terrorism (Murphy 2012a).

In Europe, moreover, the problems associated with these associative and preparatory offences are compounded by the EU definition of terrorism itself. This definition is also expansive, defining terrorist acts as those committed with the aim of: 'seriously intimidating a population, or unduly compelling a Government or international organisation to perform or abstain from performing any act, or seriously destabilising or destroying the fundamental political, constitutional, economic or social structures of a country or an international organisation' (Article 1(1)). The list of offences goes beyond violence to include serious property damage 'likely to result in major economic loss' (Article 1(1)(d)), a move which has been criticised, particularly when interpreted in the context of the broadly drafted 'unduly compelling' a government (Douglas-Scott 2004). While drafted more tightly than the UK provisions, it does appear broader than the definitions adopted by most of the UN

[4]Council of the European Union (2002/475/JHA).

conventions on terrorism and indeed the US Patriot Act (Zedner 2013; Roach 2011, 2013).

The European Arrest Warrant (EAW)—'the jewel in the crown of the EU's response to the terrorist attacks' (Douglas-Scott 2004, p. 223)—probably represents one of the most prominent, yet possibly also the most controversial, of the EU counterterrorism measures (Van Sliedregt 2010). While proposals for the EAW predated the events of 9/11, negotiations between Member States on this sensitive area were so protracted that it really only became 'politically palatable' (Murphy 2012b, np) in the period after the attacks. Indeed, while the proposal had already been under preparation by officials for a period of 2 years, national views on the most basic features of the instrument were 'very, very far apart' (Kaunert 2007, p. 396) until the events of 9/11. The measure, adopted in a Framework Decision of 13 June 2002, revolutionised laws relating to extradition in the EU, effectively transforming what was once a detailed judicial procedure with strict legal requirements such as the dual criminality rule into an administrative 'box ticking exercise' (MacGuill 2012). The procedure is now a summary one whereby the merits of the request are taken on trust and the receiving Member State is obliged to execute an EAW unless one of the very limited grounds of objection is applicable. The considerable efficiencies gained by the measure (particularly the reduction in delays) have been noted by the European Commission (2011), something which, given that justice delayed is often justice denied, may well work in ease of requested persons. Yet the benefits in terms of expeditious hearings must also be considered against strong concerns voiced about disproportionality, violations of procedural rights, poor detention conditions and the imprisonment of innocent persons (Hammarberg 2011; European Parliament 2014). While space constraints do not permit a full examination of the concerns voiced, two observations relevant to the current argument can be made. First, as with the FDCT discussed above, it is surprising given the ostensible respect for human rights principles proclaimed in various EU legal instruments that the prospect of serious breaches of human rights was not expressly stated as a ground on which extradition could be refused, an omission which has led to highly variable protection of rights across Member States (Magyar 2012; Anagnostopoulos 2014). Another significant concern is with net-widening or 'function creep' (Argomaniz et al. 2015) which was evident from the legislation's inception: while it was presented to Member States and to the public as a key counterterrorist measure it included within its scope a long list of (32) offences, many of which, such as road traffic offences, are not even offences of specific intent. Unsurprisingly, this has resulted in the majority of requests being issued for ordinary rather than terrorist offences as well as the systematic use of the EAW procedure for minor offences (European Parliament 2014). This is unfortunate given the severely damaging effect which the disproportionate use of the EAW can have on individuals sought by requesting states; not only may they may be taken away from their homes, families and employment for a lengthy period, perhaps for years, but they will in all likelihood be denied bail by virtue of very fact of being a resident of another country (Fennelly 2007).

It should not be forgotten that the EU has also played a role in the implementation of UN Security Council Resolutions. EC Regulation 2580/2001 implemented UNSC Resolution 1373 (2001) and also instituted the EU's own autonomous counterterrorist restrictive measures regime (Cameron 2003; Hoffmann 2008). Initially, the EU adopted a highly secretive and legally complex approach to the blacklisting process which, alarmingly, appeared to preclude judicial review (Amnesty International 2005). This approach, described by Murphy (2012a) as 'counter-law' or 'law against law', was subsequently amended in response to a series of judgments from the European Court of Justice, requiring procedural amendments to ensure both access to effective judicial review and the provisions of reasons for a suspect's initial listing (Guild 2008; Lang 2011). The most recent Directive from the EU has also incorporated the measures contained in Resolution 2178 above in relation to foreign terrorist fighters, with largely negative consequences for human rights standards in European countries (Council of the European Union 2017). In January 2017, for example, Amnesty International, in a report focusing on Europe, expressed its concern that counterterrorism measures adopted in the aftermath of UNSC Resolution 2178 'have been steadily dismantling [the European human rights system], putting hard won rights at risk' (Amnesty International 2017, p. 7), citing concerns about abuse of the definition of terrorism, the use of secret evidence and the criminalisation of various forms of expression.

## 4 Conclusion: Rights, Criminology and the Siren Call of Security

As observed by Roach (2015, p. 2) it is impossible to understand counterterrorism law without understanding the demands supranational laws and institutions place on states. These demands have clearly intensified since the tragic events of 9/11, which not only served to underline the urgency of effective cooperation in this field, but have perhaps also presented a 'window of opportunity' for regional and international bodies to assert their authority in the justice field (EU) and/or expand their law-making powers (UN). As illustrated by the discussion above, these laws and policies have largely had negative implications for fundamental human rights with strong drives towards pre-emptive action (blacklisting) and the proliferation of pre-cursor crimes (e.g. financing, travel, support). Rather than a 'shield' against the expansion of the penal state, therefore, this legislation better fits with the concept of supranational and international bodies as a 'sword' (Dumortier et al. 2012), advancing the reach of the criminal law, particularly for those protestors and opposition groups who may be caught up in the ambiguities of the broad definition of terrorism.

The above observations raise two important points with relevance to criminology. The first concerns accountability and law-making in the international sphere. If Powell (2007) is correct in her contention that a 'culture of authority' has replaced the 'culture of justification' more commonly associated with international human rights law, the question may be posed as to how appropriate limits may be placed on actions taken by executive bodies such as the UN Security Council. In a European context institutional dynamics will assume a new relevance with the entry into force of the Lisbon Treaty and the now increased capacity of the Parliament in decision-making in sensitive areas such as counterterrorism (Servent 2010). In this new context there may well be greater opportunities for the European Parliament to 'de-securitise', particularly given its previous criticisms of legislative overreaching in the 2008 Framework Decision and its recent report calling for EAW reform (European Parliament 2014). Questions regarding legitimacy and accountability apply with even more force to the more indirect means of enforcing UN Security Council Resolutions adopted by intergovernmental institutions such as the Financial Action Task Force. The strong pressure applied by this body to countries such as Brazil to enact counterterrorism laws points up the complexity of the governance field in this area and the difficulty in rendering all of the institutional actors involved democratically transparent and legitimate. This is all the more so when there is little public or media scrutiny of their activities. As Bowling and Sheptycki (2012, p. 1) have remarked in their recent study of international policing bodies more broadly, discussions around these global shifts in governance have largely taken place in 'behind the closed doors of international bureaucracies'.

The second point concerns the prioritisation of security concerns over core human rights values in the decade or so since the attacks of 9/11. While both the EU and the UN may strongly endorse human rights values and standards in their respective charters and recommendations, these are less in evidence in the counterterrorism sphere. The failure of the European Council to include formal safeguards protecting fundamental rights in the 2008 amendments to the Framework Decision on Counter-terrorism, even in the face of objections from the European Parliament (2008), is a case in point. Similarly revealing is the absence of any reference to human rights in the Framework Document on the EAW and the recent Security Council Resolution (2178) on foreign terrorist fighters. With human rights emissaries such as the Special Rapporteur on counterterrorism and human rights perenially part of the rearguard action in the security field, progress is delayed, incremental and, oftentimes, overtaken by events (witness Martin Scheinin's (2014) disappointment at Resolution 2178).

The failure of human rights to act as an effective bulwark against excessive securitisation recalls earlier work by Zedner (2007) and others (Krasmann 2012) regarding the limits of the human rights idiom as a means of resisting the siren call of 'security' and the emerging paradigm of preventive justice. One of the most substantial of these criticisms is the concern that the discourse on human rights 'presupposes what has yet to arise, namely a common concern about governmental encroachment in the name of security and a willingness of all parties to join in that discourse' (Krasmann 2012, pp. 381–382). On the above analysis this appears highly plausible, even in relation to international organisations from which the international protection of human rights originated and which still advance their protection as one of their fundamental goals. From a criminological perspective, one potential way forward from the seemingly intractable problem of securitisation and its relation to human rights regimes is perhaps to acknowledge a role for critically oriented criminological inquiries such as governmental criminology in the analysis of *how* both sovereign and supranational powers work against recognition of rights and human rights violations. As Lippert (2016) argues, an examination of human rights from within criminology may provide more detail on the subjectivities driving these developments and therefore identify potential sites for progressive intervention. While 'more agnostic than normative' (Lippert 2016, p. 88) in relation to human rights, the unique province of criminology is its ability to reconcile policies aimed at twenty-first-century 'super-terrorism' (Lazarus and Goold 2007) with the pursuit of security of a more anodyne kind. Indeed, it is perhaps in this more sociologically informed analysis that the beginnings of a process of social contestation of securitisation and its associated effects may be found (Hamilton and Berlusconi 2018).

## References

Amnesty International (2005) Human rights dissolving at the borders? Counter terrorism and EU criminal law. Amnesty International EU Office, Brussels

Amnesty International (2017) Dangerously disproportionate: the ever-expanding national security state in Europe, London.

Anagnostopoulos I (2014) Criminal justice cooperation in the European Union after the first few 'steps': a defence view. ERA Forum 15(1):9–24

Argomaniz J (2009) Post-9/11 institutionalisation of European counter-terrorism: emergence, acceleration and inertia. Eur Secur 18(2):151–172

Argomaniz J, Bures O, Kaunert C (2015) A decade of EU counter-terrorism and intelligence: A critical assessment. Intell Natl Secur 30(2–3):191–206

Banks C, Baker J (2016) Comparative, international and global justice. Sage, California

Bowling B, Sheptycki J (2012) Global policing. Sage, London

Cameron I (2003) European Union anti-terrorist blacklisting. Human Rights Law Rev 3:225–256

Chaves M (2015) EU's harmonization of national criminal law: between punitiveness and moderation. Eur Public Law 21(3):527–553

Coleman R, Sim J (2005) State. In: McLaughlin E, Muncie J (eds) Sage dictionary of criminology. Sage, London

Coolaset R (2016) Counterterrorism and counter-radicalisation in Europe. In: Coolaset R (ed) Jihadi terrorism and the radicalisation challenge: European and American experiences. Routledge, London

Council of the European Union (2017) Directive (EU) 2017/541 of the European parliament and of the council of 15 March 2017 on combating terrorism and replacing council framework decision 2002/475/JHA and amending council decision 2005/671/JHA

Daems T (2013) Punishment and the question of Europe. In: Daems T, van Zyyl SD, Snacken S (eds) European penology? Hart Publishing, Oxford

De Hert P, Gutwirth S (2005) Grondrechten: vrijplaatsen voor het strafrecht? Dworkins Amerikaanse trumpmetafoor getoetst aan de hedendaagse Europese mensenrechten. In: Haveman RH, Wiersinga HC (eds) Langs de randen van het strafrecht. Wolf Legal Publishers, Nijmegen, pp 141–175

De Souza Costa R (2015) Brazil. In: Roach K (ed) Comparative counter-terrorism law. Cambridge University Press, Cambridge

Douglas-Scott S (2004) The rule of law in the European Union: putting the security into the area of freedom, security and justice. Eur Law Rev 29(2):219–242

Dumortier E, Gutwirth S, Snacken S et al (2012) The rise of the penal state: what can human rights do about it? In: Snacken S, Dumortier E (eds) Resisting Punitiveness in Europe? Routledge, Abingdon, Oxon, New York

European Commission (2007) Report from the Commission based on Article 11 of the Council Framework Decision on combatting terrorism of 13 June 2002. COM (2007) 681

European Commission (2011) Report from the Commission to the European Parliament and the Council On the implementation since 2007 of the Council Framework Decision of 13 June 2002 on the European arrest warrant and the surrender procedures between Member States. COM/2011/0175

European Commission (2014) Report from the Commission to the European Parliament and the Council on the implementation of Council Framework Decision 2008/919/JHA of 28 November 2008 amending Framework Decision 2002/475/JHA on combating terrorism. COM/2014/0554

European Parliament (2008) Report on the proposal for a Council Framework Decision amending Framework Decision 2002/475/JHA on combating terrorism (COM(2007)0650)

European Parliament (2014) Resolution of 27 February 2014 with recommendations to the Commission on the review of the European Arrest Warrant. A7-0039/2014

Fennelly N (2007) European Arrest Warrant: Recent Developments. Address to the Academy of European Law Conference. EU Courts in the Area of Freedom and Justice: Recent Developments, Trier 14–15 June 2007

Gearty C (2017) Is the human rights era drawing to a close? Eur Human Rights Law Rev 5:425–431

Guild E (2008) The uses and abuses of counter-terrorism policies in Europe: the case of the “terrorist lists”. J Common Mark Stud 46:173–193

Haas M (2008) International human rights: a comprehensive introduction. Routledge, Abingdon

Hamilton C (2017) The European Union: sword or shield? Comparing counterterrorism law in the EU and USA after 9/11. Theor Criminol. https://doi.org/10.1177/1362480616684195

Hamilton C, Berlusconi G (2018) Counterterrorism, contagion and criminology: the case of France. Criminol Crim Just. https://doi.org/10.1177/1748895817751829

Hammarberg T (2011) Overuse of the European Arrest Warrant - a threat to human rights. The Council of Europe Commissioner’s Human Rights Comment. http://commissioner.cws.coe.int/tiki-view_blog_post.php?postId=124

Hayes B (2008) Britain’s Financial Guantanamo. http://www.europe-solidaire.org/spip.php?article10041

Hoffmann J (2008) Terrorism blacklisting: putting European human rights guarantees to the test. Constellations 15:543–560

Human Rights Watch (2018) Overreach: how new global counterterrorism measures jeopardize rights. World Report 2017. https://www.hrw.org/world-report/2017/country-chapters/global. Accessed 10 April 2017

Kaunert K (2007) Without the power of purse or sword: the European arrest warrant and the role of the commission. J Eur Integr 29(4):387–404

Krasmann S (2012) Law’s knowledge: on the susceptibility and resistance of legal practices to security matters. Theor Criminol 16(4):379–394

Lang J (2011) EU counter-terrorism: security, justice, democracy and opportunity for all? http://www.e-ir.info/2011/08/14/eu-counter-terrorism-security-justice-democracy-and-opportunity-for-all/

Lazarus L, Goold BJ (2007) Security and human rights: the search for a language of reconciliation. In: Goold BJ, Lazarus L (eds) Security and human rights. Hart Publishing, Portland, pp 1–24

Lepard B (2012) International law and human rights. In: Cushman T (ed) Handbook of human rights. Routledge, Abingdon

Lippert RK (2016) Governmentality analytics and human rights in criminology. In: Weber L, Fishwick E, Marmo M (eds) The Routledge international handbook of criminology and human rights. Routledge, London

Loader I, Percy S (2012) Bringing the 'outside' in and the 'inside' out: crossing the criminology/IR divide. Global Crime 13(4):213–218

Loader I, Sparks R (2007) Contemporary landscapes of crime. In: Maguire M, Morgan R, Reiner R (eds) Oxford handbook of criminology. OUP, Oxford

MacGuill J (2012) European Arrest Warrant in Ireland-An Uneven Playing Field. Paper delivered at European Arrest Warrant and EU-US Extradition Conference, Irish Centre for European Law, Trinity College Dublin, 19 June 2012

Magyar G (2012) The European Arrest Warrant: A Current Evaluation. Paper presented at seminar on the pre-Lisbon instruments: Special focus on the European Arrest Warrant. European Centre for Judges and Lawyers (European Institute of Public Administration), Cracow, 16 February 2012

Monar J (2005) Anti-terrorism law and policy: the case of the European Union. In: Ramraj VV, Hor M, Roach K (eds) Global anti-terrorism law and policy. Cambridge University Press, Cambridge

Muncie J (2005) The globalization of crime control–the case of youth and juvenile justice: neo-liberalism, policy convergence and international conventions. Theor Criminol 9(1):35–64

Murphy C (2011) EU Counter-Terrorism & the Rule of Law in a post-'War on Terror' World. In: Scheinin M (ed) European and United States Counter-Terrorism Policies, the Rule of Law and Human Rights, RSCAS Policy Paper 2011/03. http://www.cesruc.org/uploads/soft/130221/1-130221192106.pdf

Murphy C (2012a) EU counterterrorism law: pre-emption and the rule of law. Hart Publishing, Oxford

Murphy C (2012b) The constitution of EU counterterrorism law. www.ejiltalk.org/the-constitution-of-eu-counter-terrorism-law/. Accessed 16 July 2012

Ní Aoláin F (2017) Report of the Special Rapporteur of the Human Rights Council on the promotion and protection of human rights and fundamental freedoms while countering terrorism, 27 September. http://www.ohchr.org/Documents/Issues/Terrorism/A_72_43280_EN.pdf. Accessed 10 April 2018

Oliveira de Sousa CH (2014) A criminal law approach to terrorism in Brazil. Unpublished Masters thesis. Naval Postgraduate School, Monterey, California

Powell CH (2007) The legal authority of the United Nations Security Council. In: Goold BJ, Lazarus L (eds) Security and human rights. Hart Publishing, Portland

Roach K (2011) The 9/11 effect: comparative counter-terrorism. Cambridge University Press, Cambridge

Roach K (2013) Introduction: comparative counter-terrorism law comes of age. In: Roach K (ed) Comparative counter-terrorism law. Cambridge University Press, Cambridge

Roach K (2015) Comparative counter-terrorism law. Cambridge University Press, Cambridge

Scheinin M (2014) Back to post-9/11 panic? Security Council resolution on foreign terrorist fighters. https://www.justsecurity.org/15407/post-911-panic-security-council-resolution-foreign-terrorist-fighters-scheinin/. Accessed 10 April 2018

SECILE (2013) Catalogue of EU Counter Terrorism Measures Adopted since 11 September 2011. http://secile.eu/

Servent AR (2010) Point of no return? The European Parliament after Lisbon and Stockholm. Eur Secur 19(2):191–207

Sheppele KL (2011) The migration of anti-constitutional ideas: the post-9/11 globalization of public law and the international state of emergency In: Choudhry S (ed) The migration of constitutional ideas. Cambridge University Press, Cambridge

Snacken S (2010) Resisting punitiveness in Europe. Theor Criminol 14(3):273–292

Snacken S, Dumortier E (2012) Resisting punitiveness in Europe? Routledge, New York

Snacken S, van zyl Smit D (2013) European penology and penal policy-making. In: Daems et al (eds) European Penology? Hart Publishing, Oxford

Szasz P (2002) The security council starts legislating. Am J Int Law 96:901

Talmon S (2005) The security council as world legislature. Am J Int Law 99:175

Telesur (2016) UN and Social Movements Condemn Brazil's new Anti-Terror Law. https://www.telesurtv.net/english/news/UN-Brazils-Anti-Terror-Bill-Could-Be-Used-Against-Activists-20160227-0008.html. Accessed 10 April 2018

United Nations (2010) Promotion and protection of human rights and fundamental freedoms while countering terrorism, 6th August. A/65/258

Van Sliedregt E (2010) European approaches to fighting terrorism. Duke J Comp Int Law 20:222–235

Weber L, Fishwick E, Marmo M (2014) Crime, justice and human rights. Palgrave Macmillan, London

Zedner L (2007) Pre-crime and post-criminology? Theor Criminol 11(2):261–275

Zedner L (2013) Review of 9/11 effect. Univ Toronto Law J 63(4):161–165

# EU Law-Making Process in Criminal Matters After Lisbon. In Search of a *Better* EU Criminal Policy

**Noelia Corral-Maraver**

**Abstract** For years the European Union has been concerned about the quality of legislation and better regulation. This has been observed for a long time in various programmatic and working documents of the different EU institutions. It aims to fighting against the criticisms of over-legislation, excessive bureaucracy and obsolescence of European legislation, which undermine the credibility of the Union itself. On the other hand, this concern is also due to a sincere attempt to achieve better norms that harmonise or unify the Member States' legislation. In recent times this interest has also focused on the criminal norms elaborated in the area of Freedom, Security and Justice.

In any case, despite the efforts made to date, the quality of EU legislation still can be improved. In this context, it would be desirable to provide legislative rationality—from the field of Legisprudence—for the elaboration of European criminal legislation. A good starting point for this would be the development of a model of supranational legislative rationality that establishes rationality criteria that can be used in European Criminal Law.

**Keywords** European Union · Criminal Policy · European Criminal Law · Law-making · Legal Rationality · Legisprudence

## 1 Introduction

Criminal policy is a field that gradually is gaining adherents among scientific doctrine. This is due to the fact that, despite the efforts of criminal-legal dogmatic academics to achieve a rational application and interpretation of Criminal provisions, it can be observed that the results of some legislative actions are not easy to interpret or justify from a dogmatic approach. Hence, it is necessary to address the actions of

N. Corral-Maraver (✉)
Basque Institute of Criminology, University of the Basque Country, San Sebastian, Spain
e-mail: noeliamaria.corral@ehu.eus

 
J. Becerra (ed.), *Criminal Law-Making*, Legisprudence Library 7,
https://doi.org/10.1007/978-3-030-71348-5_4

the legislator themself. The study of criminal policy is aimed at this purpose, and it makes use of the so-called Science of Legislation (also called *Legisprudence*), which studies legal provisions from different perspectives. The ultimate goal is to achieve a high level of rationality in the elaboration of criminal legislation.

This awareness of the need for greater legislative rationality which is mostly assumed by the doctrine in many States—but not to the same extent by the legislators—is weakened when we focus on the international context. This situation must change, taking into account that, in an increasingly globalised world, Criminal Law has begun to be understood from a global perspective. For years now, Criminal Law—or at least a significant part of it—is promoted by international organisations. Among them, it is worth noting the United Nations Security Council, which often produces resolutions related to criminal policy on various issues—such as organised crime, drug trafficking or terrorism-, that is mandatory for State parties to the Charter of the United Nations. The European Council is also important, which encourages legislative harmonisation among the member states through conventions.

The role of the European Union (EU) is also quite relevant. For many years the EU has had competence—now shared with the Member States ex Article 4 of the Treaty on the Functioning of the European Union (TFEU)—to harmonise national criminal legislation both in the field of substantive and procedural law (Articles 82 and 83 TFEU).

Therefore, nowadays the criminal policy of the 27 Member States can no longer be fully understood without taking into account the EU criminal policy. The current tendencies in this context do not give rise to optimism, since they generally contribute to the emergence of an increasingly harsher criminal legislation.[1] For this reason, in this paper a brief approximation will be made to the way in which the EU criminal legislator elaborates its legislation. New lines of action and improvements can only be proposed after having identified the possible shortcomings and weaknesses of the EU procedure.

## 2 Law-Making Processes. Core Issues

By referring to a legislative process it can be understood as if this only refers to procedures that take place within the corresponding legislative chamber. However, in order to correctly analyse the law-making process it is not enough to base the study solely on this moment, but attention must also be paid to other stages and places. Commonly, the doctrine establishes three phases in the legislative procedure: pre-legislative, legislative and post-legislative.[2] Although in reality the Law-making process is quite dynamic, this sequential model is useful to study and systematise all

[1]See, Corral-Maraver (2016), Corral-Maraver (2018), pp. 203–248.

[2]Díez Ripollés (2013), p. 18; Becerra Muñoz (2013), pp. 288–292, 329; Rodríguez Ferrández (2016), pp. 109 et seq.

the proceedings, phases and actors involved.[3] In the following analysis of the EU criminal legislative procedure, I will follow this scheme divided into three phases, which—despite certain variations with respect to the national systems—is fully applicable to the EU.

First of all, it should be noted that for several years in the EU various legislative procedures have coexisted. These have always presented a remarkable complexity derived from the joint participation of several institutions in them. The divergences between the different procedures were related to diverse issues, such as the matter to be regulated, the institution that had the right of initiative, the majorities needed to adopt the norm, the role of the European Parliament, etc. These procedures changed at the same time that the process of European integration progressed. Among them, it is worth highlighting the consultation procedure, which for years was the ordinary legislative procedure, the conciliation procedure and the codecision procedure.

The latter procedure was introduced by the Maastricht Treaty in 1992 and has been the most important and most used since its creation. This procedure was positively received by the doctrine, as it helped to relieve the EU's democratic deficit by attributing greater powers to the European Parliament and, thus, achieve a greater institutional balance. It is a long and complex procedure, structured in several phases. After the Treaty of Lisbon, it has become the ordinary legislative procedure and most of the areas of competence of the EU are regulated through it, including judicial and police cooperation in criminal matters.[4] It will be this procedure, therefore, which will be the subject matter herein.

## 3 The Ordinary Legislative Procedure in the European Union. Pre-Legislative Phase

In this study, the pre-legislative phase is understood as the one that begins with the emergence of a social issue and ends with the presentation of a legislative proposal. In the pre-legislative phase, we distinguish the emergence of an interest, the establishment of the political agenda, creation of an action plan and formation of a legislative proposal as differentiated sub-phases.[5] This is perhaps the most diffuse phase, since a large part of it lacks institutionalisation and the actors and proceedings are difficult to identify and follow. Nevertheless, it is crucial to understand the law-making procedures, because sometimes what is done here is simply formally ratified later in the legislative phase.[6]

[3]Becerra Muñoz (2013), pp. 287–288.

[4]Escobar Hernández (2006), pp. 181 et seq.

[5]See Díez Ripollés (2013), pp. 20 et seq.

[6]Cobb and Elder (1983), p. 12.

## 3.1 Emergence of Social Interest and Agenda-Setting

In the first place, to begin the legislative cycle, it is necessary for some social agent to detect the existence of certain social dysfunction, which reveals the need to intervene in an area of social reality. We are facing a social dysfunction when we feel the need—real or imagined but plausible—to intervene and change a given situation.[7] Of course, some issues are more susceptible to awaken interest, empathy and attention than others—such as dramatic events with high levels of morbidity, or issues related to daily experiences—and, therefore, more suitable for accessing and staying in the social agenda.[8] When this persistent social dysfunction has become a social discomfort, it is when mass social media step in and contribute to categorising said discomfort as a social issue. This must be defined and made visible to a plurality of people, thus increasing the possibilities to include it in the political agenda.[9] All these are informal and ill-defined processes, so it is often difficult to detect the emergence of a certain idea and the reasons that make it enter the political agenda.[10]

If we focus specifically on the EU's agenda-setting processes, differences can be observed with those occurring in Member States.[11] Thus, in the European Union we cannot speak of a single political agenda, but rather each institution maintains its own agenda which are usually not identical and, even within the same institution, multiple agendas can coexist. There are often topics of special interest that can be included in the agenda of various institutions at the same time.[12]

Moreover, both the public agenda and the mass media agenda are weaker in the EU than on a national level. Political disinterest in European affairs, perhaps caused to some extent by the great EU institutional complexity, difficult to understand for the average citizen, and by language barriers, have promoted that in practice there is a weak public opinion with regards to Europe.[13] There are also no proper European

---

[7]It should be noted that a social issue is actually a construction or interpretation of reality and that, besides the construction of an issue, there may be various interests, which are not necessarily related to its resolution, such as partisan interests, personal political success, institutional interests, etc. See, Kingdon (2011), pp. 109–114; Cobb and Elder (1983), pp. 82–83; Edelman (1988), pp. 12–36; Díez Ripollés (2013), pp. 20–21.

[8]Díez Ripollés (2013), pp. 22–23; Cobb and Elder (1983), p. 116; Edelman (1988), pp. 90, 99.

[9]Díez Ripollés (2013), pp. 27–28; Cobb and Elder (1983), pp. 141, 150, 157.

[10]Kingdon (2011), pp. 71–73. Although, as this author points out, it is not so important to know the origin of the idea as other factors that contribute to the good reception of this idea among the actors of the legislative process.

[11]Recently, remarkable efforts to study the European political agenda have been made. In this sense, the *European Union Policy Agendas Project* must be highlighted, which has developed a database and tried to analyse the European Council's agenda, as well as the *Comparative Agendas Project*, focused on the comparative analysis of the political agendas of the different Member States. See, http://www.policyagendas.eu/ and http://www.policyagendas.eu/. Accessed 29 July 2019.

[12]Lelieveldt and Princen (2011), p. 208; Princen (2007), p. 29; Costa and Brack (2014), pp. 335–338.

[13]This is particularly reflected in the low participation rates for elections to the European Parliament. See, Princen (2007), p. 31; Lelieveldt and Princen (2011), pp. 108–111.

media, but they are still nationally focused and do not tend to prioritise European issues. On the other hand, EU political representatives are less subject to control than national representatives. In the European Parliament there are direct elections, but the campaigns remain focused from a national point of view, and the Council and the Commission are only chosen indirectly.[14] Due to all of the above, most of the issues trying to access the EU political agenda and reach the legislative process arise from the EU institutions themselves. The major drivers of the European political agenda are therefore the European Council and the Commission.[15]

In any case, in order for an issue among the thousands of existing issues to access the EU political agenda, it must get attention and to do this some relevant actors must be attracted to support the cause and exclude potential opponents to it.[16] Unlike what can often happen in the Member States, here the actors often run away from political confrontation. The way to define a specific issue,[17] the administrative venues and interinstitutional relations[18] and the political moment[19] are determining factors for an issue to enter the political agenda and to predetermine its approach.[20]

Once the issue enters the agenda, it must be included in some of the various work programmes of the EU institutions. In this regard, it is worth highlighting the political programmes of the European Council and the *multiannual political guidelines* of the Commission. This last document establishes the political priorities for the 5-year term of office of the Commission. These political lines will be specified later in the annual work programme of this body.[21]

There is no doubt that legislative planning in the Union is more detailed and developed than that of the States, although there is still some improvisation with regards to some issues.[22]

---

[14]Princen (2007), p. 31; Princen (2011), p. 940.

[15]Hardacre and Akse (2015), pp. 50–53; Szapiro and Kaeding (2013), pp. 164 et seq.

[16]Princen (2011), pp. 928 et seq.

[17]In criminal matters, it has been common to frame the issue as intimately linked to the common values of all Europeans and to turn it into a question of identity. However, not all issues are susceptible to this method.

[18]These can highly determine the content of the political agenda, more than what happens on a national level. Thus, pressures from one institution on another can make a certain issue access the agenda or be removed from it.

[19]In particular, the dramatic events which have acted as a *focusing event* have also played a great role in the EU in order to allow an issue enter the legislative agenda quickly or to increase its priority. Thus, the focus on terrorism after the 9/11 attacks in the USA is paradigmatic. Terrorism was not an EU priority until that moment. The same phenomenon took place more recently due to the Charlie Hebdo terrorist attacks and the attack in Paris n November 2015, which triggered the process of Directive 2017/541.

[20]Lelieveldt and Princen (2011), pp. 220–225; Princen (2007), pp. 29–30, 33, 45; Princen (2011), pp. 933–934, 940; Costa and Brack (2014), p. 233.

[21]Szapiro and Kaeding (2013), p. 171.

[22]See in this sense Corral Maraver (2018), pp. 216–217, 242. See also, inter alia, Pérez Bernárdez (2012), pp. 174, 178 et. seq.; Ordóñez Solís (2003), pp. 475–476; Argomaniz (2010), pp. 127 et seq.

### 3.2 *Pre-Legislative Works Within the European Commission. Right of Initiative*

The European Commission is a hardly comparable legislative and executive body. It is the largest body in the EU, staffed with more than 33,000 workers.[23] The Commission has the right of legislative initiative in the ordinary legislative procedure and in some special legislative procedures. Thus, it will be the body in charge of referring the issue from the political agenda into a legislative initiative.

After the Treaty of Lisbon, the initiative is currently practically monopolised by the Commission. However, in criminal matters it is possible—although not usual—that the legislative proposal comes from a group of Member States. Other institutions, such as the European Parliament or Council, have a sort of right of indirect initiative. Thus, they can request the Commission to submit a legislative proposal (Articles 225 and 241 TFEU), although the Commission is not obliged to take the request into account.

Furthermore, Article 11.4 of the Treaty of the European Union (TEU) and Article 24 TFUE regulate the so-called European citizens' initiative, which allows one million citizens of at least a quarter of the Member States,—with the current situation being seven Member States—to propose the development of bills in any field to the Commission. Again, the Commission is not obliged to legislate and, to this date, this mechanism has had little success.[24] Ultimately, in spite of all the aforementioned possibilities, practically all the directives approved in recent years in criminal matters have been processed at the initiative of the European Commission. In theory, this is supposed to guarantee greater care and objectivity in the Law-making of the initiatives than if these were in the hands of the States or of the Council. However, the Commission's neutrality is questionable and its labour leads a greater bureaucratisation of legislative initiatives.

### 3.3 *Public Consultations and Reports*

Within the Commission's services, the dossier is assigned to an administrative unit, located within the General Directorate that is in charge of the proposal, which in criminal matters will be the General Directorate of Migration and Home Affairs.

There it is common to develop several studies and reports to assess the necessity of the legislation and the technical details. In this sense, for years it have proceeded

---

[23]Hardacre and Akse (2015), p. 16.

[24]The initiatives can be consulted in: http://ec.europa.eu/citizens-initiative/public/initiatives/successful (Accessed 29 July 2019). In view of the limited success of this mechanism, as regulated by Regulation EU/211/2011, the EU has recently approved a new Regulation EU/2019/788 of April 17, 2019, on the European citizens' initiative, replacing the previous one. This aims to make the European citizens' initiative more accessible and user-friendly.

to carry out consultations, through the so-called green and white papers,[25] although this instrument has fallen into disuse lately.

Currently, the organisation of numerous citizen Internet-based consultations is common. These were published on the website *Your Voice in Europe*, but recently this space has been replaced by a link to another page that includes all the Commission's consultations.[26] They aim to obtain opinions from a wide spectrum of stakeholders, including jurists, authorities, companies, academics, international organisations, civil society and the general public. The consultations are usually made through a not very extensive questionnaire available in all the official languages and they usually remain open for about 3 months. These questionnaires usually include various sorts of questions and a brief state of play, an analysis of the issue and some attached documents. By reading of these questionnaires, a series of observations can be inferred, such as that the formulation of some questions is excessively complicated for the average citizen or that some of them are designed to be answered in the affirmative. In addition, although most of the consultations are translated, there are still some that are available exclusively in English, which could hinder access for some interested parties.

Other types of online consultations, such as interviews with companies or external reports by study groups, agencies or consultancies can also be carried out or commissioned. However, these resources are not common in legislative initiatives in substantive Criminal Law.[27] These are most commonly informal meetings, forums or conferences in which the Commission brings together experts from different areas

---

[25]The green papers consist of a document—published on the Directorate's website—that contains a proposal from the Commission in relation to a given matter. Lobbyists or interested stakeholders generally have a deadline to respond and give their opinion on the matter. On the other hand, the white papers are similar to the last, but they contain more specific legislative proposals. See Hardacre and Akse (2015), pp. 29–30. Green papers have been common in criminal matters in recent decades. In this regard, it is worth mentioning the following: Green Paper on the protection of minors and human dignity in audio-visual and information services (COM/96/0483 final); Green Paper on criminal-law protection of the financial interests of the Community and the establishment of a European Prosecutor (COM/2001/0715 final); Green paper—Compensation to crime victims (COM/2001/0536 final); Green Paper from the Commission—Procedural Safeguards for Suspects and Defendants in Criminal Proceedings throughout the European Union (COM/2003/0075 final); Green Paper on mutual recognition of non-custodial pre-trial supervision measures (COM/2004/0562 final); Green paper on the approximation, mutual recognition and enforcement of criminal sanctions in the European Union (COM/2004/0334 final); Green Paper Strengthening mutual trust in the European judicial area—A Green Paper on the application of EU criminal justice legislation in the field of detention (COM/2011/0327 final). White papers on this subject have been less common, although some examples can also be found, such as the White Paper on exchanges of information on convictions and the effect of such convictions in the European Union (COM/2005/0010 final).

[26]The most recent—open or closed—consultations can be found here: https://ec.europa.eu/in-fo/consultations_es . Accessed 29 July 2019.

[27]Except in Directive 2017/1371/EU, on the fight against fraud to the Union's financial interests by means of criminal law, for which an external study was committed: "Study on the legal framework for the protection of EU financial interests by criminal law", from February 2012 (Contract JUST/2011/EVAL/FW/1023/A4).

and stakeholders. These can be bilateral or multilateral. Among them, informal meetings called *open hearings* stand out. They are events with civil society actors and public administrations. Said open hearings last one or two days, but due to the large number of participants (up to 300 people) the discussions remain on a very superficial level.[28]

For years now, the Commission has been preparing the so-called *impact assessment reports*, accompanying the legislative proposals; these reports must include all the consultations carried out. The administrative unit in charge of the initiative must prepare the impact assessment report.

The impact assessment system was launched on the basis of a communication from the Commission in 2002.[29] In the following years, pilot reports were developed[30] and, from the Interinstitutional Agreement on Better Law-making (2003/C321/01), the three institutions decided on a more frequent use of impact assessment reports for all the most relevant legislative proposals.[31] In 2009, as a result of an external evaluation of the impact assessment system commissioned by the Commission, a new modification of the guidelines[32] took place. A communication by the Commission in 2015 insisted on the idea of improving impact assessment reports and extending them to non-legislative initiatives.[33]

There is no specific indication for which legislative initiatives must be accompanied by an impact assessment report. The guidelines only refer proposals that are the most relevant and that may have a great economic, social and environmental impact. Based on these criteria, it should logically be inferred that this report should always be made in criminal matters' initiatives, given its impact on fundamental rights and its special link with national sovereignty. In fact, in terms of substantive Criminal Law,[34] impact assessments have usually been carried out in almost all the directives approved after the entry into force of the Treaty of Lisbon.

---

[28]Szapiro and Kaeding (2013), p. 180; Hardacre and Akse (2015), p. 29.

[29]See particularly, Communication from the Commission on impact assessment (COM (2002) 276 final). Also consult other communications: European Governance: Better Law-making (COM (2002)275; Action Plan "Simplifying and Improving de Regulatory Environment" (COM(2002) 278; Towards a reinforced culture of consultation and dialogue–General Principles and Minimum Standards for Consultation of Interested Parties by the Commission" (COM(2002)704); and The Collection and Use of Expertise by the Commission: Principles and Guidelines" (COM(2002)713).

[30]Muñoz de Morales Romero (2010a), pp. 494–495.

[31]See Interinstitutional Agreement on better law-making (2003/C 321/01); Akse (2013), p. 31.

[32]See Impact assessment guidelines of 15th January 2009 (SEC (2009) 92), that replaces the former Commission Guidelines of 2005. More recently, the *Better Regulation Guidelines* (SWD(2015) 111 final).

[33]See Communication from the Commission to the European Parliament, the Council, the European Economic and Social Committee and the Committee of the Regions "Better regulation for better results - an EU agenda" (COM(2015) 215 final).

[34]For supposed reasons of urgency, the Commission has dispensed the impact assessment with regards to Directive 2017/541/EU, on combating terrorism and replacing Council Framework Decisions 2002/475/JHA and amending Council Decision 2005/671/JHA.

In order to prepare the impact assessment report, the Commission must collect reports, obtain data and make diverse consultations with the aim of proposing different policy options, comparing them and deciding which are the most convenient. Depending on the issue, different kinds of consultation can be done.[35]

Finally, all these data must be reflected in the impact assessment report, which must not exceed 30 pages (excluding graphs and annexes). The report must be written for a non-expert audience[36] in German, French or English—although it is usually written in the latter-. There should also be a summary (no more than 10 pages) translated into all the official languages.[37] The process of preparing the report requires at least 1 year or 18 months.[38]

The development and progressive generalisation of an EU prelegislative evaluation system through impact assessment reports deserves a general positive consideration, since it makes possible the participation of multiple actors in the decision-making process, such as experts and stakeholders representing public or private interests,[39] and allows the Commission to collect information that it probably would not have available otherwise. However, on the other hand, these reports used have a poor methodology and inconsistency when trying to justify the various options for criminalisation.[40] Sometimes it seems that the reports are made as a mere process of justification of previously-adopted political decisions. In spite of everything, significant efforts to improve the system in recent years should be highlighted.[41]

### 3.4 *Interest Groups Within the European Union*

The EU and, especially, the European Commission has always been favourable on integrating interest groups, considered as representatives of civil society, into the legislative process.[42] This is partly due to the Commission's aim to strengthen its own political position and find support for its initiatives.[43]

---

[35]There are guidelines on how to make the consultations, what to take into account, how to formulate the questions, etc. The same guidelines warn that not all stakeholders have the same strength and that the results of the consultation will not always be exactly representative of a state of opinion. See Impact assessment guidelines of 2009 (SEC (2009) 92), p. 20.

[36]See critically, Akse (2013), p. 50.

[37]See Impact assessment guidelines of 2009 (SEC (2009) 92), pp. 9–10.

[38]See Akse (2013), pp. 121, 125–126.

[39]For the same opinion, emphasising that this favours the principles of proportionality and *ultima ratio*, see Muñoz de Morales Romero (2010a), pp. 495–497.

[40]Íbid, p. 496.

[41]More information can be consulted in Corral Maraver (2020).

[42]See Rodríguez Torres (2016), pp. 3, 11–13.

[43]See Costa and Brack (2014), pp. 216–218, 226–227.

The large number of professionals who act and even have an office in Brussels with the aim of influencing the EU institutions is well known. This amount has been increasing in parallel to the acquisition of competences by the European Union, due to the fact that there are increasingly more areas in which they can influence.[44] Quantifying the exact number of lobbies is not easy. It is estimated that the number is between 10,000 and 30,000 lobbyists (individuals) and between 3500 and 4000 groups.[45] Of all these interest groups, most are trade federations which represent some kind of industry, followed by commercial consultancies,[46] international or national companies and trade unions, which can be integrated into federations or act on their own. Likewise, albeit with less importance, NGOs and civil society associations can be found. Finally, it is worth highlighting the expert study groups or *Think Tanks*, which try to initiate debates on several topics.

The lack of transparency lobbying in the legislative process is frequently criticised, because the meetings that take place are not made known and the degree of their real influence is not measured. To mitigate the criticism, in 2011 a Joint Transparency Register by the European Commission and Parliament was established.[47] This is a voluntary registration for those groups involved in European law-making, although registration is encouraged.[48] In 2017 there was a proposal to create a mandatory common register.[49] Given the shortcomings of the Transparency Register, the concern for the influence of the lobbies in the EU has caused an increase in some independent work groups that seek to provide greater transparency regarding EU lobbying.[50]

---

[44]See Rodríguez Torres (2016), pp. 4–10.

[45]Lelieveldt and Princen (2011), pp. 129–130. For these authors, 15,000 lobbyists would be closer to the reality.

[46]To try to alleviate this strength imbalance, the European Commission spent part of its budget to support some of the groups, especially NGOs and civil society associations, which usually have less resources to organise on a European level. In this way, the Commission allows other types of interests to be represented, although it seems that it tends to mainly fund groups that support its policies. In addition, this action does not completely eliminate the issues of the small interest groups when they move in a transnational scenario. See Mazey and Richardson (2006), pp. 286, 288–289; Lelieveldt and Princen (2011), pp. 137–138, 148.

[47]See This agreement shall replace the agreement between the European Parliament and the European Commission of 23 June 2011, replaced by the Agreement between the European Parliament and the European Commission on the transparency register for organisations and self-employed individuals engaged in EU policy-making and policy implementation of 16 April 2014. Document available in: https://eur-lex.europa.eu/legal-content/EN/TXT/?uri=CELEX:32014Q0919(01) (Accessed 29 July 2019).

[48]See Hardacre and Akse (2015), p. 218; Lelieveldt and Princen (2011), p. 148; Rodríguez Torres (2016), pp. 17–18.

[49]Proposal for an Interinstitutional Agreement on a mandatory Transparency Register (COM(2016) 627 final). Available at: http://eur-lex.europa.eu/legal-content/en/TXT/?uri=CELEX:52016PC0627 (Accessed 29 July 2019).

[50]It is worth noting the *Corporate Europe Observatory*, which is a working group aimed at controlling the EU's economic lobby, which it believes fosters social inequality and the degradation of the environment; it is also responsible for monitoring the phenomenon of revolving doors; and

Within the Commission there are also numerous expert groups–about 800 at the present-. 95% of them are informal, and only 5% are formally constituted, created by the Commission. Given the growing relevance of these groups, the Commission also created a register of expert groups, in order to ensure transparency.[51] To comply with the advisory role in the field of Criminal Law in 2012, a group of experts in criminal policy was formally constituted.[52] This group must advise the Commission in the elaboration of criminal norms and provide empirical data. The group is permanent and consists of up to 20 independent high-level legal experts of different nationalities, combining academics with practical professionals. The election of the experts of this group is at the discretion of the Commission. In practice, group meetings are scarce, being held once or twice a year and, according to some of its participants, despite being interesting, there is a disparity of approaches between the academic and practical members, and between all of them and the experts of the Commission itself. Therefore, although the Commission's concern to establish a permanent group in criminal policy is remarkably positive, the real influence of this on the law-making process does not seem to be too high.[53] Experts outside the European institutions, such as academic groups or professionals in various fields, can also be consulted, as has occurred in some directives regarding EU substantive Criminal Law.[54]

In summary, nowadays it is quite difficult to assess the incidence of these diverse interest groups in the elaboration of substantive Criminal Law and, therefore, greater transparency must be achieved in the near future in order to gain more formal legitimacy in the Law-making process.

*Integrity Watch* created within the NGO Transparency International, to make the lobbying information in the EU institutions more accessible. More information available at: http://corporateeurope.org/ and http://www.integritywatch.eu/ (Accessed 29 July 2019).

[51]It can be consulted at: http://ec.europa.eu/transparency/regexpert/index.cfm (Accessed 29 July 2019).

[52]Commission Decision of 21st February 2012 on setting up the expert group on EU criminal policy (2012/C 53/05) (register number: E02760).

[53]There are also other Commission's expert groups that may eventually be consulted on criminal matters. For instance: Procedural criminal law (E00636), Commission stakeholder expert group on public procurement (E02807), EU High Level Group on combating racism, xenophobia and other forms of intolerance (E03425), Expert group on the rights of the child (E02884), Forum on organised crime prevention (E00622), Expert Group on Policy Needs for Data on Crime (Crime Statistics) (E02837), Expert Group Trafficking in Human Beings (E02722).

[54]This happened in the case of Directive 2017/1371/EU on the fight against fraud to the Union's financial interests by means of criminal law, for which the Commission requested the *Max-Planck-Institut für ausländisches und internationales Strafrecht* of Freiburg drafted a report. See Wade, M. (2011), *Evaluating the needs for and the needs of a European Criminal Justice System*, Freiburg. Report available in: http://www.mpicc.de/shared/data/pdf/euroneeds_report_jan_2011.pdf (Accessed 29 July 2019).

### 3.5 *Drafting and Approval of the Legislative Proposal*

Once all the consultations have been made and the impact assessment report has been prepared, the legislative proposal document is drawn up. The Commission is not bound by the result of any of the previous consultations, although it must publish the results of all of them. The administrative unit in charge of the proposal must take into account the opinion of all the Commission's departments that may have a legitimate interest in it, particularly of the General Secretariat and the Legal Service.

The draft proposal must follow the usual format of the EU drafting style guidelines. Once this administrative control has been overcome, the proposal must be validated on a political level; that is, it must receive the approval of the College of Commissioners. When the text receives a green light, it is sent to the EU legislators, namely the European Parliament and the Council.

## 4 The Ordinary Legislative Procedure in the European Union. Legislative Phase

The legislative phase goes from the moment in which the proposal is sent to the legislator until it is approved, published in the official journal and comes into force. This phase is usually highly institutionalised and regulated.

At the same time, the Commission sends the proposal to the legislators and to the Member State's national parliaments so that the latter can pronounce on its conformity with the principle of subsidiarity,—the so-called *early warning* mechanism[55]-. In doing so, States maintain some power to intervene in the legislative process. Another way to allow the participation of the Member States in the ordinary legislative procedure only applicable in criminal matters—substantive and procedural—is the *emergency brake* mechanism, which enables the legislative process to be paralysed (Articles 82.3 and 83.3 TFEU).[56]

[55]The early warning mechanism is regulated by Protocol No. 2 on the application of the principles of subsidiarity and proportionality (Articles 6 and 7), annexed to the Treaty of Lisbon. This is an external control that seeks to monitor compliance of EU legislation with the principle of subsidiarity. This principle is important in the EU level because it determines its powers in the areas of shared competence, as is the case of Criminal Law and, thus, the Union should only legislate when regional or local authorities cannot do so with the same effectiveness. According to this, within a period of 8 weeks from the reception for the proposal, national parliaments may send a reasoned opinion to the presidents of the three institutions in which they assess the compliance of the legislative proposal with the principle of subsidiarity. Since the report is optional, it is common to issue it only when an infringement of that principle is detected. See, inter alia, Aranda Álvarez (2013), Camisón Yagüe (2012), Gattermann and Hefftler (2015), Peters (2009), Auel and Christiansen (2015).

[56]Through this mechanism, any Member State can consider that a certain draft directive in criminal matters affects its national fundamental rights. In that case, the Member State can request to stop the procedure and the submission of the proposal to the European Council. A period of 4 months is then

The legislative proposal is also sent at the same time to the European Economic and Social Committee (EESC) and the Committee of the Regions (CoR), advisory bodies that have the power to eventually issue reports.[57]

The codecision procedure or ordinary legislative procedure is regulated in Article 294 TFEU and developed in the respective rule of procedure of the EU institutions. This process consists up to 3 readings: first reading, second reading and third reading or phase of conciliation. The most relevant is the first reading because this phase does not have a deadline for the adoption of the decision, thus offering more flexibility. Therefore, the vast majority of files are adopted at first reading, regardless of whether the process is fast or stuck for months or years.[58] The second reading is similar to the first one, but it already establishes a period of three months to reach an agreement, which can be extended by one month upon request. If an agreement on the proposal is not reached within that period, the third reading or conciliation phase begins. At this point, given the discrepancies between the Parliament and the Council, a conciliation committee is convened. It consists of a delegation from Parliament and another from the Council, composed of 28 members each. This phase of the procedure is exceptional and their movements are difficult to follow, because the meetings are held behind closed doors and documentation is rarely made public. Once the committee has been convened, another six-week term is established, which can be extended up to eight weeks, so that an agreement on the proposal can be reached. If the agreement is not possible, the legislative act is considered not adopted and the Law-making process ends.

In the Law-making process, Parliament works through parliamentary committees formed by MEPs belonging to the various EP political groups, while the Council does so through its working groups, which are composed of national representatives (up to four representatives per Member State) and by a representative of the European Commission. Specifically, for the area of substantive Criminal Law

---

opened for the European Council to reach an agreement on the proposal. This mechanism has both supporters and detractors, since on one hand it can be considered as a way of preserving constitutional legal traditions and, on the other hand, can be seen as an assignment to the Member States of a veto power and as a way to foster nationalism and intergovernmentality.

[57]See Mangas Martín and Liñán Nogueras (2010), p. 237.

[58]According to data from the legislature 2009–2014, 85% of the files are decided during the first reading and 8% in the so-called early second reading. Only 5% of them were concluded after a complete second reading and less than 2% reached conciliation and a third reading. There are no major differences depending on the area of activity. From the available data of the previous legislature (July 2014–April 2017) it appears that 75% of the files are adopted during the first reading, 23% during the early second reading and 2% in the second reading, without any file reaching the conciliation phase. In criminal matters, most of the directives up until now have also been approved during the first reading. Of the 50 files in which the European Parliament LIBE Committee—in charge of criminal matters legislation—was involved, 86% were adopted during the first reading and 14% during the early second reading, without any of them requiring the exhaustion of the second reading or reaching the conciliation phase. See Activity Report on the Ordinary Legislative Procedure available at http://www.europarl.euro-pa.eu/ordinary-legislative-procedure/en/ordinary-legislative-procedure.html (Accessed 29 July 2019).

there is a working group called DROIPEN. Both bodies, the Parliament and Council, begin to work on the proposal sent by the Commission in parallel, suggesting amendments to it.

However, despite all that has been said, in practice it is important to point out that the deliberations are made through informal appointments and behind closed doors. These meetings are called *trilogues* and there participate representatives of the three institutions. These are traditional in the EU, being an existing institutional practice since the creation of the codecision procedure, although it is not regulated in the treaties. These informal meetings are held mainly for efficiency reasons. They intend to facilitate and accelerate the legislative process, identifying the controversial points in each institution and working to reach agreements.[59] However, the opacity of these meetings generates great suspicion and criticism. The main one is that this system allows to leave in the background political deliberation, turning the parliamentary debate into a merely formal and superfluous activity. In addition, the lack of transparency is evident, since what is discussed in the *trilogues* is unknown to non-participants and the most relevant working documents—which would provide a great deal of information—are rarely available;[60] the most important is a four-column document in which each coloumn expresses the position of an institution regarding the matter (proposal of the Commission, position of the EP Committee, position of COREPER, and possible agreement text).[61] It is not even possible to follow when exactly the meetings take place, since the most that can be found on the institutions' websites regarding a certain procedure is a brief allusion saying "follow up in *trilogues*".

For all these reasons, the European Parliament has modified its rule of procedure to establish rules of conduct or good practices in the *trilogues*.[62] Also, recently, a surprising judgment of the Court of Justice of the European Union (CJEU) of March 22, 2018 (Case T-540/15) has ruled that the EU is obliged to provide the documents handled in the *trilogues*.[63] The European Ombudsman, previously, in May 2015,

[59]See Rasmussen and Reh (2013).

[60]These documents are not usually available in the European Parliament Public Register. It is possible to request them on the basis of Regulation (EC) 1049/2001 of the European Parliament and of the Council of 30th May 2001 regarding public access to the European Parliament, Council and Commission's documents, but there is a possibility that they will not be forwarded. See infra.

[61]See Hardacre and Akse (2015), p. 164.

[62]Ibid, pp. 160–162. See also, Joint declaration on practical arrangements for the codecision procedure (2007/C 145/02), recitals 7, 8 et 9.

[63]The judgement is based on a claim by Mr. Emilio De Capitani, who requested information on an ongoing legislative process from the European Parliament. Specifically, he requested the four-column document used in the *trilogues*. The Parliament only sent him partial information, refusing to transmit the information in the fourth column, which is the possible compromise text, because it considered it would undermine the legislative process. The Parliament's decision was based on Article 4.3 of Regulation (EC) 1049/2001, which allows denial of access to documents in the case they are for internal use or related to an institution that has not yet made a decision on a procedure, if its disclosure seriously impairs the decision-making process. This does not apply in the case that such disclosure has a higher public interest. The CJEU ruled in favour of Mr. De Capitani, pointing

made an inquiry regarding transparency in the EU law-making process (Case OI/8/2015/JAS) and, consequently, a request to the EU institutions highlighting the need to provide transparency to these meetings, publishing their dates, agendas and participants.[64]

Once an agreement has been reached on the normative proposal, regardless of whether it takes place in the first, second or third reading, and when the document has been ratified in the respective bodies—the plenary in the European Parliament and the respective meeting of the Council—, the presidents of the Parliament and the Council proceed to sign the legislative act. When the legislative proposal is of special relevance or there is a special political interest in it, the signature act can be public and open to the press.[65]

A final legislative review—following the existing legislative technique guides—and the translation of the proposal to all official languages must be carried out. However, in any case, this does not avoid certain incoherencies and systematic issues in the final texts. Once all the steps have been taken, the final text is sent for publication in the Official Journal of the EU.

## 5 The Ordinary Legislative Procedure in the European Union. Post-Legislative Phase

### *5.1 Preliminary Notes*

Finally, the post-legislative phase extends from the entry into force of the legislation until it is evaluated and, eventually, subject to a new pre-legislative phase. The legislative evaluation must take place sometime after the legislation has been elaborated and its effects have already been produced, because only then can it be concluded whether or not it achieves the proposed objectives.[66] If the evaluated legislation has shortcomings or inconsistencies, this may lead to the beginning of a new legislative process.

This phase of the legislative process is more variable in terms of its duration and main features. In States with a broad evaluative or technocratic culture, there is usually more interest in the systematic evaluation of the legislations to check their effectiveness, while this interest is lower in the systems that do not have such culture.

---

out that, given the usual use of *trilogues* in EU Law-making processes, it cannot be presumed, unless there are reasons that justify it, that providing these documents when required damages the legislative process.

[64]See more information at https://www.ombudsman.europa.eu/en/decision/en/69206 (Accessed 29 July 2019).

[65]See *Guía del Parlamento sobre el procedimiento legislativo ordinario,* pp. 26–30. Available at https://www.consilium.europa.eu/media/29856/qc0415816esn.pdf (Accessed 29 July 2019).

[66]Subirats (1992), pp. 139–144; Díez Ripollés (2013), p. 58; Becerra Muñoz (2013), pp. 323, 331; Rodríguez Ferrández (2016), pp. 107–108.

In the European Union, there has been an increasing interest for the *ex-post* evaluation of legislation for some time now. This attention is reflected in various instruments, such as, among others, the White Paper on European Governance of 2001 (COM(2001) 428 final) or the Interinstitutional Agreement on Better Law-making of 2003 (2003/C 321/01), and it also reached criminal matters; Article 70 TFEU mentions the need to have periodic assessments of the EU policies and, in particular, in the area of the Area of Freedom, Security and Justice. More recently, the Commission's Communication "*Better regulation for better results - an EU agenda*" (COM(2015) 215 final)[67] called for the evaluation of existing legislation and, furthermore, indicated that each new norm should be accompanied by a prevision of future evaluation; the subsequent Interinstitutional Agreement on Better Law-Making, of 13th April 2016,[68] also highlights the ex-post evaluation as a way to improve the quality of legislation in the EU. The latter document invites the Commission to draft an annual evaluation programme, to provide systematic evaluations in EU Legislation, as well as to encourage it to include specific evaluation clauses in the provisions. Such evaluations should be based on the principles of effectiveness, efficiency, relevance, coherence and added value, and emphasis is placed on the use, where possible, of scientific evidences.

In any case, the post-legislative evaluation phase in the EU is not as institutionalised and developed in practice as it seems. Nowadays there are various types of legislative evaluations, such as those carried out by the Commission, which is the EU body normally in charge of this task, and the evaluations carried out by other actors.

## 5.2 *Post-Legislative Evaluation by the European Commission*

Among the different legislative evaluations carried out by the Commission, the most relevant are the infringement reports, which monitor the inobservance of the harmonisation duties by the Member States. After the transposition deadline, the Member States are obliged to notify the Commission of the legislative measures eventually adopted to comply with European law. For this reason, the European Commission draws up a report on the monitoring of the application of EU law each year, which analyses the degree of compliance of the Member States when adapting EU legislation.[69] In addition, administrative infringement procedures are commonly

[67]Document available at http://ec.europa.eu/smartregulation/better_regulation/documents/c-om_2015_215_en.pdf (Accessed 29 July 2019).

[68]Document available at http://eurlex.europa.eu/legalcontent/EN/TXT/PDF/?uri=OJ:L:20-16:123:FULL&from=EN (Accessed 29 July 2019).

[69]The infringement reports are available at http://ec.europa.eu/atwork/applying-eu-law/infringements-proceedings/annual-reports/index_en.htm (Accessed 29 July 2019).

carried out by the Commission and the CJEU, which can lead to significant economic penalties for non-compliant countries.

Until the entry into force of the Treaty of Lisbon, Criminal Law was located within the third pillar, meaning that this matter could not be susceptible to be controlled through the infringement procedure. The Treaty of Lisbon puts an end to this disadvantageous situation and allows European Criminal Law provisions to also be subject to control. However, it would happen after a transitional period of 5 years, which ended on 1st December 2014. During this time, it was still not possible to proceed against the Member States, but after that time the Commission acquired full powers.[70] For this reason, since 2015, in its annual infringement reports, the Commission has declared the initiation of non-compliance procedures due to the lack of transposition of the third pillar instruments. Moreover, in recent years, it has done the same with regards to the infringement of criminal law directives approved after the Treaty of Lisbon.

In addition, the European Commission sometimes promotes *ad hoc* evaluations in certain legislations and programmes, including many in the field of Criminal Law. Thus, under the third pillar, the Commission tried to carry out various evaluations of some legislations—mainly framework decisions—although this control was a *dead letter* as the Commission had no competence to act in case of infringement at the time. Besides, these evaluations were not especially developed and still had serious shortcomings,[71] since they were based almost exclusively on verifying States' compliance with their transposition obligations, without taking into account other rationality criteria that may also be of importance,[72] such as efficacy, effectiveness, coherence, compliance with fundamental rights...

Nowadays, the directives, particularly those that were approved in matters of substantive Criminal Law after the Treaty of Lisbon, usually include a post-legislative evaluation clause. There is no general rule regarding the deadline to carry out these evaluations, although it is common to establish a period of between 4 and 5 years after the directive comes into force. This normally means a period of about 2 to 3 years following the end of the transposition deadline to the States. This seems to be a very short period if it aims to assess not only the implementation but also whether the norm is effective and achieves the desired objectives.

Unfortunately, taking into account the short time that has passed since the approval of many of the substantive Criminal Law directives, we still do not have many post-legislative evaluation reports, and we will still have to wait a few years in order to examine and assess the way in which these are carried out. It is desirable that future evaluations be more developed, moving beyond the assessment of Member States' implementation, as well as taking into account other rationality criteria.

---

[70]See Protocol No. 36 on transitional provisions. See also Mitsilegas and Carrera (2014), pp. 22, 32.

[71]See Nieto Martín (2010), pp. 234–235.

[72]See Sánchez Lázaro (2016), pp. 247–254.

### 5.3 Other Types of Evaluation

Although the most part of the post-legislative evaluation in the EU is in the hands of the Commission, they can also be carried out by other entities. Among them the so-called *peer reviews* can be highlighted, which are conducted by experts of different Member States to assess the implementation of a specific European policy in another Member State. This kind of evaluation has fallen into disuse in recent years.[73]

There are also occasional evaluations carried out by independent expert groups. Often this task is on behalf of the European institutions themselves, but it can also arise spontaneously. This type of evaluation is very varied and can be carried out by academic networks, groups of professional experts, European agencies, interest groups, NGOs, etc.[74] They are not made regularly and their quality is changing or uneven, sometimes lacking a proper methodology and rationality guidelines.

## 6 Concluding Remarks

As we can observe, the ordinary legislative procedure of the EU is more complex and developed than that of many Member States. In the EU, there is a greater concern to institutionalise the various proceedings and phases and to include deliberative elements and transparency requirements in the law-making process. Hence, it can be affirmed that, compared to most national legislators, the European legislator is much more rational. This is partly due to the fact that the EU law-making is a considerably more technocratic system and, therefore, the way to elaborate legislation is different and certain tendencies—related to punitive populism—still affect the EU but not as significantly.

This does not necessarily mean that the EU law-making process is perfect or immune to punitivism. The analysis of the legislative procedure carried out in this paper unveils some shortcomings that must be taken into account.

The most prominent shortcomings in the pre-legislative phase are the deficient technique of elaboration of impact assessment reports or even their non-elaboration in some cases, due to alleged reasons of urgency. It must be remembered that there are many countries whose legislators do not even consider making this impact assessment report and that is why the European practice is positive and should consolidate and extend. However, it must also be pointed out that nowadays these reports are, to a large extent, made to justify criminalisation in a field that has been previously decided at a political level, not paying enough attention to the report's quality itself. For this reason, there is a risk that the impact assessment reports end up

[73]Nilsson (2006), pp. 117–118.

[74]See, inter alia, Muñoz de Morales Romero (2010b), pp. 39–45.

becoming just another bureaucratic proceeding within the EU Law-making procedure.

In the legislative phase, the main criticism is the secrecy of the *trilogue* meetings, which prevent knowing how EU provisions are really elaborated in practice. Moreover, the special mechanisms envisaged by the Treaty of Lisbon, namely the emergency brake and the early warning system or order to provide more legitimacy and rationality, have proved to be ineffective either in monitoring the adequacy of European criminal legislations to national constitutional traditions or in monitoring compliance of these with the principle of subsidiarity, respectively.

The post-legislative evaluation phase also presents serious problems. On the one hand, the shortcomings derivative of any type of ex-post evaluation in the criminal field, such as methodological difficulties, or the complexity of designing an evaluation system that fulfils a series of requirements: independence, transparency, interdisciplinarity, etc. On the other hand, the existence of a multilevel regulatory system in the EU also handicaps the evaluation. This means that the evaluator must firstly decide which legislation is to be evaluated: the European legislation, the national implementation legislation, or both. Then, the contents to be assessed must also be considered, that is, whether the focus should be solely on the control of the effectiveness of the legislations or other contents should be taken into account. Currently, there is no clear and satisfactory methodological development in the EU evaluations, which continue to focus mostly—or exclusively—on the control of compliance by the Member States, that is, on effectiveness and not efficiency criteria. This means that the EU evaluation system is almost entirely focused on the national transposition legislation, neglecting the European legislation itself. In doing this, the EU considers the Member States exclusively responsible for the issues regarding the European criminal policy. However, it avoids being self-critical and considering that maybe in some cases European criminal legislation may present defects that make national compliance difficult and deficient. The fact that most of the normative evaluations are carried out by the European Commission—the same body that draws up the legislative proposals—and not by an independent body is also an issue, since the lack of independence does not guarantee quality and objective evaluations.

In short, there is no doubt that the EU legislative procedure is better than that of many Member States, nor that the EU is making remarkable efforts with regards to the improvement of law-making. Nevertheless, there is still a lot to be done. It is necessary to focus on the Science of Legislation, carrying out studies in order to improve the quality of EU decision-making and achieving greater doses of rationality. As previously stated,[75] it is therefore convenient to create and develop a model of supranational criminal legislative rationality, which could be applicable to the EU sphere. This model would make it possible to organise and systematise all the relevant content that should be taken into account in the elaboration of criminal

[75]Corral Maraver (2020).

legislation and in the ex post evaluation[76]—ethical, pragmatic, efficiency or effectiveness issues, legal-formal issues, etc.—and it would guarantee a better quality of analysis in the different phases of the EU legislative procedure.

I believe that, despite all the limitations of any theoretical model, if in the pre-legislative phase and perhaps in the post-legislative phase, the technicians of the European Commission and the EU legislators follow a structured rationality model, this would make them focus on at least certain relevant rationality contents that are not currently effectively addressed. This could finally contribute to the development of a high-quality or *better* criminal policy.

## References

Akse E (2013) Influencing the preparation of EU legislation: a practical guide to working with impact assessments. John Harper Publishing, London

Aranda Álvarez E (2013) La alerta temprana en el procedimiento legislativo de la Unión Europea. Una reflexión sobre su utilidad. Desde la reciente experiencia española. Revista de Derecho Comunitario Europeo 44

Argomaniz J (2010) El proceso de institucionalización de la política antiterrorista de la Unión Europea. CIDOB d'Afers Internacionals 91

Auel K, Christiansen T (2015) After Lisbon: National Parliaments in the European Union. West European Politics

Becerra Muñoz J (2013) La toma de decisiones en política criminal. Bases para un análisis multidisciplinar. Tirant lo Blanch, Valencia

Camisón Yagüe JA (2012) Las cortes generales y el control del principio de subsidiariedad: una visión práctica. Los dos primeros dictámenes negativos en el marco del procedimiento de alerta temprana. Dykinson, Madrid

Cobb R, Elder CD (1983) Participation in American politics. The dynamics of Agenda-Building. The John Hopkins University Press, Baltimore

Corral Maraver N (2016) La irracionalidad de la política criminal de la Unión Europea. InDret 4

Corral Maraver N (2018) La legislación penal contra el terrorismo en la Unión Europea y en España. Algunas reflexiones a raíz de la Directiva 2017/541/UE. Cuadernos de Política Criminal 126

Corral Maraver N (2020) Racionalidad legislativa y elaboración del Derecho penal de la Unión Europea. Tirant lo Blanch

Costa O, Brack N (2014) How the EU really works. Ashgate Publishing

Díez Ripollés JL (2013) La racionalidad de las leyes penales, 2nd edn. Trotta, Madrid

Edelman M (1988) Constructing the political spectacle. The University of Chicago Press, Chicago

Escobar Hernández C (2006) Instituciones de Derecho Comunitario. Tirant lo Blanch, Valencia

Gattermann K, Hefftler C (2015) Beyond institutional capacity: political motivation and parliamentary behaviour in the early warning system. West Eur Polit 38(2)

Hardacre A, Akse E (2015) How the EU hnstitutions work and... how to work with the EU Institutions, 2nd edn. John Harper Publishing, London

Kingdon JW (2011) Agendas, alternatives and public policies, 2nd edn. Longman, Boston

Lelieveldt H, Princen S (2011) The politics of the European Union. Cambridge University Press, Cambridge

[76]Substantially following the model proposed by Díez Ripollés (2013), pp. 91–98, 109–162.

Mangas Martín A, Liñán Nogueras DJ (2010) Instituciones y Derecho de la Unión Europea, 6th edn. Tecnos, Madrid
Mazey S, Richardson J (2006) The Commission and the lobby. In: Spence D, Edwards G (eds) The European Commission. John Harper Publishing, London
Mitsilegas V, Carrera S (2014) The end of the transitional period for police and criminal justice measures adopted before the lisbon treaty. Who monitors Trust in the European Justice Area? Centre for European Policy Studies, CEPS
Muñoz de Morales Romero M (2010a) Deberes de motivación y de argumentación del legislador penal europeo en torno a los derechos fundamentales. In: Díez-Picazo L, Nieto Martín A (coords) Derechos fundamentales en el Derecho penal europeo
Muñoz de Morales Romero M (2010b) Evaluación Legislativa y Racionalidad en el Ámbito Penal Europeo (y Nacional). Revista General de Derecho Penal 14
Nieto Martín A (2010) El Derecho penal europeo: una aproximación a sus problemas actuales. In: Arroyo Zapatero, Nieto Martín A, Piratas, mercenarios, soldados, jueces y policías: nuevos desafíos del Derecho penal europeo e internacional. Ediciones de la Universidad de Castilla-La Mancha
Nilsson HG (2006) Eight years of experiences of mutual evaluation within the EU. In: Weyembergh A, De Biolley S (cords) Comment évaluer le droit pénal européen? Institut d'Estudes Européennes, Editions de l'Université de Bruxelles, Bruselas
Ordóñez Solís D (2003) El Espacio Judicial de Libertad, Seguridad y Justicia en la Unión Europea. Revista de Estudios Políticos (Nueva Época) 119
Pérez Bernárdez C (2012) El collage de la política antiterrorista de la Unión Europea: una aproximación jurídica. In: Pérez González M (dir) Lucha contra el terrorismo, Derecho Internacional humanitario y Derecho Penal Internacional. Tirant lo Blanch, Valencia
Peters J (2009) The role of National Parliaments. Checks and balances between EU and Member States. In: Verhey L, Kiiverf P, Loeffen S (eds) Political accountability and European integration. Europa Law Publishing, Groningen
Princen S (2007) Agenda-setting in the European Union: a theoretical exploration and agenda for research. J Eur Public Policy 14(1)
Princen S (2011) Agenda-setting strategies in EU policy processes. J Eur Public Policy 18(7)
Rasmussen A, Reh C (2013) The consequences of concluding codecision early: trilogues and intra-institutional bargaining success. J Eur Public Policy 20(7)
Rodríguez Ferrández S (2016) Evaluación legislativa en España: su necesaria aplicación en los procesos de aprobación de las reformas penales. In: Nieto Martín A, Muñoz de Morales Romero M, Becerra Muñoz J (eds) Hacia una evaluación de las leyes penales. Marcial Pons, Madrid
Rodríguez Torres C (2016) Marco regulatorio de las actividades de los lobbies en la Unión Europea. Revista General de Derecho Europeo 39
Sánchez Lázaro FG (2016) Evaluación y Derecho Penal Europeo: sobre el modelo de evaluación de la Comisión Europea. In: Nieto Martín A, Muñoz de Morales Romero M, Becerra Muñoz J (eds) Hacia una evaluación de las leyes penales. Marcial Pons, Madrid
Subirats J (1992) Análisis de políticas públicas y eficacia de la administración. Ministerio para las administraciones públicas, Madrid
Szapiro M, Kaeding M (2013) The European Commission: a practical guide. John Harper Publishing

# From Lobbying to Corruption: The Strategies of Interest Groups to Influence the Law-Making Process

**Patrícia Carraro Rossetto**

**Abstract** There is a widespread view that interest groups are key features of contemporary democracies. Through those political participation channels, citizens articulate their political preferences and interests, express their support and demands to the government, and seek to influence the public decision-making process.

Interest groups with ambitions to influence public policy can choose from a wide range of strategies to accomplish this aim. Therefore, the purpose of this article is threefold. On the one hand, it serves to shed some light on the strategies used by interest groups to influence the democratic law-making processes. On the other hand, it offers useful insights into the relationship and differences between lobbying, political financing, and corruption. Finally, the article offers some brief comments on the measures proposed by the OECD to prevent undue and corrupt influence on decisionmakers.

The article is based on three main assumptions. Firstly, private organised interests seeking to influence the policy-making process is part of the complex political game. Secondly, lobbying is deemed as an intrinsically legitimate political action, even though it shall be carefully regulated by legislation for the sake of transparency, openness, and accountability. Lastly, corruption is defined as the abuse of entrusted power for private gain and the criminal offences included in this concept range from bribery to trading in influence.

**Keywords** Political participation · Interest groups · Lobbying · Political financing · Political corruption · OECD recommendations

---

P. C. Rossetto (✉)
Department of Criminal Law, Universidad de Málaga, Malaga, Spain



J. Becerra (ed.), *Criminal Law-Making*, Legisprudence Library 7,
https://doi.org/10.1007/978-3-030-71348-5_5

## 1 Introductory Remarks

Every democratic political system has some ways for citizens to participate in the political life. The electoral process enables the most common forms of involvement in the political process. During elections, citizens may run for political office, seek to convince others how to vote, attend political debates and rallies, contribute to campaigns, express their opinion to pollsters, and turn out to cast their ballots for partisan candidates.[1]

The democratic political participation, however, extends far beyond elections. In fact, it usually involves a wide range of individual and collective actions, including the participation in protests and demonstrations, partaking in political discussions and debates, communication with elected representatives, affiliation with political parties, and, finally, involvement with civil society organisations, such as social movements and interest groups.[2] Hence, it is not an overstatement to say that interest groups are key features of contemporary democracies. Through these political participation channels, citizens can articulate their political values, preferences and interests, express their support and demands to the government, and seek to influence the public policy. Since democratic politics is a process in which several political actors compete with one another for political access and influence, the methods and strategies used by interest groups to reach the political agenda gain crucial relevance.

Interest groups with ambitions to influence the public decision making-process can use different strategies—or a combination of them—to accomplish this goal. Broadly speaking, their standard repertoire includes *indirect strategies* based on public appeals through the media and the mobilisation of group members and citizens to *direct strategies* targeting bureaucrats, parliamentarians, and political parties. In this particular context, a distinction has been made between legitimate methods, such as lobbying and political funding, and illegitimate tactics, such as influence peddling and bribery.

Against this background, the aim of this article is threefold: to shed some light on the strategies used by interest groups to influence the democratic law-making processes, to provide useful insights into the connections and differences between lobbying, political financing, and political corruption, and to offer some brief comments on the measures proposed by the OECD to prevent undue and corrupt influence on decisionmakers.

In order to achieve these purposes, the paper is structured as follows:

Firstly, a concept of interest groups is provided. This analysis is followed by a summary of the main strategies used by organised special interest to exert influence on policymakers. Some general thoughts about lobbying, political financing, and political corruption are then outlined. Essentially, three central theoretical assumptions anchor these epigraphs. The first assumption is that private organised interests

---

[1] Almond et al. (2010), pp. 60–62. About the political role of the people between elections, see, Przeworski (2010), pp. 111–117.

[2] Diamond and Morlino (2005), pp. 16–17.

seeking political access and influence is inherent to the complex political game. In fact, I assume that policies are typically the outcome of a political process that might involve both representatives and non-elected political actors, notably mass media and interest groups. Second, lobbying is deemed as an intrinsically legitimate political action, even though it shall be carefully regulated by legislation for the sake of transparency, openness, and accountability. Finally, political corruption is defined as the abuse of entrusted political power for private gain and the criminal offences included in this concept range from bribery to trading in influence.

## 2 On the Concept of Interest Groups

An interest group is any voluntary association of social actors "who manifest conscious desires concerning the authoritative allocation of values".[3] In pluralistic political systems, it consists of a set of individuals and organisations that, having their activity totally or partially oriented to influence the outcome of public proceedings, engage in activities related to the aggregation and articulation of special preferences and interests, the promotion of issues on the social and political agenda, and the mobilisation of citizens on public policy matters.[4]

In the political field, interest groups differ from social movements inasmuch as they are institutionalised and formalised collective political actors, have relatively stable organisational structures, advocate for a more specific issues or policies, and are able to build and maintain group cohesiveness in order to achieve their policy purpose and scope.[5] Hence, to a certain extent, interest groups resemble political parties: both have a formal organisational capacity. Nevertheless, unlike political parties, interest groups do not seek to conquer the political power by nominating candidates and winning general elections, they do not represent or promote general interests, nor are their members subject to group discipline or electoral accountability. In this sense, interest groups share common features with social movements: both political participation channels represent special interests and seek to influence, and not to obtain control of, the political decision-making process.[6]

Contemporary democracies are marked by a steadily growing number and diversity of interest groups.[7] Generally, these best-organised components of civil society

[3]Lapalombara (2015), p. 18.

[4]About the concept of interest groups, see Almond et al. (2010) pp. 64–68; Binderkrantz (2005), p. 699; Eising (2008), p. 05; Jordana (2015).

[5]For a definition of *collective political actor*, see Mitnick (1993), p. 12.

[6]Regarding the differences and similarities between political parties, interest groups and social movements, see, Schattschneider (2017), pp. 187–205; Ibarra and Letameda (2015).

[7]Indeed, Schattschneider (2017), p. 27, states that the prodigious growth of interest group associations is one of the principal distinguishing marks of a democratic regime. "Nothing could be more mistaken that to suppose that the parties monopolise the impulse to organise politically; the parties do not operate in an organisational vacuum".

share some crucial characteristics: they are independent from the State, they have established some formal organisational capacity, they have the ability to mobilise resources and act collectively, and they aspire to defend and advance one or multiple special interests.[8] Among the main functions performed by interests groups in order to consolidate the democratic political systems, the following can be highlighted: the representation of social pluralism, the articulation and aggregation of special interests, as well as the political socialisation, integration, and participation.[9]

Operating in the same society, it is possible to identify two broad categories of interest groups: the institutional and the associational groups. On one side, the *institutional groups* are public and private organisations that, despite formed to achieve broader goals, be they social, economic, professional, or cultural, pursue to exert influence on decision-making proceedings involving specific issues or single results, such as the passage of one bill or the reverse of a particular executive ruling. Included in this category are business corporations, churches, bureaucracies, armies, and the legislative, executive, and judicial branches, either as institutional bodies or as smaller groups within them.[10] *Associational interest groups*, on the other hand, are created explicitly to articulate, represent, and promote common interests, preferences, beliefs or ideologies. Indeed, trade unions, chambers of commerce, professional bodies, and others advocacy groups, including international non-profit organisations, fall within this category.[11] Usually, these organisations tend to pursue policies rewards that serve their own needs or the needs of their members. Nevertheless, a special subset of associational groups struggles to bring about broader issues and collective outcomes, such as human rights, social justice, environmental quality, empowerment of women, and consumer protection.[12]

It is noteworthy that, despite the similarities between these groups, significant asymmetries arise from differences in terms of social and economic clout, financial means, constituency size, overall solidity of organisational structures, internal workings, resource mobilisation efforts, media presence, and logics of action.[13] Ultimately, the intrinsic characteristics of the groups themselves can play a central role in improving their capacity to achieve members' commitment, to reach crucial policy information, to appropriately express their interests and concerns to the pivotal decisionmakers, and to gain enough legislative support. As we know, these

[8]Diamond (2008), p. 164; Schattschneider (2017), pp. 30–31.

[9]Diamond (2008), pp. 164–168. For more on the roles and importance of interest groups to the consolidation of democracy, see Straßner (2006), pp. 11–16.

[10]On similar lines, see Almond et al. (2010), pp. 66–67. According to Eising (2008), p. 05, it makes sense to conceive such actors as *interest organisations* that are equivalent to interest groups, even though their *raison d'être* is usually not the aggregation and representation of some constituency preferences and interests.

[11]On this topic, see Almond et al. (2010), p. 67; Von Alemann and Eckert (2006), pp. 04–05.

[12]In this sense, see Almond et al. (2010), pp. 66–67; Diamond (2008), p. 157.

[13]Almond et al. (2010), p. 67; Jordana (2015).

attributes are fundamental for increasing the likelihood of being heard and thus for attaining their desired policy outcome.[14]

# 3 The Organised Special Interest Strategies to Influence the Decision-Making Process

Considering that a greater range of organised special interests are now directly making demands on policymakers, the understanding of the dynamic and implications of the strategic choices used by these competing groups become significantly more relevant.

Studies on the political behaviour of interest groups has pointed out the systematic variation in the strategies interest groups typically engage in to exert influence on public policies. According to Binderkrantz, interest groups with ambitions to influence the public decision-making process can use a wide range of indirect and direct strategies as part of their action repertoire to accomplish this goal.[15] The *indirect strategies* are based on public appeals by means of the mass media or the mobilisation of group membership and citizens. Thus, on the one hand, interest groups might influence political processes by shaping the manner in which issues are perceived and debated in the public, either through massive propaganda campaigns or advocacy advertisements via mass and social media.[16] On the other hand, they might pressure policymaking institutions by mobilising group membership and citizens through activities such as online petitions, social protests, legal demonstrations, general strikes, and civil disobedience.[17] In turn, *direct strategies* are associated with actions targeting parliamentarians, government officials, and political party leaders. In attempting to wield influence and power over politicians and decisionmakers, interest groups could employ both legitimate and illegitimate

---

[14]On a similar line, Almond et al. (2010), p. 67. Regarding this point, Schattschneider (1960), pp. 20–43, highlights the biases of the pluralistic pressure systems. According to the author, "the flaw in the plurasit heaven is that the heavenly chorus signs with a strong upper-class accent. Probably about 90 per cent of the people cannot get into the pressure system" (p. 35).

[15]Binderkrantz (2005), pp. 695–696. Following this author, in this paper I avoid the usual connotations of the words *insider* and *outsider,* as well as the assumption that outsider strategies are inferior to insider strategies. Instead, I prefer to distinguish between *direct strategies*, whereby interest groups approach public decision-makers, and *indirect strategies,* whereby influence on public policy is sought in more indirect ways. With regards to the strategies interest groups tend to employ in order to influence EU institutions and processes, see Eising (2008), pp. 16–18.

[16]Schattschneider (2017), p. 188. For the author, the method of propaganda differs from the method of pressure. According to Schattschneider, "propaganda and pressure can be combined by powerful organised interests and minorities, but they should not be confused. The distinguish mark of pressure tactics is not merely that *it does not seek to win elections* but that in addition *it does not attempt to persuade a majority.* A pressure group is not a minority becoming a majority. (...) Pressure politics is a method of short-circuiting a majority" (p. 189).

[17]Binderkrantz (2005), p. 696.

strategies. While legitimate strategies are linked to regular political financing and a great deal of lobbying and counter-lobbying activities, the illegitimate strategies, otherwise, are related to activities seeking corrupt and undue political influence, among which illegal political campaign financing, influence peddling, and bribery[18] can be highlighted.

Given the close relationship between the direct strategies that could be used by groups to advance their special interests, it is worth clarifying any misunderstandings regarding them. Hence, in the following sections, I aim to provide useful insights into the connections between lobbying, political financing, and political corruption.

## *3.1 Lobbying*

Interest groups engage in lobbying decision-makers in order to achieve policy outcomes that are close to their specific policy preferences.[19] Deemed a legitimate and useful element of democratic political systems, lobbying encompasses efforts to exert direct influence on public policy-making process and is based on both the right to petition the government and the right to be heard before decisionmakers in situations that affect special interests.[20]

In law-making proceedings, lobbying can embrace any legal attempt to influence the acts or votes of legislators, government officials, or staff members on behalf of or against a proposed or pending legislation. The advocacy activities included in such an attempt can range from contacting with public officials who participate in the formulation of specific legislation to attending public hearings or committee meetings, providing technical information, advice or assistance to legislators, helping to draft legal acts, inciting group supporters to write letters to representatives, and, in countries such as the United States, making monetary contributions or raising funds for political campaigns.[21]

Lobbying activities can be fulfilled directly by employees of the interest group (*in-house lobbyist*), or rather by intermediaries specifically hired for that purpose, that is, by individuals or organisations whose primary line of business is lobbying (*professional* or *consultant lobbyist*).[22] In any case, some qualitative studies support the conclusion that an effective and successful lobbyist requires a range of personal

[18]For a summary of the strategies used by interest groups to gain political access, see Almond et al. (2010), pp. 70–74; Binderkrantz (2005), pp. 694–699, 710–711.

[19]Klüver (2011), p. 483; Bennedsen and Feldmann (2002), p. 919.

[20]In this sense, OECD (2012), p. 23. About the distinctions between the right to be heard and the pressure tactics see, Schattschneider (2017), pp. 203–204.

[21]Indeed, according to Milbrath (1958), p. 339, "the lobby process is fundamentally a communication process". In this sense, see OECD (2009), p. 18. For further information about lobbying practices, see, Thomas and Hrebenar (2008), p. 04; Nownes and Freeman (1998), p. 91; Ridao (2017), pp. 21–22.

[22]See Álvarez Vélez and De Montalvo Jääskeläinen (2014).

qualities and professional competences, including, among others, aptitudes such as persistence, patience, politeness, self-confidence and credibility, a high capacity for information-gathering, communication, and negotiation, ability to form and develop direct and solid relationships with key political players, keen knowledge of legislative processes, procedures and—both formal and informal—political rules, and, finally, significant expertise on issues related to their advocacy mandate.[23] Despite a lack of qualitative empirical evidence in favour of this approach, these studies claim that all these personal and professional skills enable lobbyists to access the political arena more easily and to communicate the perspectives and concerns of their employers or clients more effectively to public officials and political representatives, both in the intermediate and upper echelons of legislative and government branches.[24]

Based on the foregoing considerations, it can be concluded that, unlike influence peddling and bribery, lobbying activity is not inherently illegal. Lobbying is rather a form of political action that could guarantee the communicative conditions of an inclusive political process of opinion- and will-formation, since it potentially enables a true balance and conciliation of all competing interests, preferences and values at stake.[25] It must be remembered that, according to Habermas, these are precisely the conditions under which democratic procedures of deliberation and decision-making could be presumed to generate reasonable and legitimate collectively binding decisions.[26] On a similar line, it is important to bear in mind that, since decision-makers increasingly lack the resources and technical background to delve into the detailed implications of a policy under consideration, lobbyists could be seen as political actors who could provide them useful advice on complex technical issues, as well as information on the state of public opinion regarding policy measures. Providing such valuable insights and data, lobbyists can contribute to a more informed decision-making process and, thus, to a more effective public policy, improving the performance of democratic political systems.[27]

Notwithstanding their undeniable relevance, lobbying and lobbyists continue to work under the weight of public suspicion and even outright distrust.[28] Broadly

[23]In this sense, see McGrath (2006), pp. 69–78. Other studies claim that lobbying effectiveness also depends on other factors. Bennedsen and Feldmann (2002), p. 942, for instance, affirm that lobbying effectiveness depends on the legislative structure in which the interest group operates. On the other hand, Klüver (2011), pp. 484–486, 502 claims that its success depends on the strength and size of the lobbying coalition and on the characteristics of the policy issue at stake.

[24]Bertrand et al. (2014), pp. 3887–3888. With regards to this point, Von Alemann and Eckert (2006), p. 05, argues that although the original target of lobbying was the parliamentarians. However, nowadays the preferred targets of lobbying activities are the government and the corresponding ministerial bureaucracy, given the undeniable prominence of the government regarding legislative initiative and policy implementation.

[25]On a similar line, see McGrath (2006), p. 69; Felli and Merlo (2006), p. 181.

[26]See Habermas (1994), p. 03.

[27]For more information about this assumption, see Klüver (2011), pp. 487–488.

[28]McGrath (2008), p. 20.

speaking, there are two reasons for this unfavourable picture. Firstly, there is a huge misunderstanding with regards to the very concepts of lobbying and lobbyists. Indeed, lobbying is commonly mistaken with the exploitation of personal and long-standing connections to exert corrupt or undue influence on public officials, while the lobbyist is wrongly viewed—and framed in mass media reports—as a "fixer" or as a "middleman", that is, as a person who is able to resolve "issues" for clients through corrupt means.[29] Secondly, lobbying activities are usually carried out in an opaque, permissive and unaccountable political environment, which may lead to unfair advantages for vocal vested interests at the expense of the wishes of the whole community or, at least, at the cost of the interests of less organised groups, who struggle to have their voices heard in policy development circles, whether in Parliament or in the Administrations.[30] In the worst case scenario, this environment increases the likelihood that lobbying activities cross the line of legality and legitimacy, becoming an intent to exert illicit influence on public decision-making through corrupt means. Certainly, these circumstances counteract the potential positive effects of lobbying activities and, ultimately, deny the very legitimacy of interest group dynamics.

In view of the significant downside risks of lobbying and given that some lobbyists are proving exceptionally creative in circumventing the rules of the democratic political game, the widespread claim that lobbying activities must be subject to legal regulation for the sake of transparency, fairness, integrity, and accountability in the law-making process[31] is more than justified. In fact, as long as all potential affected groups and interested parties are granted fair and equitable access to the development and implementation of public policies, the legitimacy of lobbying and, consequently, of interest groups shall not be seriously challenged.

In order to help States to achieve this aim, the OECD address a series of interrelated issues that might logically guide the development of a framework for a legislation or government regulation on lobbying. According to the organisation, this framework requires the consideration of five key building blocks.

The first building block focuses on the development of an appropriate framework. This set of recommendations draws attention to the fact that a framework for fostering trust in public decision-making while preserving the benefits of the free flow of information to decision-makers by lobbyists should begin with clarifying and better understanding the nature of public concerns, especially those related to issues such as the accessibility to decisionmakers, the integrity of political decision-making proceedings, and the perceived conduct in lobbying. Additionally, regulations and legislative provisions related to lobbying must respect and conform to the prevailing

[29]For the cases of Poland and Hungary, see McGrath (2008), pp. 19–20.

[30]Ridao (2017), p. 23. Accordingly, Von Alemann and Eckert (2006), pp. 07-09 put into question the black and white approach to lobbying, since it misrepresents the real problem regarding lobbying activities: the intermediate area between these two extremes, which is characterised by the fact that they do not encompass criminal offence, but rather forms of behaviour constituting misconduct.

[31]For further information, see Transparency International (2015, 2017).

political culture, the established democratic practices, constitutional tradition, and the administrative context in each jurisdiction. In any case, those standards and rules should be consistent with the wider regulatory framework that promotes good governance across the public and private sectors, which must include, inter alia, provisions criminalising undue influencing of public decision-making, such as influence trafficking, bribery and other corruption offences, clear codes of conduct and ethical standards for public officials when contacted by lobbyists, as well as measures that prevent the "revolving door" phenomenon.[32]

The second building block puts emphasis on the importance of clearly defining the scope of the lobbying policy or regulation. In particular, it is considered that public authorities must strive to clarify what actors and activities are deemed to be lobbyists and lobbying and, moreover, to provide proper descriptions of reasonable exclusions and exemptions. According to the recommendations, in order to generate a level playing field for all interest groups intending to influence political decisions, lobbying activities should be broadly and inclusively defined and the specificities of the competing interest groups should be taken into account. Besides, definitions can be refined by specifying that certain classes of actors or activities are excluded from the policies or regulations. For instance, communication that is already on public record, such as formal presentations to legislative committees, and representatives of other governments as they act in their official capacity could be excluded from the definitions.[33]

The third building block examines the necessity to establish clear and suitable standards, rules, and procedures for collecting and disclosing pertinent but parsimonious information on key aspects of lobbying, such as its intent, beneficiaries and targets. According to the OECD, an effective disclosure system should provide officials and citizens with sufficient information to clearly identify lobbying activities and objectives, as well as the interests being represented. For that purpose, efforts must be made to establish policy or regulation in order to disclose information on who is trying to influence public decisions, which may include lobbyist registration and periodical reporting of lobbying activities. In addition, it is necessary to set up supportive transparency measures and mechanisms that enable public scrutiny without implying an indiscriminate openness or an excessive demand for information.[34]

The fourth building block deals with the standards of conduct for lobbyists to foster a culture of integrity in lobbying. The recommendations encourage self-regulation in the form of professional codes to be developed by associations of lobbyists or professional bodies. Professional codes would state ground rules for lobbyists in their relations with public officials, other lobbyists, their clients, and the public, as well as the sanctions that could be applied in the case of failure to conform to these rules. However, when the perceived conduct of lobbyists raises significant

---

[32]For further information, see OECD (2009), pp. 21–25.

[33]For further information, see OECD (2009), pp. 25–26.

[34]For further information, see OECD (2009), pp. 26–29.

public concern, maintaining trust in the government's decision-making process would require public authorities to set professional and ethical standards of conduct for lobbyists. The goal of such standards of conduct is to promote the principles of good governance, more particularly, integrity, honesty, transparency, accuracy of information, and avoiding conflicts of interest. [35]

Finally, the fifth building block revolves around the enforcement mechanisms that ensure compliance with standards and rules. According to the OECD, putting a regulation into effect requires the involvement of all key actors, in particular public officials and lobbyists, to establish a common understanding of the expected standards in daily practice. Additionally, ensuring both voluntary and mandatory compliance entails the design and application of carefully balanced incentives and sanctions in a coherent spectrum of strategies and practices for supporting implementation through communication, education, formal reporting, leadership, managerial directives, incentives, sanction and co-ordination. Lastly, effective enforcement of lobbying policies or regulations entails dissuasive and proportional sanctions and depends on the cooperation of the public officials who are lobbied. Moreover, it requires States to provide administrators of lobbying policies or regulations with independence, operational competence, and sufficient resources to effectively carry out their responsibilities.[36]

## 3.2 *Political Financing*

The financing of political parties and electoral campaigns is another legitimate mechanism of political participation that is used by interest groups to exert influence over public policies.

As we know, a political party is a political organisation, which is formed for the purpose of winning elections in order to obtain general control of the government.[37] Since political parties play a crucial role in the performance of democratic political functions and they need appropriate funding in order to carry out their core activities, it is of particular relevance to examine their sources of income.[38]

Certainly, money means a great deal in political parties.[39] Beyond political campaigns, political parties spend their resources on maintaining permanent offices and staff, engaging in political mobilisation, socialisation and integration, organising rallies and other events, carrying out policy research, and promoting political

[35]For further information, see OECD (2009), pp. 29–30.

[36]OECD (2009), pp. 30–34.

[37]Schattschneider (2017), p. 187. For other definitions of political parties, see Almond et al. (2010), pp. 81–82; Lapalombara (2007), p. 144; Strøm (1990), p. 574; King (1969), pp. 113–117; Katz and Mair (1999), pp. 21–22.

[38]Diamond and Morlino (2005), p. 18.

[39]Diamond and Morlino (2005), p. 18.

propaganda.[40] Hence, Western political systems have struggled to provide sources of private and public funding for political parties that enhance democratic values on the decision-making process without encouraging the sale of officeholders and political parties to wealthy interest groups and individuals.[41] Among the main sources of income are regular membership and affiliation fees, profit of party-owned business and investments, such as the sale of party literature and newspapers, funds from the government budget in the form of public subsidies, public non-financial resources, and donations from individuals and organisations.[42]

Although private and societal contributions were originally the main sources of income for political parties and candidates, a set of specific social, cultural and political conditions, mainly the general decline in the levels of political participation and the increase in the costs of permanent parties and electoral activities cause political parties to move away from civil society towards the State, using their control of the centres of political decision-making to provide themselves with all necessary resources to survive and prosper in the political arena.[43]

Thus, as Piccio and Van Biezen pointed out, the public funding of the political process in the form of State subsidies has gradually become a widespread phenomenon, with Hungary and Spain among the countries that contribute most resources to political parties and electoral campaigns.[44] Broadly speaking, public funding encompasses the allocation of direct and indirect subsidies to political parties. While *direct public funding* includes pecuniary benefits, often in the form of State subventions, *indirect public funding* refers to resources with a monetary value that the States provide to political parties, including tax exemptions, free political broadcasts in the media, access to public buildings, provisions of goods, and so on.[45]

In literature on political parties, public financing is usually justified by the following arguments. Firstly, it potentially strengthens political pluralism, ensuring broader levels of ideological diversity and more equitable conditions in electoral competitions. Secondly, it is essential to the sound functioning of democracies, providing political parties with the necessary financial resources to bear the increasing costs of their permanent and electoral activities. Moreover, it guarantees the independence and the impartiality of candidates and political parties, meaningfully

[40]In this sense, see Pinto-Duschinsky (2002), p. 70; Koole (2014), pp. 45–47.

[41]Rose-Ackerman and Palifka (2016), p. 356.

[42]Regarding this point, see Rodríguez Teruel (2016), pp. 136–137; Mendilow (2018), pp. 01–03.

[43]Katz and Mair (1999), pp. 15–16; Rodríguez Teruel (2016), pp. 136–137.

[44]Based on empirical evidence, Piccio and Van Biezen (2018), p. 70 observe that "the relative importance of State subsidies as a source of party income is considerable: across European democracies, the state contributes on average nearly 60 per cent of total party income. There is variation between countries of course. The state reportedly provides only around 30 per cent of total party income in Germany and the Netherlands, for example, against nearly 80 percent in Hungary and Spain. The UK is situated at the lowest end of the scale, with the state contributing to a mere 10 per cent of party income (amongst others in the form of so-called policy development grants)". In this sense, see Sawer and Gauja (2016), pp. 06–07.

[45]OECD (2016), pp. 44–45.

reducing the influence of wealthy donors and powerful interest groups on public policy and legislative outcomes. It can also be used to promote gender equality in politics, linking the allocation of public aid to the enforcement of electoral quotas and the nomination of women as candidates. Finally, it fosters the institutionalisation of legal mechanisms to advance party transparency and accountability, since the allocation of public resources usually requires more strict regulations and rules to prevent fraud, corruption and other illegal activities in political fundraising and spending.[46]

Notwithstanding the foregoing, under the surface public funding systems often work rather differently from the democratic values of equity, inclusiveness, and fair play. Indeed, some studies indicate that the steady increase in State subventions to political parties and candidates is linked to the emergence of a new type of political party: *a cartel party*. According to Katz and Mair, the cartel party is characterised by a close symbiosis between parties and the State, by a high level of party reliance on public resources, and also by a pattern of collusion and cooperation between all, or almost all, relevant political parties.[47] In this configuration, political parties gradually become agents of the State, securing themselves large amounts of money and resources and, at the same time, posing some important barriers for minority parties and newly organised political alternatives that struggle to participate fully in electoral competitions. In this sense, the State "becomes an institutionalised structure of support, sustaining insiders while excluding outsiders".[48]

In short, the rent-seeking relationship of political parties with the State can be as much a concern as the reliance of political parties on private money: both might be detrimental to political equality and thus to the general public's good. On the one hand, empirical research suggests that, under some circumstances, public financing could completely determine the dominant parties in the long run, despite the preferences of interest groups or society. One important caveat is that the effect of public financing depends strongly on the amount of State aid. If it is too small, its long-term effect will be insignificant. On the contrary, if it is high enough, it may entirely jeopardise long-term electoral competition.[49] On the other hand, an exclusive reliance on private-sector funds can have a direct influence on the way public policies and legislative regulations are conceived, enacted, and implemented, thus negatively impacting the performance of political systems and the distribution of power in democracies.

On this matter, empirical analysis reveals that electoral donations and contributions to political parties and candidates are usually used by wealthy donors to build long-term relationships with key political leaders and, as a result, to receive preferential treatment and benefits in terms of favourable regulations, awards of

[46]For further information, see OECD (2016), pp. 06–07.

[47]Katz and Mair (1999), p. 16.

[48]Katz and Mair (1999), pp. 15–16.

[49]Cuoco Portugal et al. (2007), pp. 148–149, 169–170.

government contracts, fewer controls, and favourable administrative decisions.[50] In fact, according to Offe, in several developed countries political donations are commonly granted by powerful economic agents to the two largest and most powerful political parties. In doing so, these political actors increase the likelihood of their interests being duly considered by political decision-makers and, in addition, guarantee themselves the power to "sanction" candidates and political parties who fail to reciprocate by simply discontinuing said donations.[51] Thus, even entirely legal contributions from wealthy interests are a source of concern, since money is often given with the expectation that it will be reciprocated in some way.[52]

Given the significance of political parties and the role that money plays in politics, there is a broadly shared and long-standing consensus that political financing must be subject to a strong legal and regulatory framework. However, despite efforts taken over the years, the increasing number of scandals concerning corruption and illegal campaign contributions and expenditures is an indication that States have largely failed to develop optimal and sustainable models of political financing. Hardly a month goes by without a political party being accused of corruption or some political financing negligence across the globe.[53] Some of these accusations encompass corporations and interest groups spending a lot of resources in an effort to exert undue influence on political leaders and to assure preferential treatment in the distribution of public resources at the expense of the general public. Many others, however, involve claims of illegal expenditure, secret slush funds, and contributions from disreputable sources, activities disobeying political finance regulations, allegations of corrupt dealings related to political financing, including buying voters, as well as cases of fraud, embezzlement, misappropriation or improper use of party and campaign funds.[54]

According to the OECD, the political financing framework may be built on four main pillars: the promotion of a level playing field, the assurance of transparency and accountability, the creation and consolidation of a culture of integrity, and the guarantee of compliance and review.[55]

To promote a level playing field, States should guarantee a regulation of political finance that focuses on the full electoral cycle, including the pre-campaign phase, the campaigning period itself, and the period once the elected official takes office. Against this background, it is absolutely necessary to implement measures to guarantee the balance between direct and indirect public contributions, to limit privileged access to State resources by ruling parties and candidates, to impose

---

[50]Evertsson (2018), pp. 50–51.

[51]Offe (2004), p. 89.

[52]In this sense, see Mendilow (2018), p. 03; Rose-Ackerman and Palifka (2016), p. 357; Peters and Welch (2009), pp. 159–160.

[53]For an example of campaign finance scandals, see Rose-Ackerman and Palifka (2016), pp. 356–359.

[54]For further information, see Pinto-Duschinsky (2002), pp. 69–74.

[55]OECD (2016), p. 27.

clear limits on political contributions and spending, and to forbid certain types of private contributions, in particular contributions from foreign donors, from anonymous sources, and from corporations with government contracts or partial government ownership. In addition, it is important to consider that certain shortcomings in the regulations are particularly vulnerable to exploitation by powerful special interests. Loans, membership fees and third-party funding, for instance, can be used to circumvent the regulations of private funding.[56]

Besides that, to assure transparency and accountability, States should require for political parties and candidates to disclose information on how they raise and spend money, since such information can facilitate better informed voter decisions, as well as an effective oversight of political finance. Comprehensive disclosure of financial information contributes to greater transparency and accountability, serving as a deterrent measure to minimise the impact of undue influence. No oversight mechanism, however, is complete without civil society and media scrutiny. Therefore, the political finance information must be organised in an intelligible and user-friendly way, submitted and published in a standardised, machine-readable format, and made publicly available for their analysis. Only then will civil society and media be able to play their watchdog role, ensuring effective electoral and social accountability.[57]

Similarly, in order to foster a culture of integrity among political parties, public officials and donors, States should promote a comprehensive approach to integrity and good governance, including issues such as the adoption of enforceable codes of conduct, conflict of interest policies for high-risk categories of public officials, disclosure of selected private interests (assets, liabilities, income sources and amount, paid and un-paid outside positions, gifts and previous employment) and the public availability of such information, the legal regulation of lobbying practices, including the disclosure of lobbyist contributions to political campaigns, structured approach to risk assessment, and the introductions of whistle-blower protection mechanisms. However, promoting a culture of integrity in the public sector is only part of the equation. In order to mitigate the risks of money in politics, a culture of integrity can and should also be promoted among private donors. It is therefore of great importance to design policy instruments to promote responsible lobbying and business practices, including measures to prevent corruption and cartel formation.[58]

Lastly, to safeguard compliance and reviews, States should ensure an independent and efficient oversight of political finance. For this purpose, States may choose from a variety of non-exclusive institutional arrangements. They can either establish an independent oversight body tasked with the supervision of political finance or allocate the responsibilities for monitoring and enforcing political financing regulations among different government bodies and agencies. In order to strengthen investigatory capacity, some countries can also closely advance cooperation between enforcement bodies, while others can promote internal auditing within their

[56]OECD (2016), pp. 27–28, 30, 35–64.

[57]OECD (2016), pp. 28, 30, 65–77.

[58]OECD (2016), pp. 28–29, 79–93.

structure. In any case, the proper functioning of supervisory bodies must consider the following factors: (1) independent appointment of its members (independence from both political parties and the executive at the same time) and security of their tenure; (2) independent budget providing sufficient resources; (3) specialised expertise of personnel and methodologies to discover illegal funding of political parties and candidates; (4) clear mandate and legal power to conduct investigations, refer cases for prosecution, and impose dissuasive and enforceable sanctions; (5) educational and training support programmes for political parties to encourage compliance with the legal regulation.[59]

## 3.3 *Political Corruption*

Political corruption is one of the major challenges that contemporary democracies are facing today.[60] Cross-national studies support the argument that corruption leads to adverse consequences for economic performance and growth by perverting competitive bidding procedures, improving delay in the distribution of permits and licenses, generating anti-competitive market distortions, reducing incentives to private investments in strategic sectors, particularly foreign direct investments, and increasing inefficiency in the allocation and flow of public goods and services.[61] Likewise, the available data suggests that corruption and, notably, political corruption, is a determining factor for the low rates of human development and welfare. This is largely due to the fact that predatory behaviour by corrupt politicians distorts the composition of government expenditure, with education and health spending being adversely affected by this sort of malfeasance. Furthermore, corruption is associated with poverty and the unequal distribution of income and wealth, ineffective tax collection and administration, as well as low quality and the slow implementation of environmental policies.[62] Finally, strong empirical evidence shows that political corruption affects the fiduciary relationship between rulers and citizens, corroding public trust in democratic institutions and political processes, undermining the rule of law, and ultimately, delegitimising the State. As Maciel and Sousa highlight, if "citizens are unable to see through the mechanisms of politics and understand how decisions are made, but have the feeling that these systematically serve a restricted group of powerful individuals and businesses, they tend to believe

---

[59]OECD (2016), pp. 30–31, 95–109.

[60]Díez-Picazo (2000), pp. 20–21.

[61]For further information, see Mauro (1995), pp. 683, 695–706; Bardhan (1997), pp. 1323–1329; Ades and Di Tella (1999), pp. 991–992; Emerson (2006), pp. 193–195, 211.

[62]For further information, see Mauro (1998), pp. 263–267, 277–278; Baughn et al. (2010), p. 15; Pellegrini and Gerlagh (2006), pp. 335–336, 348; Transparency International (2013).

the democratic process has departed from its natural condition and evolved into something else that has little to do with the fostering of the public interest".[63]

In this context, the following question arises: *what is corruption?*

Corruption has been traditionally defined as the *abuse of public office for private gain.*[64] Not accidentally, the legal literature on corruption was restricted to the analysis of criminal offences against public administrations, encompassing theoretical debates on the delimitation of the protected legal good, on the meaning of the elements that constitute the corruption offences, on the questions regarding the application of regulatory and legal acts, as well as on issues relating to investigation techniques, criminal evidence, and criminal procedures. Additionally, relevant theoretical and empirical studies in the field of political economy and political science shared a broad consensus that the better mechanisms for preventing and curbing corruption would be the aggravation of sanctions regarding corruption offences, the imposition of limits to the use of discretionary power, and the reduction of State intervention in the economy through measures such as the privatisation of public companies and market deregulation.[65]

In spite of their previous significance, these assumptions have gradually been replaced by a more comprehensive and sophisticated notion of corruption. Thus, in contemporary literature, we can distinguish between two principal meanings of the term.

In the first sense, corruption is defined as the *abuse or misuse of entrusted power for private gain.* As Rose-Ackerman and Palifka pointed out, this definition captures the principal-agent problem at the root of all types of corruption, either in private or public realms.[66] Hence, in this sense, political corruption involves the violation of a regulatory system that delegates to representatives discretionary power, resources, capacity and information to pursue the tasks that are expressions of the interests of the sovereign people. The key term of this concept is *entrusted power*, which refers to the tasks one is expected to perform according to certain rules, regulations and procedures. If the representatives abuse said entrusted power, those rules, regulations and procedures are broken, and the citizens' stated goals are subverted. Corruption, therefore, can entail the explicit exchange of money, gifts in kind, favours for rule breaking, or payment for benefits that should legally be costless. Likewise, it can imply the use of political position, influence in government, or connections with public authorities to obtain favours or preferential treatment for a third party in exchange for money or other valuable resources. Finally, in a broader sense, it can also implicate the misappropriation of entrusted public funds as well as the practice of nepotism or patronage in political appointments.[67]

---

[63]Maciel and Sousa (2018), p. 658.

[64]In this sense, Treisman (2007), p. 211; Heidenheimer (1993), pp. 3–13; Friedrich (2009), p. 15.

[65]For further information, see Lambsdorff (2009), pp. 389–392.

[66]Rose-Ackerman and Palifka (2016), pp. 06–08.

[67]In this sense, see Rose-Ackerman and Palifka (2016), pp. 06–08. Despite embracing the principal-agent approach, Della Porta and Vannucci (2012), pp. 07–12, claim that we can only speak of

Instead, in the second sense, corruption is associated with more or less *complex networks of corrupt exchanges*, which are sustained by governance structures and enforcement mechanisms that regulate and coordinate corrupt transactions among different agents, overcoming their tendency to free ride and lowering the transaction costs of such illegal dealings.[68] In addressing this issue, Della Porta and Vannucci stress that transaction costs are higher in corruption than in ordinary markets, since the search for a counterpart, the gathering of relevant and reliable information, the negotiation and bargaining of corrupt agreements, the exchange of commodities and political rents, as well as the monitoring, implementation, and potential enforcement of corrupt dealings are extremely risky and costly in terms of time and money.[69] So, corrupt exchanges could only flourish and spread across different societies and environments if it is underpinned by a *hidden order*, that is, by a set of institutional arrangements that help such opaque, secret, and illegal dealings to become an acceptable, viable and profitable alternative for rational agents.[70] In fact, where political corruption is widespread, it is possible to observe the existence of internalised codes, practices and informal norms that neutralise the moral costs of illegal behaviours and favour corruption, pre-existing networks based on reciprocity and trust, rational investments in increasing the reputation of honesty in illegal transactions, as well as the presence of brokers or middlemen that intervene to facilitate and enforce corrupt agreements.[71] All these mechanisms and institutions are components of a "complex organisational architecture that facilitates the implementation of corrupt exchanges, enforcing hidden agreements and reducing transaction costs".[72]

The reality of political corruption, therefore, can take several forms. Among others, it can embrace activities such as the acceptance of money in return for an unauthorised favour or the promise of a favour in the event of election to an office, the direct and secret purchase or sale of a parliamentarian's vote on important pieces of legislation by a powerful entrepreneur or interest group, the use of social power and political connections to obtain favours or preferential treatment for third parties in exchange for a payment, the practice of revolving doors, or the use of political appointments based on familiar patronage.[73] However, corruption can also stratify, involving a complex network of politicians, government officials, political parties,

---

corruption "when a third actor enters into, and distort, the relations between agent and principal". So, in its elementary logic, corruption would be a three player-game. According to the authors, "the intervention of a client or a briber pushes the agent to sidestep the constrains and controls imposed by norms and procedures. The corrupter, by offering resources such as money or other utilities, succeed in obtaining favorable decisions, reserved information, or the broader protection of his interests" (p. 09).

[68]Della Porta and Vannucci (2005), pp. 154–155; Della Porta and Vannucci (2012), p. 23.

[69]Della Porta and Vannucci (2005), p. 153.

[70]Della Porta and Vannucci (2005), pp. 154–155; Della Porta and Vannucci (2012), p. 23.

[71]For further information, see Della Porta and Vannucci (2012) passim.

[72]Della Porta and Vannucci (2012), p. 34.

[73]In a similar vein, see Pinto-Duschinsky (2002), p. 71; Maciel and Sousa (2018), pp. 655–659.

interest groups, and brokers, as well as the exchange of (small and large) sums of money in order to secure favourable outcomes for few individuals and organisations or to obtain control over decision-making processes and public resources.[74]

Having said that, a distinction has been made between attempts of a single interest group to exert undue influence on legal, regulatory, and policy proceedings through corrupt activities and illegal political financing practices and a more comprehensive phenomenon known as *State capture*, a form of grand corruption which occurs when political elites and powerful interests conspire to distort and manipulate decision-making proceedings and the democratic rules of the game in order to secure themselves particular advantages from government policies or legislative and regulatory outcomes.[75] According to Hellman and Kauffman, State capture may be defined as "the efforts of firms to shape the laws, policies, and regulations of the State to their own advantage by providing illicit private gains to public officials".[76] Thus, capture is the "opposite of inclusive and fair policy-making, and always undermines core democratic values".[77] In the legislative field, this capture may involve a great deal of legal and illegal activities, including payments of bribes to representatives, informal lobbying, trading in influence, donations to political parties and prospective candidates, the use of slush funds, patronage appointments, and the practice of revolving doors.[78] All these activities can translate into mechanisms for buying political influence, jeopardising the general performance and, thus, the very legitimacy of democratic political systems.[79]

On this matter, the OECD has elaborated a set of recommendations for policymakers to identify and mitigate State capture risks. Building on previous works on integrity, conflicts of interest, lobbying and political financing, its report provides integrated and mutually reinforcing strategies based on transparency, stakeholder engagement, accountability, and organisational integrity. Amongst the principal measures are the regulation of lobbying activity and political financing, the setting up of accountability mechanisms, the conduction of compliance audits on political fundraising and spending, the creation of meaningful opportunities (including online) for the public to participate in the political decision-making processes,

---

[74]Della Porta and Vannucci (2012), pp. 01–02.

[75]Therefore, while most types of corruption are directed toward changing how existing laws, rules, or regulations are implemented with regards to the bribe payer, state capture refers to corrupt efforts to influence how those laws, rules, and regulations are formed. Bribes to parliamentarians to "buy" their votes on important pieces of legislation, bribes to government officials to enact favourable regulations or decrees, bribes to judges to influence court decisions - these are the classic examples of grand corruption through which firms can encode advantages for themselves into the basic legal and regulatory structure of the economy.

[76]Hellman and Kauffman (2001).

[77]For further information, see OECD (2017), pp. 09–10, 13–27.

[78]Maciel and Sousa (2018), p. 667.

[79]Transparency International (2014), p. 02.

and the disclosure of relevant information regarding the financial assets, liabilities and interests of public officials and representatives.[80]

# 4 Concluding Remarks

Based on the above considerations, the following conclusions shall be drawn:

1. Interest groups are key features of contemporary democracies. Through these political participation channels, citizens can articulate their political values, preferences and interests, express their support and demands to the government, and seek to influence the public policy.
2. Private interests seeking to influence public decision-making process through legal and legitimate means, such as lobbying or the financing of political parties and electoral campaigns, is part of the complex political game.
3. Lobbying is a form of political action that could guarantee the communicative conditions of an inclusive political process of opinion- and will-formation, since it potentially enables a true balance and conciliation of all competing interests, preferences and values at stake.
4. Political financing is a legitimate mechanism of political participation that enables political parties to carry out their democratic functions.
5. Lobbying activities and political financing practices shall be carefully regulated by legislation for the sake of transparency, openness, and accountability.
6. The legislation or government regulation regarding lobbying and political financing should be based on good governance principles, including integrity, honesty, transparency, accuracy of information, and avoiding conflicts of interest.
7. In a narrow sense, corruption is defined as the abuse or misuse of entrusted power for private gain, encompassing offences such as bribery, fraud, embezzlement, misappropriation, and trading in influence.
8. Corruption is also associated with more or less complex networks of corrupt exchanges, which are sustained by governance structures and enforcement mechanisms that regulate and coordinate corrupt transactions among different agents, overcoming their tendency to free ride and lowering the transaction costs of such illegal dealings.
9. Finally, a distinction has been made between attempts of a single interest group to exert undue influence on legal, regulatory, and policy proceedings through corrupt activities and illegal political financing practices and a more comprehensive phenomenon known as *State capture*, a form of great corruption which occurs when political elites and powerful interests conspire to distort and manipulate decision-making proceedings and the democratic rules of the game

[80]For further information, see OECD (2017), pp. 53–79.

in order to secure themselves particular advantages from government policies or legislative and regulatory outcomes.

10. In the legislative branch, this capture may involve a great deal of legal and illegal activities, including payments of bribes to representatives, informal lobbying, trading in influence, donations to political parties and prospective candidates, the use of slush funds, patronage appointments, and the practice of revolving doors.
11. Efforts to prevent and curb the capture of the State must include integrated and mutually reinforcing strategies based on transparency, stakeholder engagement, accountability, and organisational integrity.

**Acknowledgements** The author would like to thank José Luis Díez Ripollés, Heloísa Estellita and the anonymous reviewers for their critical comments on earlier versions of this article.

## References

Ades A, Di Tella R (1999) Rents, competition, and corruption. Am Econ Rev 89(4):982–993

Almond GA, Powell GB, Dalton RJ, Strøm K (2010) Comparative politics today: a world view, 9th edn. Longman, Nueva York

Álvarez Vélez MI, De Montalvo Jääskeläinen F (2014) Los lobbies en el marco de la Unión Europea: una reflexión a propósito de su regulación en España. Teoría y Realidad Constitucional 33:53–376

Bardhan P (1997) Corruption and development: a review of issues. J Econ Literature 35 (3):1320–1346

Baughn C, Bodie NL, Buchanan MA, Bixby MB (2010) Bribery in international business transactions. J Bus Ethics 92(1):15–32

Bennedsen M, Feldmann SE (2002) Lobbying legislatures. J Polit Econ 110(4):919–946

Bertrand M, Bombardini M, Trebbi F (2014) Is it whom you know or what you know? An empirical assessment of the lobbying process. Am Econ Rev 104(12):3885–3920

Binderkrantz A (2005) Interest group strategies: navigating between privileged access and strategies of pressure. Political Stud 53:694–715

Cuoco Portugal A, Bugarin M, Dal Bó E (2007) Electoral campaign financing: the role of public contributions and party ideology (with comments). Economía 8(1):143–177

Della porta D, Vannucci A (2005) The governance mechanisms of corrupt transactions. In: Lambsdorff JG, Taube M, Schramm M (eds) The new institutional economics of corruption. Routledge, London

Della Porta D, Vannucci A (2012) The hidden order of corruption: an institutional approach. Ashgate, Surrey

Diamond L (2008) The spirit of democracy: the struggles to built free societies throughout the world. Henry Holt and Company, New York

Diamond L, Morlino L (2005) Introduction. Assessing the quality of democracy. The Johns Hopkins University Press, Baltimore

Díez-picazo LM (2000) La criminalidad de los gobernantes. Editorial Crítica, Barcelona

Eising R (2008) Interest groups in EU policy-making. Living Rev Eur Governance 4:04–32

Emerson PM (2006) Corruption, competition and democracy. J Dev Econ 81:193–212

Evertsson N (2018) Corporate contributions to electoral campaigns: the current state of affairs. In: Mendilow J, Phélippeau E (eds) Handbook of political party funding. Edward Elgar Publishing, Northampton

Felli L, Merlo A (2006) Endogenous lobbying. J Eur Econ Assoc 4(1):180–215
Friedrich CJ (2009) Corruption concepts in historical perspective. In: Heidenheimer AJ, Johnston M (eds) Political corruption: concepts & contexts, 3rd edn. Transaction Publishers, New Brunswick
Habermas J (1994) Three normative models of democracy. Constellations 1(01):01–10
Heidenheimer AJ, Johnston M, Levine VT (1993) Terms, concepts, and definitions. Political corruption: a handbook. Transaction Publishers, New Brunswick
Hellman J, Kauffman D (2001) Confronting the challenge of state capture in transition economies. Finance Dev 38(3):31–35. https://www.imf.org/external/pubs/ft/fandd/2001/09/hellman.htm
Ibarra P, Letameda F (2015) Movimientos sociales. In: Caminal Badia M, Torrens X (eds) Manual de ciencia política. Tecnos, Madrid
Jordana J (2015) Asociaciones de interés y acción colectiva. In: Caminal Badia M, Torrens X (eds) Manual de ciencia política, 4th edn. Tecnos, Madrid
Katz RS, Mair P (1999) Changing models of party organization and party democracy: the emergence of the cartel party. Party Politics 1(5):05–28
King A (1969) Political parties in Western Democracies: some sceptical reflections. Polity 2 (2):111–141
Klüver H (2011) The contextual nature of lobbying: explaining lobbying success in the European Union. Eur Union Politics 12(4):483–506
Koole R (2014) Dilemmas of regulating political finance, with special reference to the Dutch case. In: van Biezen I, ten Napel H-M (eds) Regulating political parties: European democracies in comparative perspective. Leiden University Press, Leiden
Lambsdorff JG (2009) The organization of anticorruption: getting incentives right. In: Rotberg RI (ed) Corruption, global security, and world order. Brookings Institution Press, Washington, DC
Lapalombara J (2007) Reflections on political parties and political development. Party Politics 13 (2):141–151
Lapalombara J (2015) Interest groups in Italian politics. Princeton University Press, Princeton
Maciel GG, Sousa L (2018) Legal corruption and dissatisfaction with democracy in the European Union. Soc Indicators Res 140:653–674
Mauro P (1995) Corruption and Growth. Q J Econ 110(3):681–712
Mauro P (1998) Corruption and the composition of government expenditure. J Public Econ 69:263–279
Mcgrath C (2006) The ideal lobbyist: personal characteristics of effective lobbyists. J Commun Manag 10(1):67–79
Mcgrath C (2008) The development and regulation of lobbying in the new member states of the European Union. J Public Aff 8(32):15–32
Mendilow J (2018) Introduction: the party funding paradox and attempts at solution. In: Mendilow J, Phélippeau E (eds) Handbook of political party funding. Edward Elgar Publishing, Northampton
Milbrath LW (1958) The political party activity of Washington lobbysts. J Politics 20(2):339–352
Mitnick BM (1993) Political contestability. In: Mitnick BM (ed) Corporate political agency: the construction of competition in public affairs. Sage Publications, Newbury Park
Nownes AJ, Freeman P (1998) Interest group activity in the states. J Politics 60(1):86–112
OECD (2009) Lobbyists, governments, and public trust: volume 01. Increasing transparency through legislation. OECD Publishing, Paris
OECD (2012) Lobbyists, governments and public trust: volume 02. Promoting integrity through self-regulation. OECD Publishing, Paris
OECD (2016) Financing democracy: funding of political parties and election campaigns and the risk of policy capture. OECD Publishing, Paris
OECD (2017) Preventing policy capture: integrity in policy decision making. OECD Publishing, Paris
Offe C (2004) Political corruption: conceptual and practical issues. In: Kornai J, Rose-Ackerman S (eds) Building a trustworthy state in post-socialist transition. Palgrave Macmillan, New York

Pellegrini L, Gerlagh R (2006) Corruption, democracy, and environmental policy: empirical contribution to the debate. J Environ Dev 15:332–354
Peters JG, Welch S (2009) Gradients of corruption in perceptions of public American life. In: Heidenheimer AJ, Johnston M (eds) Political corruption: concepts & contexts, 3rd edn. Transaction Publishers, New Brunswick
Piccio DR, Van Biezen I (2018) Political finance and the cartel party thesis. In: Mendilow J, Phélippeau E (eds) Handbook of political party funding. Edward Elgar Publishing, Northampton
Pinto-Duschinsky M (2002) Financing politics: a global view. J Democracy 4:69–86
Przeworski A (2010) Democracy and the limits of self-Government. Cambridge University Press, New York
Ridao J (2017) Los grupos de presión: análisis de la regulación del lobby en la UE y España. Tirant lo Blanch, Valencia
Rodríguez Teruel J (2016) Dinero público y ciudadanos ausentes: la financiación de los partidos en España. In: Llera Ramo FJ (ed) Desafección política y regeneración democrática en la España actual: diagnósticos y propuestas. Centro de Estudios Políticos y Constitucionales, Madrid
Rose-Ackerman S, Palifka BJ (2016) Corruption and government: causes, consequences, and reform. Cambridge University Press, New York
Sawer M, Gauja A (2016) Party rules: promises and pitfalls. In: Gauja A, Sawer M (eds) Party rules? Dilemmas of political party regulation in Australia. ANU Press, Canberra
Schattschneider EE (1960) The semisovereign people: a realist's view of democracy in America. Holt, Rinehart and Winston, New York
Schattschneider EE (2017) Party government: American government in action. Routledge, New York
Straßner A (2006) Funktionen von Verbänden in der modernen Gesellschaft. Aus Politik und Zeitgeschichte 15-16:10–17
Strøm K (1990) A behavioral theory of competitive political parties. Am J Political Sci 34 (2):565–598
Thomas CS, Hrebenar RJ (2008) Understanding interest groups, lobbying and lobbyists in developing democracies. J Public Aff 8:1–14
Transparency international (2013) Literature review on costs of corruption for the poor. U4 Expert Answer 382
Transparency International (2014) State capture: an overview. Anti-corruption helpdesk. https://www.transparency.org/files/content/corruptionqas/State_capture_an_overview_2014.pdf
Transparency International (2015) Lobbying in Europe: hidden influence, privileged access. Transparency International Publishing, Berlin. https://www.transparency.org/whatwedo/publication/lobbying_in_europe
Transparency international (2017) Defining lobbyists and regulation lobbying in Europe. Transparency International Publishing, Anti-Corruption Helpdesk. https://knowledgehub.transparency.org/assets/uploads/helpdesk/Defining_lobbyists_and_regulating_lobbying_in_Europe_2016.pdf
Treisman D (2007) What have we learned about the causes of corruption from ten years of cross-national empirical research? Ann Rev Political Sci 10:211–244
Von Alemann U, Eckert F (2006) Lobbyismus als Schattenpolitik. Aus Politik und Zeitgeschichte 15-16:03–10

# Part II
# Rationality Standards and the Legislative Phase

# Does Public Opinion Matter for Criminal Law? Revisable Life Imprisonment in Spain and Its Relationship with Social Demands

**Fernando Miró-Llinares and Ana B. Gómez-Bellvís**

**Abstract** Since the 1980s, criminological and legal literature has dealt both theoretically and empirically with the phenomenon of punitive populism. In Spain, from 2003 to 2019, punitivisim has had a prominent role with 33 modifications to the Spanish Criminal Code. These included the introduction of revisable permanent prison for the most serious crimes, which was explicitly justified in the legal system by the social support for this punishment. In this sense, the political power has claimed the need to maintain and increase the scope of this punishment in our country based on certain opinion polls whose methodology and results have been seriously questioned by some empirical studies. All of this has reopened the debate among experts on whether citizens should be considered when making legislative decisions that directly affect the values of a democratic state in general and fundamental rights in particular. This paper addresses the question of the data obtained on public opinion and reflects on whether this should be incorporated into criminal law.

**Keywords** Revisable life imprisonment · Social demand · Democracy · Penal populism · Legitimacy

This paper has been produced in the framework of the project 'NEXO. Criminology, empirical evidence and Criminal policy. On the use of scientific data for decision-making in relation to the criminalisation of conducts -Reference: DER2017-86204-R, funded by the State Research Agency (AEI)/Ministry of Science, Innovation and Universities and the European Union through the European Regional Development Fund-FEDER- 'A way to make Europe'. This work has also received funding from the grants for pre-doctoral contracts for the training of doctors 2018 (FPI) from the Ministry of Science, Innovation and Universities and with co-funding from the European Social Fund, with reference PRE2018-083939.

F. Miró-Llinares · A. B. Gómez-Bellvís (✉)
Department of Legal Sciences, Universidad Miguel Hernández, Elche, Spain
e-mail: fmiro@umh.es; ana.gomezb@umh.es

 
J. Becerra (ed.), *Criminal Law-Making*, Legisprudence Library 7,
https://doi.org/10.1007/978-3-030-71348-5_6

## 1 When the Reason Is Argued But Not Discussed: Criticism of 'Revisable Life Imprisonment' Beyond Its Constitutionality and Preventive Effectiveness

For decades, the harshening of sentences in most Western societies has been a matter of concern for academics dedicated to the study of criminal law policies.[1] In the analysis of this trend it is common to find a diagnosis based on what has been called 'punitive populism'.[2] This phenomenon, as is well known, is based on the hypothesis that the punitive drift in criminal policy is due to either citizens' demands for harsher penalties from politicians (punishment from 'below', or also 'democracy-at-work'), or to politicians' self-interested use of certain particularly high-profile crimes to offer changes in criminal laws and thus increase their electoral support (punishment as a 'top-down' process).[3] In any case, the phenomenon of punitive populism has a negative connotation regarding particularly severe penal legislation policies despite the fact that, in many societies in which it has been identified, crime rates are not worrying enough to justify punitive increases either in terms of prevention or of necessity.[4] Some examples of this type of legislation can be found in Canada's controversial 'Three Strikes Law' enacted on the basis of demands by a group of victims supported by certain politicians and a subsequent referendum;[5] the Crimes and Disorder Act 1998 in the United Kingdom clearly in the spirit of listening to public opinion on issues relating to crime and disorder;[6] or, revisable life imprisonment (hereafter RLI) in Spain that seems to have arisen as a consequence of social demands in the face of especially high-profile crimes.[7]

The emergence of this type of criminal law and the citizen-based justification provided by legislators has rekindled the debate on whether it is acceptable to take public opinion into account when designing and implementing criminal law. At the risk of falling into a dichotomous fallacy, for the moment, it can be said that such a debate has settled on two clearly identifiable positions: those academics who argue that citizen participation in criminal legislative policy produces such drastic and perverse effects that it is necessary to keep them separate;[8] and, those who

[1]Specifically, as Larrauri (2006) explains, this harshening of legislation and the consequent increase in the prison population has been detected since the 1980s. Garland (2001). Also, see Tonry (2007) and Duus-Otterström (2018).

[2]Bottoms (1995).

[3]Matthews (2005) and Wood (2014). However, the term 'democracy-at-work' is also used to refer to the link between social demands and the enactment of criminal laws (See Frost 2010).

[4]Hutton (2005) and Beckett and Snodgrass (2012).

[5]Greenberg (2002).

[6]Johnstone (2000).

[7]Miró Llinares (2019b), Gómez-Bellvís and Falces (2010). On the role of the media see Varona Gómez (2011).

[8]Thus, for Zimrig and his collaborators, the more democracy, the more severe the penal systems. They therefore understand that the solution to this is to move legislative policy away from the

understand that in accordance with democratic principles, the citizenry should not only participate, but should do so more than it already does[9] and we should even aim for a deliberative democracy model.[10]

It is striking, however, that two important nuances are missing from the debate and should perhaps be taken into consideration. The first relates to how this supposed social demand is constructed. As argued in a previous paper,[11] in academic arguments defending the isolation of criminal policy, it is taken for granted that there really is a social demand for harsher penalties and that this is directly related to the modification of criminal law. It is argued precisely against the legislator's reason for increasing state punishment, against making decisions based on society. However, the existence of this social demand is not disputed by the academics that claim to isolate criminal law from the public opinion, despite the fact that the social demand argument is based on pre-existing circumstances. The second nuance that is ignored in this debate is that it is not the same if a social demand comes directly from society or, rather, is created by the political power itself. In Spain, all these questions—whether there is consensus on the punishment of particularly serious crimes, whether there is a specific punitive social demand, whether this is a social demand that has been constructed by the public authorities or the media, and whether it is sufficient to justify a reform of this magnitude- have arisen as a result of the implementation of RLI. Regarding the latter, in 2015 Spanish legislators decided to introduce this penalty under the pretext of needing to strengthen trust in the justice system and to ensure citizens perceive the penalties for the most serious crimes as just.[12] It is not the first time that our Criminal Code has been amended to increase penalties or criminalise new conducts under the justification of alleged social demand or concern. However, it cannot be said that we are merely facing a further modification because, although it is true that our Criminal Code already provided for very long sentences, the very idea of life imprisonment in our country is at least an important qualitative change.[13] In fact, the Spanish legislator has revived a punishment that academia thought we had moved beyond since the beginning of the twentieth

pressure of society and leave it in the hands of experts (Zimrig and Johnson 2006). In Spain, Silva Sánchez (2018).

[9]Johnstone (2000).

[10]Dzur (2012), Green (2006), Varona Gómez (2018) and Rowan (2015).

[11]Miró Llinares (2019b).

[12]Specifically, the Explanatory Memorandum of the Law stated: 'The need to strengthen confidence in the Administration of Justice makes it necessary to make available to it a legal system that guarantees foreseeable judicial resolutions that, in addition, are perceived in society as just. To this end, following the model of other countries of our European context, a revisable life imprisonment is introduced for crimes of extreme severity, in which citizens demanded a sentence proportional to the act committed'.

[13]Nistal Burón (2015).

century,[14] and despite the fact that, in terms of official data,[15] Spain is among the European Union countries with the lowest rates of violent crime (and yet we have one of the harshest criminal codes[16]). As might be expected, practically all criminal law scholars were strongly against this type of punishment for very different reasons, of which perhaps the most relevant are those regarding the unconstitutionality of the measure based on the violation of both article 15 of the Constitution which prohibits inhuman or degrading punishment, and article 25.2 which establishes the legislative mandate to orientate punishment towards resocialisation. In addition, there were opposing views based on the ineffectiveness and needlessness of this punishment in terms of prevention. Along with these criticisms, there was strong criticism of the legislator for relying on the citizenry to introduce such a far-reaching change in our Criminal Code instead of relying on arguments considered 'rational' or instrumental. This has led to the emergence of voices warning of the dangers of incorporating society's—punitive?—demands into criminal legislation,[17] but also of others that doubt citizens' punitivism and that, in any case, express the need to take social opinions into account for their democratic value,[18] as well as for their effect on normative compliance.[19] This is obviously not a new debate, since it cannot be isolated from the eternal discussion on the material legitimacy of the state's exercise of *Ius Puniendi*, but today the discussion also encompasses the specific scope that citizen participation can have in the construction of criminal law, that is to say, the (more or less direct) way in which it must manifest itself and the role of experts and, in particular, of criminal law scholars in the delimitation of what could be called the 'correct criminal law' based on principles and guarantees from social and democratic rule of law.[20] It is the latter, a much more profound debate, that cannot be entirely resolved in the present paper. However, there is a more humble twofold goal, related only to the issue of RLI: on the one hand, to cast doubt on the main justification used by the legislator to introduce this penalty in the Spanish legal system, that is, to cast

[14]González Collantes (2013).

[15]For example, by 2016 and according to statistical data provided by Eurostat, Spain was the fourth country with the lowest rate of intentional homicides in the European Union, surpassed only by Slovenia, Austria and the Czech Republic. Regarding sexual assault, Spain ranked ninth among the 28 Member States of the European Union for the same year. In addition, if one looks at sexual crimes rates per 100,000 inhabitants collected from 2008 to 2016, a decrease in this time span can be observed. Available online at: https://ec.europa.eu/eurostat/statistics-explained/index.php?title=Crime_statistics/es.

[16]Díez Ripollés (2015a).

[17]Juanatey Dorado (2012) and Silva Sánchez (2018).

[18]Varona Gómez (2018).

[19]Robinson (2013) and Miró Llinares (2017).

[20]The expression 'correct criminal law' is used by Professor Silva Sánchez (2018) to refer to criminal law as a product of the work of penal dogmatics, which consists of distinguishing 'correct and incorrect criminal laws, between correct and incorrect judicial applications, as well as – in graduated terms- between some that are more correct than others'. All this through the rational analysis that only penal dogmatics has the capacity to carry out. For more on this matter, see Miró Llinares (2019a), Larrauri (2009) and Varona Gómez (2018).

doubt on the premise of social demand or social support for RLI in Spain. On the other hand, to reflect on the real importance that the existence of proven social support for this specific punishment would have and on what this would imply for the rule of law within the debate on the consideration of citizenry in the drafting of criminal laws.

## 2 Spanish Social Support for Revisable Life Imprisonment: ¿Fact or Fiction?

On the 30th of March 2015, the so-called RLI entered into force.[21] This is the most serious sentence in the Spanish legal system according to which, in the most favourable case, the person sentenced to this punishment must serve a minimum of 25 years in prison before the court can revise it and consider if they are eligible for parole.[22] Since its enactment, there has been intense social, political and academic debate. Social because Spanish society already has this penalty in its collective imagination as the answer to the most serious crimes. Political because some political parties have requested its derogation while others believe that not only is not necessary to derogate, but that the number of crimes to which this penalty is associated should be extended. And academic because practically the totality of academia has expressed its collective rejection of this type of punishment as they consider it illegitimate. The source of illegitimacy is essentially based, as has been said, on two main issues. The first is its unconstitutionality. The second is the absence of a preventive function. Regarding unconstitutionality, this has been argued both because it is understood that any form of life imprisonment (even if it is revisable) is contrary to our Constitution,[23] and because it is held to be unconstitutional on the basis of its regulation and, specifically, of the system of revision.[24] Regarding the instrumentality of punishment, the doctrine and other high-level

[21]This penalty is provided for in the following cases: murder of a victim under 16 years of age, or a person who is particularly vulnerable by reason of age, illness or disability; when the murder follows a crime against sexual freedom; when the murder was committed by someone belonging to a criminal group or organisation; multiple murder; murder of the King or Queen or Princess of Asturias; murder of the Head of a foreign State, or a person internationally protected by a Treaty, who is in Spain; genocide; and crime against humanity.

[22]In the event that they are not eligible; a new period will be imposed until the second review. In addition, the severity of the sentence is determined not only by the minimum number of years in prison, but also by the rigidity of the requirements to be met by the convicted person in order to be eligible for their first review.

[23]To the extent that it amounts to inhuman or degrading punishment (Cuerda Riezu 2011); for the absence of proportionality (Martínez Garay 2016); due to the impossibility of its adaptation to the resocialising objectives (Mir Puig 2015; Carbonell Mateu 2015, p. 215). In addition, the General Council of the Bar itself pronounced itself forcefully on its unconstitutionality.

[24]Landa Gorostiza (2017) and Yagüe (2017).

institutions, such as the State Council,[25] have strongly criticised the legislator's failure to base the introduction of RLI on necessity in terms of crime prevention with regards to specific individuals or society as a whole. In this sense, the doctrine has provided compelling reasons for its derogation, such as: (a) the available scientific evidence on the negative and irreversible consequences on the prisoner's character as a result of 15 or 20 years imprisonment,[26] which would not comply with the re-educational purposes of individual treatment;[27] or, (b) regarding general prevention in society as a whole, the little difference in terms of deterrence between RLI and the current prison sentence for 'common' murder (in the sense that common murder is not punished with RLI) which can reach up to 25 years of imprisonment.[28] However, in addition to these two debates raised by the penal doctrine, another source of illegitimacy is added, tacitly more than expressly: the introduction of RLI on the basis of social demand or social support for this measure. We have seen that the legislator's essential justification for the introduction of RLI includes the premise that society understands that this is the just and proportionate penalty attributable to the crimes for which it is intended. In the public (and academic) debate, this has been summarised in the idea that there is social demand and acceptance of the application of this sanction for the most serious crimes and for the 'most dangerous' offenders, but it has also even used specific numbers. On the 26th March 2015, in the Congress of Deputies, the *Partido Popular* (Spanish People's Party (right-wing) defended that the reform listened to citizens since, in fact, RLI had 'the support of two thirds of Spaniards; later, with RLI in force, social support seemed to rise to 80% of the population, as expressed by the then Minister of Justice. But how does the legislator come to the conclusion that there is general will in favour of this sanction, and from where do these data come?

These data come from different opinion polls carried out by consulting companies in all of which practically the same result is found: almost 80% of the Spanish population is in favour of RLI.[29] The first reference to this type of survey can be found in the public opinion study carried out by the company GAD3, which obtained precisely this percentage of support for said punishment. Looking at this study, it can be seen that these specific data came from the formulation of the following question: 'Specifically, are you in favour of revisable life imprisonment for the murderers of Diana Quer or the child Gabriel Cruz?', to which study participants had the response

[25]Council of State, Expert Opinion 358/2013.

[26]Among others, Cuerda Riezu (2011) and Serrano Gómez and Serrano Maíllo (2016).

[27]Abel Souto (2015), p. 1359.

[28]Carbonell Mateu (2015), Fuentes Osorio (2014) and Terradillos Basoco (2012). To this, considerations could be added regarding the profile of the perpetrators for whom this penalty is supposed to be imposed and which would not make it possible to predict any kind of intimidating effect.

[29]Companies such as GAD3, Simple Lógica or NC Report, among others. See, for example, the results of some of the surveys carried out and offered to the media at: https://www.cambio16.com/espana/encuestas-sobre-la-prision-permanente/.

options 'yes/no/don't know-no answer'.[30] Accordingly, it might seem indisputable that there is citizen support for the sanction, which may not constitute enough justification for it, as we will argue later, but certainly a strong argument for political debate. However, if we compare the method used with the scientific knowledge obtained over the years regarding attitudes towards punishment, it can be suspected that this method is not the most appropriate to obtain rigorous information about the social support for RLI. Criminological literature has devoted a great deal of time to analysing the way in which we must obtain such complex information with such a sensitive subject matter: society and perceptions of and attitudes towards justice.[31] Important findings to consider have been found. In this sense, scientific literature has identified certain citizen beliefs regarding the functioning of the criminal justice system, such as punishments being lenient or that the sentences actually imposed are not fully served. However, while the above is present in lay opinion, it is also true that, contrary to what one might expect, public opinion often ends up resolving scenarios in a similar or even less severe way than a judge would.[32] It has also been found that punitive attitudes are reduced when study participants are provided with information, that is, when public opinion is informed.[33] On the other hand, the presentation of the problem by the media, and therefore the context or frame offered[34] can condition beliefs about the justice system and attitudes towards it. Likewise, studies show that the type of victims of a crime is a variable that influences punitive attitudes, as well as the type of perpetrator.[35] Another interesting finding is that, regarding the most serious crimes, society demands harsher penalties and these demands are identified with real punitive attitudes.[36] Based on the latter, it could be understood that support for RLI for crimes of particular severity, found in studies such as that carried out by GAD3, would reflect the true opinion and attitudes

[30]Diana Quer and Gabriel Cruz were two victims of violent crimes. Diana Quer was an 18-year-old girl who was missing until the perpetrator was finally arrested for trying to kidnap another girl. After this arrest, it became known that the man had raped her, killed her and dumped her in an industrial warehouse inside a van where the body had been hidden for 500 days. Gabriel Cruz was an 8-year-old boy who also disappeared in strange circumstances. The case received a lot of media attention. The child's parents, as well as the father's girlfriend, appeared in the media constantly claiming that if someone was holding the child, they should release him. A short time later it was discovered that it had been the father's girlfriend who had killed and hidden the boy.

[31]The question of public opinion on the criminal justice system and punitive populism has been addressed from the stand point of scientific and social literature, especially in the international sphere, and at the very least it has called into question the phenomenon of punitive populism, even speaking of the 'myth of punitive populism'. One clearest conclusion reached by researches in this field is that punitive attitudes are a truly complex and sensitive phenomenon with may edges. See Green (2006), Maruna and King (2004), Roberts et al. (2003), Roberts and Houhg (2005), Allen (2002a), Haines (2007) and Adriaenssen and Aertsen (2015).

[32]Gelb (2008).

[33]Aizpurúa González and Fernández Molina (2011) and Varona Gómez (2016).

[34]See Varona Gómez (2011).

[35]As shown in Silver (2017).

[36]See Aizpurúa González and Fernández Molina (2016). Also, Miller and Applegate (2015).

of society. However, other positions regarding how the method used to obtain information on an attitude influences the findings can be found, especially those related to the context and configuration of the questions on which the studies are based.[37] Thus, for example, the use of the term 'paedophile' has been found to lead to the choice of higher punishments than describing the accused as having 'sexual interests in minors'.[38] In an experiment carried out by Petrinovich and O'Neill, they put the effects of framing to the test by exposing their participants to the classic railroad track dilemma, in which the decision has to be taken to move the lever and save five people. In that study, they found that the decision to move or not move the lever was more acceptable when presented in terms of saving lives rather than killing innocent people.[39] Likewise, with regards to Social Psychology, another factor that influences the elaboration of a judgment is the perspective of processing (if the information to be evaluated is presented to prosecute a third party [judge as an observer] or if, instead, it is presented to prosecute oneself [judge as an actor]), for which ample evidence[40] can be found. This indicates that in the area of moral judgments there are differences in the way one's own conduct is judged compared to that of others.[41] In a study carried out by Nadelhoffer and Feltz, in which they used the same moral dilemma as Petrinovich and O'Neill, they found that the participants valued the decision to move or not move the lever as less permissible or acceptable when they judged a third party (observer-group) than when they imagined themselves as protagonists of the decision (actor-group).[42] In short, there is sufficient scientific evidence to conclude that the type of question and the context in which it is framed have a decisive influence on the participants' answers. And not only the type of question, but also the answer options. Thus, in a study on life imprisonment, Kubiak and Allen showed that when asked about agreement or disagreement (dichotomous answer) with life imprisonment without the possibility of parole for adolescent homicides, 42.6% agreed, while, if asked about the punishment that a young man convicted of homicide should receive with six different punishment possibilities, only 5% of the sample opted for life imprisonment.[43] Considering all these findings and faced with the intense public debate that was taking place regarding this penalty and its application in especially high-profile cases, we conducted two experimental studies, taking as a reference the actor/

[37]Spellman and Schnall (2009) collect a whole series of factors that condition our judgments and relfect on their implications with decisions and jugments regarding the law. In this sense, the authors show how whether the question is asked in an abstract or concrete way, the emotional state of the participants in the studies, or the processing perspective (if the subjects prosecute themselves or a third party) in which the information is presented, can modify the results of these judgments. See Balvig (2015) and Adriaenssen and Aertsen (2015).

[38]Imhoff (2015) and Harris and Socia (2014).

[39]Petrinovich and O'Neill (1996).

[40]See Falces Delgado et al. (2011).

[41]Davinson (1983) and Spellman and Schnall (2009).

[42]Nadelhoffer and Feltz (2008).

[43]Kubiak and Allen (2011).

observer effect that Nadelhoffer and Feltz had shown in their study, and, in addition, an experimental design where the effect of framing was tested.

In the first study, Gómez-Bellvís and Falces tested the effect on the results of one group of participants judging themselves for multiple murder (allegedly punishable by RLI) and the other group judging a third party for the crime.[44] To this end, they developed a case scenario in which participants were told that a subject (or themself) had been charged with a multiple murder offence. Accordingly, the participants had to choose which maximum punishment would be just for the case. Participants were given six different possibilities of maximum penalties (maximum 20 years' imprisonment; maximum 30 years' imprisonment; life imprisonment but revisable after 15 years' imprisonment; revisable after 18 years'; revisable after 25 years'; life imprisonment without parole). They were then presented with a description of the principles and guarantees of criminal law and asked how essential it was to apply them to the case they had read. Finally, they were asked about the function of the sentence. The main results were that participants who had tried a third party who had been accused of multiple murders opted in majority (62.9%) for prison sentences of 20 or 30 years maximum. Those who understood that the just maximum sentence should be RLI opted for RLI that was revisable at 15 years, with the option of RLI at 25 years (which is our current regime for the most favourable case) particularly insubstantial. On the other hand, for the participants in the group who had to judge themselves as if they were accused of this crime, 84% understood the fair maximum penalty to be 20 years in prison. In addition, those in the self-judging group considered that it was much more imperative that the principles and guarantees of criminal law be applied to this case than those who judged a third party and they were also less retributive. Thus, this study shows how the manner in which information is written, specifically whether it is written to prosecute another person or to prosecute oneself, directly affects punitive preferences.

Later, Miró Llinares carried out the same experimental study but this time modified the certainty of the commission of the crime. That is, in the previous case scenario it was stated that a subject (or oneself) had been accused of a multiple murder. In this new experiment, 'accused' is modified to 'convicted'.[45] The purpose of this manipulation was to make participants certain of the crime committed, hypothesising that in the first study the results could be mediated by the participants' caution in the face of the uncertainty that a person has actually committed the crime. In general, this new manipulation resulted in preferences that were somewhat more punitive than in the previous case. In the case of the group judging a third person, just over 32% considered the fair maximum penalty to be 20 or 30 years imprisonment (in the previous study the percentage was almost double). As for the RLI options, there was much more variability than in the previous case. Thus, 18.5% understood that the review should take place at 15 years; 7% at 18 years; 20.2% at 25; and, 22.1 % life imprisonment without parole. With regard to the actor group,

[44]Gómez-Bellvís and Falces (2010).

[45]See Miró Llinares (2019b).

more than half of the sample, 51.4%, considered that the fair maximum sentence would be 25 years in prison, and 9.9% opted for 30 years maximum. Among the different RLI options, respondents opted above all for a revisable sentence at 15 years (12.7%), but also for life imprisonment without parole (13.5%). Although in general it is evident that the introduction of certainty regarding the commission of the crime has affected the preferences for punishment, the differences between the two groups remain statistically significant. That is, punitive attitudes increase if a third person is convicted while they decrease if participants have to judge themselves for the same actions.

Both experimental studies have certain limitations, such as the lack of representativeness of the sample. For this reason, they are not results with which it is possible or intended to generalise and conclude that this is the reality of public opinion regarding RLI. On the contrary, the objective and conclusions drawn from them, as we will describe in the following section, are: on the one hand, that there are other elements that can methodologically influence the results obtained. On the other hand, it could also be inferred that, although the support for RLI in both studies is quite different from the aforementioned 80% by GAD3. Even those who choose this type of penalty opt for revision to take place before 25 years, which is the system we currently have in our Criminal Code.

## 3 Does Public Opinion Matter for Criminal Law? No Man Is an Island

In light of the foregoing, an initial conclusion may be drawn regarding public opinion on RLI: there is currently no scientific evidence that guarantees the real existence of the supposed demand or social support claimed by both the Spanish legislator as an argument to justify the introduction of RLI in the Criminal Code, as well as by the section of academia that bases its criticism on the consideration of the presumably punitive opinion of the citizenry for modifications to the Criminal Code. As we have previously stated,[46] despite the fact that there are certain opinion studies carried out by consulting companies, we cannot take these data to be a rigorous reflection of the social perception of an issue as complex as the punishment of crimes considered particularly serious, and, specifically, of RLI. As Green argues, such opinion polls 'have practical and political meanings disproportionate to their scientific rigour. The requested and informed surveys and the so-called 'SLOPs' (Self-selected listener opinion polls) generate results that are not generalisable and are empirically questionable'.[47] In this sense, and despite the fact that the GAD3 samples are representative of the Spanish population, the type of questions used and their operationalisation generate doubts regarding their ability to describe

[46] Miró Llinares (2019a, b).

[47] Green (2006), p. 135.

reality. However, despite these suspicions, it is undeniable that the results of these types of surveys have permeated our society (and part of academia) as a result of their dissemination through the media. It seems that this 80% of social support for RLI is an unquestionable fact, that it is the reality and that it also supports both the legislator who justifies the measure, as well as academics who assume that society is punitive, thus giving rise to what Allen called 'the comedy of errors'.[48] However, as we have commented in the previous section, the experimental studies on social support for RLI show that most of the samples do not opt for any type of RLI, and among those who would prefer this type of sentence, they do so mostly in cases where the first revision takes place before 25 years in prison. In short, these results are a long way from the aforementioned 80%. However, beyond punitive preferences, these studies show that through simple manipulation that may seem innocuous *a priori*, such as receiving information written in the first person (to judge oneself) or in the third person (to judge a third person), results change. Providing information that a person has been accused or convicted of a crime also changes participants' responses.

Such manipulations and variations in judgments towards punishment could easily lead us to the conclusion that it is not possible to scientifically know the true opinion of the citizenry regarding punishment. Nevertheless, we believe that this is a hasty conclusion. At most, and in light of the results of this type of experiment, with little external validity insofar as they are not carried out on representative samples of the population but with the internal validity offered by the experimental design itself, getting closer to the citizenry's idea of justice and preferences regarding punishment is a difficult task, even more so when it comes to the use of quantitative methodologies. However, it is necessary to persist in the study of intuitions of justice, of the punitive attitudes of the community, and on all the social knowledge that allows us to approach issues as complex as social support for RLI in a rigorous manner.[49] However, in the meantime, we can only doubt the existence of Spanish society's preference for RLI, and discuss the consequences derived from such a premise.

The Spanish legislator has justified the introduction of RLI on the basis of the need to strengthen the functioning of the justice system by including sanctions that citizens perceive as fair. This could actually be based on scientific knowledge that perceived injustice has an impact on normative infringement while perceived legitimacy helps to increase compliance. But not only have we seen that there is no clear citizen perception that RLI is fairer than long-term prison, but that in order to make sense many more things would have to be demonstrated which, however, seem contrary to the criminological knowledge on compliance. Individual perception that a norm is fair influences behaviour and this interacts with other determinants such as the perception of how others act, or relative to the certainty of punishment.[50]

---

[48]Allen (2002b).

[49]Only in this way can the penal academia get out of the 'ivory tower', according with Díez Ripollés (2015b), pp. 45–47.

[50]Miró Llinares and Bautista Ortuño (2013). Also Gómez-Bellvís (2019).

Generally, the sense attributed to the importance of the substantive legitimacy factor (or individual perception that a legislation is fair), is that people tend to comply more with legislations that correspond to their own moral perceptions regarding how the punishment should be, and that this influences individual conduct more than, for example, the perceived greater severity of the sanction.[51] However, even if it were considered that a large part of the population considers RLI to be more 'morally adequate to the severity of the crime' than imprisonment, is it really credible that this, but not other diverse individual elements, could determine the commission of crimes as serious as multiple murder? In other words, is it reasonable to maintain that, given that RLI is perceived as 'more legitimate', this is going to suppose a reduction in the perpetration of these crimes, since people who think that the sanction is insufficient could decide to kill?(!) It does not seem at all reasonable to think that the decision to kill several people will be determined by the difference between a 25 year sentence and the revision of the penalty after 25 years, neither in terms of severity nor legitimacy. It may also be that the ultimate goal of strengthening confidence in the administration of justice and introducing sanctions for the most serious crimes that are foreseeable and perceived in society as just is not the prevention of these crimes, but rather other more general prevention objectives: to avoid other criminal conducts or simply to avoid society's dissatisfaction with justice institutions. However, this would be as illegitimate as it is absolutely irrational, also from a consequentialist perspective. It can therefore be said that beyond the very question of the potential unconstitutionality of RLI, the existing scientific evidence indicates that there are no reasonable grounds for maintaining this sanction in our system if the argument is based on reasons of general prevention and related to the strengthening of justice. This is because there is no certainty of such a social demand and because, even if there were one, it would in no way affect compliance with the rules that are intended to be regulated.

A different issue is that RLI should serve another purpose: prevention through inoculation, the social elimination of those who are considered to be incapable of reintegration. In that case, it may be that RLI could be more effective in preventive terms than long-term prison because of its greater inoculation potential by allowing life imprisonment. But then the problem would be, and in fact the problem is, another one: can our constitutional state accept a life sentence that implies the denial of people's dignity? Is the system for assessing the risk of recidivism really capable of deciding, without the potential for false positives and given the consequences we are dealing with, who is going to kill again and who is not? Can the State renounce other less harmful means of control for certain criminals with a prognosis for recidivism? This paper does not answer these questions with its own arguments, but we can, in a negative sense, add to the opinion that others have given.[52] If, as it

[51] Miró Llinares (2017).

[52] In particular, regarding the question of dignity, see Lascuraín Sánchez (2016); with regards to risk assessment tools, see Martínez Garay (2016), in the same book.

seems, the only preventive sense of RLI is inoculation, we are facing an involution of difficult compatibility with our Constitution.

Having said that, and to answer the question that leads this section, the existence of a social demand for the introduction of some type of sanction or the criminalisation of an action is not an irrelevant argument in terms of rational criminal policy, at least in the abstract, and not only for political considerations, but also because the social demand can grow from real preventive deficits that, in order to achieve compliance with legislations, it may be necessary to address if existing measures are not effective. As Green points out 'though rationales for re-insulating policy making from public influence may be principled and justified, they are also highly impractical. It is prudent and pragmatic to face up to the challenges posed by de-insulated policy making, and to improve the means of public consultation to ensure that whenever possible, and before it is invoked to justify policies, the public voice is more defensibly assessed than is currently the case.[53] Certainly, regarding the legal basis of RLI, whether it is coherent with our legal system or not, it is possible that the question of the existence of a social demand is not the most relevant thing. However, regarding the political decision and political-legislative rationality, the existence of a social consensus, real or not, cannot be irrelevant in a democracy. If we are talking about material legitimacy, and ultimately material validity, we must demand more from the law than legitimacy in the output. We must demand legitimacy in the inputs, in the process of shaping a law. For the latter, society cannot be irrelevant, especially if one is assuming factual arguments that have not been demonstrated, when scientific premises are poorly constructed, etc. The opposite leads us to bad legislative policy, or rather, to irrational legislative policy.[54]

However, from our point of view, regarding RLI, the question of social demand has no relevance here and specifically, because even if there were such a demand, it would have to be demonstrated that it would have direct effects on compliance, and scientific evidence indicates that this would not be the case. However,, in addition, the premise on which it is based, the social support for this sanction, is not founded, but is assumed on the basis of not very rigorous surveys. Even if it is considered that there is a social demand for its introduction, this condition cannot be considered sufficient by itself. We are aware that empirical consensuses are not necessarily sufficient by themselves for rational justification in terms of 'must be'.[55] The legitimacy of a sanction does not derive exclusively from a supposed social agreement on the preference of this sanction regarding certain crimes, but its legitimacy and justification should include reasons of coherence with the penal system itself and, of course, its compatibility with the system of guarantees and limits that make up a social and democratic State ruled by law. Thus, neither the material legitimation justified by an ideal criminal law is sufficient in itself, nor the opinion of the citizenry

[53]Green (2006).

[54]Miró Llinares (2018).

[55]Sieckmann (2016). Unless they conform to it or there is a greater premise from which they can be derived. See, on naturalist and normativist fallacies Miró Llinares (2018).

will provide legitimation for criminal law by itself. Precisely for this reason, we should not be afraid to address the effective role that citizenry should have in the process of building and legitimising the criminal system,[56] nor fear recognising that the role should be much greater than we have dogmatically attempted to attribute it.[57] Because it is obvious that it will not be what decides everything, but it clearly cannot be said to be worth nothing.

## References

Abel Souto M (2015) Cadena perpetua y delitos contra la comunidad internacional (arts. 605.1, 607 y 607 bis). In: González Cussac JL, Górriz Royo E, Matallín Evangelio Á (eds) Comentarios a la Reforma del Código Penal de 2015, 2nd edn. Tirant lo Blanch, Valencia

Adriaenssen A, Aertsen I (2015) Punitive attitudes: Towards an operationalization to measure individual punitivity in a multidimensional way. Eur J Criminol 12(1):92–112

Aizpurúa González E, Fernández Molina E (2011) Información, ¿antídoto frente al "populismo punitivo"? Estudio sobre las actitudes hacia el castigo de los menores infractores y el sistema de Justicia Juvenil. Revista Española de Investigación Criminológica 9:1–29

Aizpurúa González E, Fernández Molina E (2016) Opinión pública hacia el castigo de los delincuentes: la importancia del delito cometido. Boletín Criminológico 161

Allen R (2002a) "There Must be Some Way of Dealing with Kids": young offenders, public attitudes and policy changes. Youth Justice 2(1):3–13

Allen R (2002b) What does the public think about prison? Criminal Justice Matters 49

Balvig F, Gunnlaugsson H, Jerre K, Tham H, Kinnunen A (2015) The public sense of justice in Scandinavia: A study of attitudes towards punishments. Eur J Criminol 12(3):342–361

Beckett K, Snodgrass A (2012) Poder, política y penalidad. La punitividad como reacción en las democracias americanas. Delito y sociedad 33:1–2

Bottoms A (1995) The philosophy and politics of punishment and sentencing. In: Clarkson C, Morgan R (eds) The politics of sentencing reform. Clarendon Press, Oxford

Carbonell Mateu JC (2015) Prisión permanente revisable (arts. 33 y 35). In: González Cussac JL, Górriz Royo E, Matallín Evangelio Á (eds) Comentarios a la Reforma del Código Penal de 2015, 2nd edn. Tirant lo Blanch, Valencia

[56]Duus-Otterström (2018), Miró Llinares (2017), Robinson (2013) and Varona Gómez (2018).

[57]We will not close here a complex issue on which we have initially pronounced in Miró Llinares (2019a). We do anticipate what is already obvious: that regarding the issue of citizen participation in issues previously reserved for penal dogmatics and experts, crucial, as pointed out by Díez Ripollés (2015b), we are far from the position defended by Silva Sánchez (2018), and close to those defended in our context by Díez Ripollés (2015b), Varona Gómez (2018), Larrauri (2009) and Mañalich (2018), (drawing on the ideas of Ramsay 2016). We do not think, however, that it is entirely right to raise the issue as an absolute dichotomy between experts and citizens. As pointed out by Larrauri (2009), p. 18, 'the contrast between experts and public opinion is excessively simple'. Dogmatics and citizenship are necessary, both are legitimised in their competence and criminal law will be done better with both. Having said that, if you ask us who should be closer to whom, in the configuration of how criminal law comes about, in the sense of who should be asked to participate actively and who has the legitimacy to decide its conformation, we think it is time for the citizenry to be the protagonist rather than the experts: the democratic requirement obliges the dogmatic to get closer and not to move away from the citizenry, from its real needs and understandings of the justice of society, certainly not the other way around.

Cuerda Riezu A (2011) La cadena perpetua y las penas muy largas de prisión: por qué son inconstitucionales en España. Atelier, Barcelona
Davinson PW (1983) The third-person effect in communication. Public Opinion Q 47(1):1–15
Díez Ripollés JL (2015a) Delitos y penas en España. Catarata, Madrid
Díez Ripollés JL (2015b) La política criminal en la encrucijada. BdeF, Buenos Aires
Duus-Otterström G (2018) Retributivism and public opinion: on the context sensitivity of desert. Criminal Law Philos 12(1):125–142
Dzur AW (2012) Participatory democracy and criminal justice. Criminal Law Philos 6(2):115–129
Falces Delgado C, Bautista Ortuño R, Sierra Díez B (2011) El efecto tercera persona: el papel de la calidad de los argumentos y el tipo de estimación. Revista de Psicología Social 26(1):133–139
Frost A (2010) Beyond public opinion polls: punitive public sentiment & criminal justice policy. Sociol Compass 4(3):156–168
Fuentes Osorio JL (2014) ¿La botella medio llena o medio vacía? La prisión permanente: el modelo vigente y la propuesta de reforma. ReDCE (21):309–345
Garland D (2001) The culture of control. Oxford University Press, Oxford
Gelb K (2008) Myths and misconceptions: public opinion versus public judgement about sentencing. In: Freiburg A, Gelb K (eds) Penal populism, sentencing councils and sentencing policy. Willian Publishing, Devon
Gómez-Bellvís AB (2019) Crónica de una ineficacia anunciada: Un estudio sobre los factores asociados al cumplimiento en el ámbito de la propiedad intelectual. Indret 1:20
Gómez-Bellvís AB, Falces C (2010) Los efectos del contexto en la expresión de las actitudes punitivas: el caso del apoyo ciudadano a la prisión permanente revisable. Revista Electrónica de Criminología 1:1
González Collantes T (2013) ¿Sería inconstitucional la pena de prisión permanente revisable? ReCrim 2013:6–23
Green DA (2006) Public opinion versus public judgment about crime. Correcting the 'comedy of errors'. Br J Criminol 46(1):131–154
Greenberg DF (2002) Striking out in democracy. Punishment Soc 4(2):237–252
Haines A (2007) Juvenile crime and punishment in Bucharest, Romania: a public opinion survey. Internet J Criminol. https://goo.gl/6dDiTX
Harris AJ, Socia KM (2014) What's in a Name? Evaluating the effects of the 'Sex Offender' label on public opinions and beliefs. Sexual Abuse J Res Treatment. https://doi.org/10.1177/1079063214564391
Hutton N (2005) Beyond populist punitiveness? Punish Soc 7(3)
Imhoff R (2015) Punitive attitudes against pedophiles or persons with sexual interest in children: does the label matter? Arch Sexual Behavior 44(1):35–44
Johnstone G (2000) Penal policy making. Elitist, populist or participatory? Punish Soc 2 (2):161–180
Juanatey Dorado C (2012) Política criminal, reinserción y prisión permanente revisable. ADPCP 65
Kubiak SP, Allen T (2011) Public opinion regarding juvenile life without parole in consecutive statewide surveys. Crime Delinquency 57(4):495–515
Landa Gorostiza JM (2017) Prisión permanente revisable, prisión de muy larga duración, terrorismo y Tribunal Europeo de Derechos Humanos. In: Landa Gorostiza JM (ed) Prisión y alternativas en el nuevo Código Penal tras la reforma de 2015. Dykinson, Madrid
Larrauri E (2006) Populismo punitivo... y cómo resistirlo. Jueces para la democracia 55:9
Larrauri E (2009) La economía política del castigo. Mientras Tanto (110/111):113–135
Lascuraín Sánchez LA (2016) No solo mala: inconstitucional. In: Arroyo Zapatero L, Lascuraín Sánchez JA, Pérez Manzano M (eds) Contra la cadena perpetua, vol 16. Ediciones de la Universidad de Castilla La Mancha, Cuenca
Mañalich JP (2018) El principialismo político-criminal como fetiche. Revista de Estudios de la Justicia 29:59–71

Martínez Garay L (2016) Predicción de la peligrosidad y juicio de constitucionalidad de la prisión perpetua. In: Arroyo Zapatero LA, Lascuraín Sánchez JA, Pérez Manzano M (eds) Contra la cadena perpetua, vol 16. Ediciones de la Universidad de Castilla La Mancha, Cuenca
Maruna S, King A (2004) Public opinión and community penalties. In: Bottoms T, Rex S, Robinson G (eds) Alternatives to prison: options for an insecure society. Willan, Cullompton
Matthews R (2005) The myth of punitiveness. Theor Criminol 9(2):175–201
Miller RN, Applegate BK (2015) Adult crime, adult time? Benchmarking public views on punishing serious juvenile felons. Criminal Justice Rev 40(2):151–168
Mir Puig S (2015) Derecho penal. Parte general, 10th edn. Reppertor, Barcelona
Miró Llinares F (2017) La función de la pena ante el "paso empírico" del Derecho penal. Revista General de Derecho Penal 27:6
Miró Llinares F (2018) Hechos en tierra de normas. Una introducción epistemológica a la relevancia de la realidad fáctica en el Derecho penal. In: Suárez López JM, Barquín Sanz J, Benítez Ortúzar I, Jiménez Díaz MJ, Sainz-Cantero Caparrós JE (eds) Estudios Penales y Criminológicos. En homenaje al Prof. Dr. H. C. Mult. Lorenzo Morillas Cueva. Dykinson, Madrid
Miró Llinares F (2019a) Recensión a Jesús-María Silva Sánchez, Maulum passionis. Mitigar el dolor del Derecho penal, Atelier, Barcelona, 2018. ExLibris (1)
Miró Llinares F (2019b) La demanda social de la prisión permanente revisable: ¿Premisa fundada? ¿Argumento irrelevante? ¿Razón suficiente? La Ley Penal 138:10
Miró Llinares F, Bautista Ortuño R (2013) ¿Por qué cumplimos las normas?: Sobre la disuasión en materia de seguridad vial. Indret (4)
Nadelhoffer T, Feltz A (2008) The actor-observer bias and moral intuitions: adding fuel to Sinnott-Armstrong's fire. Neuroethics 1(2):133–144
Nistal Burón J (2015) La duración del cumplimiento efectivo de la nueva pena de prisión permanente revisable introducida por la Ley Orgánica 1/2015, de 30 de marzo, de reforma del Código Penal. Revista Aranzadi Doctrinal 6:27–39
Petrinovich L, O'Neill P (1996) Influence of wording and framing effects on moral intuitions. Ethol Sociobiol 17(3):145–171
Ramsay P (2016) A democratic theory of imprisonment. In: Dzur A, Loader I, Sparks R (eds) Democratic theory and Massa incarceration. Oxofrd University Press, Nueva York
Roberts JV, Houhg M (2005) Understanding public attitudes to criminal justice. Open University Press, New York
Roberts JV, Stalans L, Indermaur D, Hough M (2003) Penal populism and public opinion. Lessons from five countries. Oxford University Press, New York
Robinson PH (2013) El papel que corresponde a la comunidad en la determinación de la responsabilidad penal y de la pena (Translated by Vicente Valiente Iváñez). Perspectiva Penal Actual 2
Rowan M (2015) Democracy and punishment: a radical view. Theor Criminol 18(1):43–62
Serrano Gómez A, Serrano Maíllo I (2016) Constitucionalidad de la prisión permanente revisable y razones para su derogación. Dykinson, Madrid
Sieckmann JR (2016) Autonomía y legitimidad democrática. Discusiones 17
Silva Sánchez JM (2018) Malum Passionis. Mitigar el dolor del Derecho penal. Atelier, Barcelona
Silver JR (2017) Moral foundations, intuitions of justice, and the intricacies of punitive sentiment. Law Soc Rev 51(2):413–450
Spellman BA, Schnall S (2009) Embodied rationality. Queen's Law J 35:117
Terradillos Basoco JM (2012) La reforma penal española de 2012. Líneas maestras. Nuevo Foro Penal 78:13
Tonry M (2007) Determinants of penal policies. In: Tonry M (ed) Crime, punishment and politics in comparative perspective, crime and justice. A review of research, vol 36. The University of Chicago Press, Chicago
Varona Gómez D (2011) Medios de comunicación y punitivismos. Indret 1

Varona Gómez D (2016) El debate ciudadano sobre la justicia penal y el castigo: razón y emoción en camino hacia un Derecho penal democrático. Marcial Pons, Madrid
Varona Gómez D (2018) Derecho penal democrático y participación ciudadana. Indret 2
Wood WR (2014) Punitive populism. Encyclopedia Theor Criminol:1–4
Yagüe C (2017) Los estándares internacionales sobre la cadena perpetua del comité europeo para la prevención de la tortura y las penas o tratos inhumanos o degradantes. Revista de Derecho Penal y Criminología 17:225–275
Zimrig FE, Johnson DT (2006) Public opinion and the governance of punishment in democratic political systems. Ann Am Acad Polit Soc Sci 605(1):265–280

# The Influence of the Law-and-Order Model in the Spanish Juvenile Criminal Law-Making Policy

**Deborah García-Magna**

**Abstract** The criminal law-and-order model, which appears to be displacing the procedural justice model in Spain, also influences the juvenile criminal system. The latest reforms in this field are a clear indicator of some of the features of the new model. The law that regulates criminal liability of minors in Spain has been modified several times (even before entering into force). The main argument for some of these reforms was the social feeling of impunity. Under the pretext of calming this social concern and even though there was not an upward trend in juvenile violent delinquency, the Spanish legislator hardened the response towards both serious and less serious crimes committed with violence or intimidation. In a clear reference to the retributive nature of the criminal sanction, the legislator mentioned the need to combine the best interests of the minor with the principle of proportionality. The main objective of this research is to undertake a critical analysis of the legislator's discourse in this field. A confrontation with reality of data on public opinion and crime, and existing empirical investigations on the effectiveness of law has been carried out. The aim is to identify some examples of the irrationality of juvenile criminal law-making policy in Spain.

**Keywords** Criminal law-making policy · Juvenile criminal system · Empirical law evaluation · Irrationality · Law-and-order model

---

D. García-Magna (✉)
University of Malaga. Criminal Law Department, Málaga, Spain
e-mail: dgmagna@uma.es

 
J. Becerra (ed.), *Criminal Law-Making*, Legisprudence Library 7,
https://doi.org/10.1007/978-3-030-71348-5_7

# 1 Introduction[1]

This study aims to analyse the rationality of criminal law-making processes, specifically in the juvenile crime field. In order to do this, the analysis will focus on the legislator's discourse during the parliamentary processing stage of two amendments which have modified the regulation of criminal liability of minors in Spain.[2] In particular, it will highlight the irrationality of Spanish legislator, mainly on ethical and teleological levels. First of all, it is necessary to assume that a rational criminal law[3] requires that the legislator not only shares and adopts the legitimizing principles of punitive intervention,[4] but also relies on sufficient willingness and capacities to incorporate said elements into the final product of the legislative process. Thus, the adequate inclusion of these principles and purposes in the law will ensure its correct subsequent enforcement and the obtainment of predicted results from principles criteria. However, in order to achieve this, on the teleological level (without underestimating the importance of other rationalities[5]), it is necessary that the law incorporates the agreed objectives following a political democratic debate that has taken the diverse amount of ethical content into consideration and confronted it with interests involved.

---

[1]This research has been carried out within the framework of the project UMA 18-FEDERJA-175, *on rights and guarantees for vulnerable persons in the Welfare State*, financed by Andalousian Department of Finance and Knowledge (*Programa Operativo FEDER Andalucía 2014-2020, convocatoria 2018*). Paper translated from Spanish by Lindsey Campbell and Deborah García Magna. A Spanish version can be found at García Magna (2018b), pp. 115–140.

[2]The Organic Law (OL) 5/2000, 12 January, regulates the criminal liability of minors between 14 and 18 years old, establishing a specific system of legal consequences, but referring to the catalogue of criminal conducts contained in the Criminal Code for adults. It has been modified on several occasions, through the Organic Laws 7/2000 (22 December); 9/2000 (22 December); 9/2002 (10 December); 15/2003 (25 November); 8/2006 (4 December) and lastly, 8/2012 (27 December). The analysis carried out in this piece of work will focus on the reforms of 2003 and 2006.

[3]Atienza Rodríguez (1997) and Díez Ripollés (2003). A development of these models can be found in Rando Casermeiro (2010), Becerra Muñoz (2013); or Rodríguez Ferrández (2016), amongst others.

[4]Within his dynamic model of criminal legislative rationality, Díez Ripollés ob. cit., (2003), pp. 136–165, groups the principles that fit into ethical rationality into three areas: principles of protection (harmfulness, fragmentarity nature, public interest, and correlation with reality), principles of liability (legal certainty, liability for the crime, personal imputation, accountability, and jurisdictionality) and principles of penalty (humanity, teleological or legitimate objectives, proportionality, and state monopoly on punishment).

[5]Díez Ripollés (2003), op.cit., pp. 95 and ff. Along with ethical rationality, teleological rationality confronts the values represented in the principles that should inform the criminal system, with characteristic arguments of the political debate, that is to say, interests of lobbies and diverse sectors of society, ideologies and interests of the parties. Pragmatic rationality, for its part, occurs when objectives set out by the law are achieved, even if it is coercively (effectiveness) and the desired effects are produced (efficacy). A law fulfils legal-formal rationality when it is coherent within itself and with the rest of the legal system. Lastly, linguistic rationality aims to correctly express the content and meaning of the law and assure satisfactory communication to its recipients.

The ethical irrationality occurs when the principle of the best interests of the child, which should mainly inspire the juvenile justice system, is undermined, enhancing in turn the principles of general prevention (both in its negative and positive meaning), and the retributive purpose of the penalty. Similarly, the principle of correlation with reality could be infringed when the legislator justifies the need for a reform by an alleged increase in juvenile crime which would have generated a growing feeling of insecurity and distrust towards laws within society, without having confirmed if this is true. On the other hand, the teleological rationality could be missing in final decisions that ignore the interests of diverse ideological forces and the real need for protection and intervention that has been expressed. Moreover, pragmatic irrationality could also be present when the legislator expands the cases in which penalties could be imposed, or provides punitive consequences that require a rise in public expenditure, but the necessary resources to apply them are not planned.

In short, regarding these kinds of irrationality, laws implying a greater use of non-custodial measures could not be effective (as it would be impossible to appropriately apply them due to insufficient resources), nor would be those that suppose a greater use of closed detention, since they do not comply with one of its main objectives: avoiding recidivism.

## 2 Objectives and Methodology

This work is based on the hypothesis that in the field of juvenile delinquency (as it happens with a highest intensity in the field of adult criminal system) the Spanish legislator is incorporating elements of a law-and-order model, that moves away from the traditional procedural justice model.[6] Therefore, along this paper, I have first briefly defined the features of said new model, to consequently identify some of them in the analysed reforms. Afterwards, the analysis has focused on the legislator's discourse, starting with the reasons given to carry out the amendments. To finish, parliamentary debates have been thoroughly studied. A classification of the arguments has been done, to allow the identification of characteristics of the law-and-order model, both with respect to the content of the arguments and its frequency of use. To carry out such analysis, the preambles of the laws and the documents including the debates at the Congress of Deputies and the Senate[7] have been taken into consideration. In particular, 16 documents have been studied in depth, including law projects, reports, special committee opinions and session's records from the law-making proceedings of Organic Law 15/2003 (4) and Organic Law 8/2006 (10).

---

[6]Garland (2001), Díez Ripollés (2004) and García Magna (2018a).

[7]All the documents can be found on the following website of the Spanish Congress of Deputies (https://www.congreso.es/web/guest/busqueda-de-iniciativas).

Before focusing on said analysis, the content of the reforms will be described and some brief notes will be provided regarding their political and media context. This will clarify why the two main parties involved in the successive reforms have more or less agreed on everything, even passing the buck of reforming the law to each other.[8] Moreover, reference will be made to the reality of juvenile delinquency before and after the approval of the reforms, in order to evaluate the veracity of the arguments put forward by the legislator. Additionally, some of the empirical evaluations carried out in Spain regarding the measures applied to minor offenders will be revised, particularly the existing body of research that focus on its link to the rate of recidivism. Now that 15 years have passed since the last reform, and having in mind the counting of data and evaluations from different researchers regarding its application, it seems appropriate to undertake this type of analysis.

## 3 The Law-and-Order Model: Main Features

The new criminal policy model that would be influencing the procedural justice model, especially in the legislative phase, can be characterised as follows:[9]

1) The control of marginalised social classes through the criminal system in a discourse of exclusion that, although it has always been present in the classic Criminal law, has been intensified by the most recent reforms. Thus, striking differences can be observed both in the duration and the type of penalties imposed, between the regulation of blue-collar and white-collar crimes.
2) The increasing feeling of insecurity. Even if most of it is triggered by all types of risk factors (labour instability, lack of assistance services, deficiencies in the health care system, non-compliance with food safety laws, environmental pollution, political corruption, etc.), the legislator addresses it from the perspective of a criminal legislative reform. Thus, citizens have the impression that the uneasiness they feel derives from crime and that all problems can be solved through legislative changes.
3) The significant role of the victims in pre-legislative processes. The re-balancing or zero-sum game rhetoric implies that guarantees recognised to the offender are perceived as a loss of rights for the victim.
4) The politicization of the criminal system and the punitive populism. It is assumed that the citizens are alarmed and not prepared to accept a rational approach to crime. Consequently, the reforms supposedly requested by society

[8]The conservative party, *Partido Popular* (PP), governed in Spain between 2000 and 2004, when the processing of the OLs 5/2000, 7/2000, 9/2000 and 15/2003 took place, while the socialist party, *Partido Socialista Obrero Español* (PSOE), governed between 2004 and 2011, initiating the OL 8/2006. As Díez Ripollés (2013), has highlighted both parties are usually quite punitive when they come into power.

[9]García Magna (2018a), op.cit.

are placed in the political agenda through intensive media coverage of certain events.

5) The rise of the afflictive component of penalties, meaning a wider use of prison, despite the fact that Spain has not significant crime figures. On one hand, the Criminal Code establishes very high penalties for those crimes most represented in prison (crimes against property or related with drugs). On the other hand, few probations are granted, so the rates of prison population are high.
6) The crime is considered a free and rational decision, disconnected from the personal and socio-economic circumstances of the offenders. They are considered responsible for their own rehabilitation, so recidivism is not seen as a failure of the system, but of the individuals themselves. As a matter of fact, it is easier to intervene with the offenders (controlling them) than with the background from which they have left and will return to when they have completed their sentence.
7) Lack of mistrust towards the punitive power of the State. Citizens now do not criticise certain reforms or proposals that maybe in a former and more guarantee-based context, would have caused opposition. In the debate between more security or more liberty, it seems that citizens clearly are in favour of the first.
8) The privatisation of the management of delinquency, especially in the field of penitentiary enforcement, with juvenile justice being a clear example of it. The responsibility of the control of disorder and a lack of trust in the system's ability to take charge of crime is transferred to society.
9) The influence of supranational instruments on the decisions of the legislator that, occasionally, cause a democratic deficit and a loss of State sovereignty. At times, punitive reforms are a result of international guidelines, but sometimes the national legislator carry out changes of greater impact than those that were required from higher instances.
10) Lastly, some experts in criminal law and criminology adopt punitive discourses and develop theories which are highly focused on security, giving support to the practices that have been outlined.

Not all of these features arise as intensely throughout each phase of the criminal law system. They are more present in areas which are exposed to public opinion and political debate, such as the pre-legislative and legislative phases. Thereafter, in moments such as police control of the crime, judicial enforcement of the law and especially penitentiary enforcement, inertia dynamics within the scope of the procedural justice system schemes and even open resistance to the change of model can be observed, representing protecting factors against the tendency towards a law-and-order criminal policy. Moreover, these characteristics have not the same intensity in the criminal system for adults and for minors, due to deep-rooted essential principles in the latter, such as special prevention and subsidiarity, represented in the principle of the best interests of the child. However, as will be highlighted in the text to follow, in the practices of some of the criminal system actors, and particularly in legislative processes that have taken place, signs of change towards a higher incidence of punitive discourse can be found.

## 4 The Penal Reforms of 2003 and 2006 as an Example of the Law-and-Order Model in the Juvenile Justice System

The change in tendency towards a law-and-order model in juvenile criminal system began to occur in 2000, through the first reform of the law (OL 7/2000), but it was accentuated with the Organic Laws 15/2003 and 8/2006.

As will be analysed further on, the law that regulates the criminal liability of minors in Spain (OL 5/2000) was reformed even before it came into effect in 2001, to include the necessity to evaluate its application concerning the more severe treatment issued for more serious crimes. In this sense, a few years later, the OL 15/2003 added a new additional provision in which the future government was given the task of applying a more firm and effective treatment to minors committing most serious crimes, once having completed said evaluation and consulted with the actors concerned. These more severe measures involved extending the time served in juvenile detention centres, and allowing judges to pass to adult prisons those minors who become 18 years old during their internment. Consequently, the 2006 legislator took charge of the task assigned in 2003 and carried out the predicted reform, translating into the law some aspects that could easily be framed in the law-and-order model.

Before evaluating such aspects, and for a better understanding of the critical analysis that will be carried out, I will briefly review the most relevant points of the laws that have reform the juvenile crime system from 2000 on:

Firstly, article 4 of the OL 5/2000 initially contained the possibility to apply it to young adults between 18 and 21 years old, on an exceptional basis.[10] Regarding the possibility of imposing closed internment, article 9 limited it to incidents committed with violence or intimidation, or implying a serious risk to life or physical integrity, and increased the maximum duration to 5 years in the case of minors over 16 years old, provided that the technical team advised on its appropriateness. As an exception to the general rule, in the case of extreme seriousness of the conduct, it was mandatory to impose closed internment of 1–5 years, and probation of maximum of 5 years, and a 1-year period of impossibility to modify, suspend or substitute the

[10]The OL 5/2000 applies to minors between 14 and 18 years old, whereas the Spanish Criminal Code is applied to adults, that is to say from 18 years of age. Minors under 14 do not have criminal liability in Spain, since they are considered immune from penal prosecution. Article 4 of the original version of the OL 5/2000, mentioned the possibility of applying the law to youngsters who had committed minor offences or less serious crimes with no violence or intimidation, nor serious danger to life or physical integrity, that had not been condemned for incidents committed once turned 18 years of age, and according to their personal circumstances and their grade of maturity.

sentence. Moreover, cases of recidivism, terrorism, homicide or murder and sexual assault are always considered extremely serious.

The OL 7/2000, approved even before OL 5/2000 came into force, incorporated an additional provision to the said law, that established a special system for those who committed the following crimes: homicide, murder, sexual assault and terrorism, or those punishable by 15 or more years of prison in the adults Criminal Code. In article 9 reference was made to this additional provision regarding offenders committing extremely serious incidents. In particular, it excluded youngsters between 18 and 21 years old from the possible application of the juvenile justice system, and for those under 18 years old it established a specific regulation: in the case of terrorism the jurisdiction would come from the National High Court; for 16 and 17 years old the duration of closed internment was extended to 8 years and the period in which it is not possible to modify, suspend or substitute the sentence was extended to half its whole length. For 14 and 15-year-olds, the internment measure imposed would be from 1 to 4 years with probation of up to 3 years; and for the aforementioned serious crimes it would be mandatory to apply the limitation periods of adults Criminal Code. Lastly, in case of committing several crimes, one of them being serious and penalised with a prison sentence of 15 or more years in adults Criminal Code, it was established that the closed internment could lead to up to 10 years for offenders of and over 16 years old, and up to 5 years for people under 16. Moreover, a new additional provision was incorporated, indicating that in 5 years (January 2006) the Government should send a report to the Congress of Deputies in which the effects and consequences of the application of the described new additional provision would be analysed and evaluated. It is important to emphasise that this evaluation was never carried out before the OL 8/2006, or it was kept secret, since it is not mentioned in the processing of the reform (when it should have been carried out already),[11] and the only known evaluation requested by the Government was carried out a long time after.[12]

The OL 9/2000, also approved before the OL 5/2000 came into force, suspended the enactment of article 4 (the application of the law to young adults between 18 and 21 years old) until the 1 January 2007.

The OL 15/2003 included a new additional provision (surprisingly incorporated during the proceedings of amendments in the Senate), following a serious crime that provoked a huge social impact (the murder of Sandra Palo).[13] This additional provision passed on the Government the task of further toughening the measures applicable for minors who commit especially serious crimes (homicide, murder, sexual assault, terrorism, etc.), and expressly stipulated that this should be done once

---

[11]Highlighted by Pozuelo Pérez (2013), p. 216.

[12]Redondo Illescas et al. (2011). Ministerio de Sanidad, Política Social e Igualdad (Ministry of Health, Social Policy and Equality).

[13]On 17 May 2003, Sandra Palo (22 years old) was violated and assassinated by four persons aged between 14 and 18, which had previously passed through the juvenile justice system on several occasions. The brutality of the incidents shocked the public. The sentence was passed on 13 October 2003, during the processing of the OL 15/2003.

the law had been evaluated, and the General Council of the Judiciary, the Public Prosecutor, regional autonomous communities, and parliamentary groups had been heard. The additional provision also mentioned some measures to toughen the regulation of these serious crimes, such as the possibility of prolonging the confinement, and serving in high security detention centres, as well as in adult's prisons when minors have reached 18 years old.

The OL 8/2006 brought a definite end to the possibility of applying the law to youngsters between 18 and 21 years old, as it completely modified the content of article 4 and changed it to include the recognition of the rights of victims and their participation in criminal proceedings. This implied that they could take part as a claimant, something that was expressly not allowed in the preamble of the original OL 5/2000,[14] as it rejected any objectives of Criminal law that were not the best interests of the child (such as proportionality or general negative prevention).

On the other hand, the requirements to impose closed internment was once again modified. Firstly, article 9 now establishes that this measure can be imposed in the case of a serious crime, less serious crimes committed with violence, intimidation or serious risk for life or integrity, any crime committed by a group, or when the minor is part of a gang, organisation or association dedicated to committing crimes. The specific regulation formerly included in the additional provision, with respect to homicide, murder, sexual assault and terrorism, as well as those crimes punishable by 15 or more years of prison in the adults Criminal Code, now it is also incorporated to article 10, applicable to crimes mentioned in article 9.2. The extension applies also to extremely serious crimes (in any case, when there is recidivism), so this originally exceptional regime is now widened to a great extent.

Another reform operated by the OL 8/2006 refers to the moment in which the minor serving an internment sentence reaches 18 years old. Until 2006, the minors continued serving their time in the youth detention centre until their sentence was completed; it was possible to pass them to prison when reaching 23 years old. The OL 8/2000 has moved this moment forward to 21 years old, in general, and to 18 years old when minor is serving closed internment or have already been in prison before.

Finally, the OL 8/2012 has incorporated crimes committed abroad into the jurisdiction of the Central Minor's Court of the National High Court.

At first glance, it is evident that some of these modifications fit in with the characteristics of the law-and-order model that has been described above. For example, a relevant toughening of the measures applied to the most serious crimes has taken place (feature 5);[15] the possibility to apply the law to youngsters between

[14]As item 8 of the said preamble establishes that, regarding minors, individuals cannot be recognised as having the right to act as claimants with full procedural rights and responsibilities.

[15]These reforms prioritise the retributive component of punishment over the special educational preventive objective of Criminal law, mentioned specifically by the OL 5/2000 in its preamble. As the Spanish Constitutional Court (*Tribunal Constitucional*) has indicated in its sentences 36/1991 and 60/1995, the measures adopted cannot be repressive, but rather orientated towards the effective reinsertion and best interests of the child. This particularly educative character, which gives way to

18 and 21 years old no longer exists, and it is now possible to serve the sentence in an adults detention centre, making the minors completely responsible for their actions, whatever the circumstances are (feature 6);[16] the victim has been introduced in the criminal proceeding (feature 3);[17] reference is made to social alarm in the preambles of laws, using incorrect data and presenting it in an inadequate manner (features 2 and 4), etc. In the parliamentary debates that will be analysed further on in this paper, some proposals indicating a political sector's tendency towards a much more severe system can be found (feature 7).[18] Moreover, in a careful analysis of the legislator's arguments, one can observe a change of objectives and principles that should inspire intervention in the juvenile justice area.[19]

considerable differences between the systems for adults and minors, is being overlooked in those reforms aimed at achieving the punishment of the minor. This happens, for example, when long sentences with a period of security are imposed, the possibility to serve sentences in adult centres is allowed, or the option to apply minors' system to youngsters under the age of 21 is discarded. Consequently, there is an excessive use of custodial measures, as noted by García Pérez (2010), pp. 8 and ff., and García Magna (2018a), ob. cit.

[16]The widespread expression "do the crime do the time" hides the idea that minors are responsible enough to know and decide what they do and that they should pay the consequences of their actions, whatever they are, therefore questioning their condition of being not totally liable for their actions. This idea can be found in the proposals to lower the age or criminal liability to 12 years old, the regulation of some crimes or forms of commission that entail the mandatory imposition of internment in closed detention centres (which only leaves the judge the possibility to decide the duration of the measure), the deactivation of the possibility to apply the law to individuals between 18 and 21 years old, or the reform that brings forward the transfer of an individual, who is serving a custodial measure, to an adult prison.

[17]As will be seen in the coming pages, the reforms carried out between 2003 and 2006 came mainly from the mobilisation of Sandra Palo's parents following her murder. Pozuelo Pérez (2013), ob. cit. p. 117 and ff., discusses this process in detail and describes how the high media coverage of the criminal proceeding transferred a great interest on this issue to public opinion and, then, along with the pressure exerted by the relatives of Sandra Palo, joined the public agenda, giving way to the two previously mentioned reforms, which included three of their four petitions.

[18]Indeed, mainly coinciding with serious crimes in which children below the age of 14 are involved, certain sectors consider the convenience of lowering the age of criminal liability to 12 or 13 years old. Similarly, the idea of minors that have committed serious crimes in the company of adults being judged in the same proceeding, before an adult court, has been considered. It is necessary to bear in mind that the age in which most criminal behaviour takes place is between 15 and 19 years old, with crimes committed at younger ages being less frequent and much less serious, as seen in Loeber et al. (2011), p. 4.

[19]Similarly, with respect to the thesis about the law-and-order model regarding minors, Pantoja (2006); Ríos Martín (2005) and García Pérez (2005). For a more detailed analysis of the impact of the law-and-order model with regards to minors, see García Magna (2018a), op.cit.

## 4.1 Background. Political and Media Context

As indicated at the start, to carry out a rationality analysis in this area, at least on the first three levels, it is essential to check: if the legislator was really starting from a hierarchy of principles other than declared; if the political actors considered the available data regarding juvenile crime and imposed measures, and the interests and ideologies represented in the parliamentary context; and, finally, if sufficient resources were provided so that the laws could be effective (ethical, teleological and pragmatic levels).

Analysis regarding which principles the legislator bases the criminal intervention on has been carried out by closely studying arguments taken from parliamentary debates. Advances have already been made to some extent in the previous section (specific content of the reforms carried out). However, on this first level of ethical rationality it is particularly significant the disregard for the principle of correlation with reality. For this reason, it is interesting to check whether the legislator's arguments responded to the reality of the crimes that aimed to modify, and whether the mandatory evaluations prescribed by law had been carried out.

With respect to the latter, it does not seem that specific research had been conducted on an institutional level. Although in the parliamentary debates one can find that Government representatives mentioned the existence of these evaluations and their conclusions, their content does not appear in the session's records. Only after the legislative proceedings of 2003 and 2006 had already been completed, the Spanish Ministry of Health, Social Policy and Equality asked Redondo's team to evaluate the efficacy of the measures and treatments applied to juvenile offenders in Spain (2011).[20] However, the results, of course, were not available and could not be considered at that moment.

Thus, it seems that the legislator did not fulfil the mandate of evaluating the effects of the law. The majority of the reports and empirical research that have evaluated the measures applicable for crimes that are subject to the 2003 reform (serious, or less serious with violence or intimidation), have been carried out after the analysed reforms. For this reason, it is hard to believe that the legislator had been able to consider this information on the occasion of a reform. Nonetheless, in general the existing evaluations positively link the alternative to custodial measures with lower rates of recidivism. On the other hand, custodial measures give negative results for this indicator, although, in these cases, social and family are also significant factors.[21] This seems to indicate that, as well as the desirability to implement less punitive measures, it is very important to provide minors a specific treatment

[20]Redondo Illescas et al. (2011), ob. cit., carry out an extensive revision of existing empirical studies on the subject. The balance is in general positive, although they note some shortcomings in the coordination between autonomous communities with regard to the registered protocols, that could be improved.

[21]Bravo Arteaga et al. (2009), Andrés Pueyo (2006) and Martín et al. (2013), where the authors suggest that the minor's own appreciation of the process should be taken into account.

according with their needs. Similarly, under the principle of diversion, empirical research on extrajudicial conflict resolution (such as mediation) show very positive results regarding recidivism.[22]

With regard to the political context in which the legislative initiative of the 2003 reform was driven, in the months preceding the promulgation of these laws various critical situations with huge media impact arose and the Government's response was called into question by numerous sectors of society. Some examples of these critical situations are: the local police protest in February 2002, which was forcefully put to an end by the National Police; the dispute with the Moroccan Government over the Islet of Perejil in July 2002; the intense parliamentary debate on the state of the nation regarding citizen's security, also in July 2002; the sinking of the Prestige oil tanker on the Galician coast in November 2002; the start of the Iraq war in March 2003; the military plane Yak-42 accident in Turkey in May 2003; the murder of young Sonia Carabantes in August 2003, allowing the clarification of the Wanninkhof case and highlighting a serious judicial mistake; various attacks by ETA[23] over both years; etc. Moreover, political parties in opposition led a strong attack towards the Government's public order and safety policies, and the police unions harshly criticised its plan to deal with street crime (*2000 Police Programme*). All of this forced the Government to announce in 2002 a new plan to fight crime. However, it was not only political opposition that led this dynamic of criticism. In fact, it is striking that during parliamentary debates for the OL 11/2003 it was the Government itself who fostered the alarming discourse regarding street crime and citizen insecurity.[24]

Concerning the reality of juvenile crime and the media context in which the reforms analysed took place, it is essential to highlight that neither the official data from Spain's Home Office, with respect to proven facts and detentions,[25] nor those from the national statistical institute with respect to convicted minors[26] indicated a rising tendency. However, in parliamentary debates an increase in juvenile crime is

---

[22]Fernández Molina et al. (2017), p. 267; Capdevila et al. (2005, 2011); Basanta Dopico (2009); García et al. (2012).

[23]ETA (an abbreviation of Euskadi Ta Askatasuna) is a formerly armed nationalist and separatist organisation in the Basque Country.

[24]While opposition deputies of PSOE focused on the government's failure in this area (Barrero López, Session's Records, Plenary session 17 June 2003, p. 24,676) and on the increase in crime rates (López Aguilar, Session's Records, Plenary session 10 April 2003, p. 12,553), the Minister of Justice, Michavila (PP), instead of calming the debate, said that the penal system had more holes than a sieve, and "criminals enter through one door and leave through another" (Session's Records, Plenary session 10 April 2003, pp. 12,540 and ff.).

[25]The official report on delinquency (*Balance de Criminalidad, Ministerio del Interior*), 2005, p.5, shows the lowering tendency in the number of known offences from 2000 to 2003. (available at http://www.interior.gob.es/documents/10180/1209813/Criminalidad+y+delincuencia.pdf/fe7be633-edf8-446f-bdeb-b1369ddc25d8).

[26]The data from the Spanish national statistical institute (*Instituto Nacional de Estadística, INE*) of registered criminal files between 2000 and 2003 indicate a lowering tendency (available at http://www.ine.es/jaxi/Datos.htm?path=/t18/p467/a2003/l0/&file=05001.px).

mentioned (particularly, regarding crimes against property), and the preamble of the OL 8/2006 itself refers to a supposed public feeling of impunity. On the one hand, studies carried out on juvenile crime noted a decrease in crimes against property.[27] On the other hand, with respect to the feeling of insecurity or concern about the possible impunity for the crimes committed by minors, there are not specific studies on this topic carried out in the months before the reforms, but the results of the opinion polls from the sociological research centre (*Barómetros de Opinión del Centro de Investigaciones Sociológicas, CIS*) found that citizen's insecurity was considered the third problem in Spain by respondents. Studies regarding public opinion at this time do not reflect special attention on these topics.[28]

Although it is difficult to obtain data (disaggregated or not) on some of the crimes subject to the analysed reforms, especially with respect to those committed in groups, for minors who are members of a gang, or those where recidivism has occurred, given that this information can only be obtained by studying sentences or the personal records of accused minors, the available data shows that the evolution of the majority of robberies committed with violence or intimidation has followed the general downward trend and started to decrease even before the reform of 2006.

## 4.2 Irrationality in the Law-Making Process. Analysis of the Legislator's Discourse in 2003 and 2006

Before thoroughly studying the legislator's discourse by looking at speeches of deputies and senators gathered from the session's records in the Spanish parliament, the preamble of the OL 8/2006 must be analysed. The following extract is particularly striking, to the extent that it refers to a supposed social demand for more severity for certain crimes, as well as a rising tendency in crimes committed by minors, which would justify the adoption of more severe measures:

---

[27]For example, the study by Serrano Tárraga (2009), analyses the evolution of detentions in Spain between 2000 (1.32%) and 2007 (1.08%), highlighting an increase in crimes against persons between 2003 (5.05%) and 2007 (9.57%). The study by Montero Hernanz, T., "La evolución de la delincuencia juvenil en España, Partes 1ª y 2ª", 2001, in *La Ley penal: Revista de Derecho penal, procesal y penitenciario,* vol. 78, observes a decrease in these crimes between 2004 and 2006. The victimisation surveys by the *Observatorio de la Delincuencia*, 2009, highlight a decreasing tendency between 1989 and 2008. A more detailed analysis is carried out in García Magna and González Cruz (2017).

[28]The June 2003 opinion polls from the *CIS* (Spanish sociological research centre: *Centro de Investigaciones Sociológicas)* (study no.2528) devotes questions 3 to 12 to citizen insecurity and the public perception of crime and the police. One of the results (question 4) is that respondents do not consider probable to become a victim of a crime (available at http://www.cis.es/cis/export/sites/default/-Archivos/Marginales/2520_2539/2528/e252800.html). According to Montero Hernanz (2011) who has gathered data from opinion polls since 2001, respondents do not express a high level of concern about these issues. Similarly, Toharía Cortés (2003).

> The statistics reveal a significant rise in crimes committed by minors which has caused a great deal of social worry and has contributed to lowering the credibility of the Law due to the feeling of impunity for the most common violations that are frequently committed by these minors, like crimes and offences against property. Along with this, it should be recognised that, fortunately, violent crimes have not increased significantly, although recent events have had a strong social impact.

The following fragment is also important because it refers to a change in the principles that should inspire the juvenile criminal system, with regard to what the law initially stated following the supranational guidelines emitted by the United Nations and the European Council:[29]

> The best interests of the child, that will continue to be a priority within the law, is perfectly consistent with the objective to expect more proportionality between the sanction and the gravity of the conduct committed. The system continues to leave in the hands of the judge the evaluation and assessment of both principles in a flexible manner and favouring an optimal individualisation of the response. Otherwise, this would lead us to understand, in a trivial way, that the best interests of the child are not only superior, but unique and exclusive compared to other constitutional assets, which should be ensured by punitive or correctional laws.

Apart from the important declaration of intent of the legislator on these lines, which will be analysed in detail along with the content of parliamentary debates, it is important to focus on the legal meaning that the preamble of laws generally has. This involves clarifying whether these arguments have to be taken as mere reasoning that have led the legislator to consider the reform, i.e. without normative value, or, on the contrary, whether they have to be interpreted as explanatory and determining provisions of the content of the law. In the latter case, it would be possible to ask the legislator to adjust the arguments to reality, and to incorporate to the law what it is stated at the preamble. Moreover, if the law deviates from what the preamble outlines or does not address reality, it should be possible to demand that the legislator rethink or reform it. However, in the first case, nothing more could be done than to highlight the inconsistencies from a critical scholar point of view, rather than from a juridical level. To resolve this problem, it is interesting to consult the constitutional jurisprudence on that subject[30] which, in summary, considers that the preambles are not strictly legal norms and that, therefore, they only have interpretive, not normative, value. This means that its content is not binding. Thus, at the

---

[29]The supranational recommendations to State members are varied but, since they are not mandatory, their compliance is left to each State. For example, regarding the United Nations, stand out the Convention on the Rights of the Child, the Minimum Rules for the Administration of Juvenile Justice (Beijing Rules), the Rules for the Protection of Juveniles Deprived of their Liberty, and the Guidelines for the Prevention of Juvenile Delinquency (the Riyadh Guidelines). In the context of European Council, the following must be highlighted: the Recommendation (87)20 on social reactions to juvenile delinquency, the Recommendation (2003)20 concerning new ways to deal with juvenile delinquency and the role of juvenile justice, and the Recommendation (2008)11 on the European Rules for juvenile offenders subject to penalties or measures.

[30]See the following sentences from the Spanish Constitutional Court: 36/1981, 12 November; 212/1996, 19 December; 173/1998, 23 July; 116/1999, 17 June; and 31/2010, 28 June.

explanatory memorandum of the law, legislator only reflects the reasoning made until reaching a decision on a legal norm. In the case of a contradiction between the preamble and the text of the law, the latter will always prevail, and the preamble would not even have integration effects which could fulfil the legal gaps of the law.[31] Although article 88 of the Spanish Constitution establishes that the legislator is obliged to motivate the bills submitted to the Congress, it is not compulsory that said motivation eventually appears as the preamble of the law which is finally passed.[32] Nevertheless, it is evident that the arguments that the legislator incorporates in the preamble enable the interpretation of the normative text in a more reliable way than if they were taken from other sources[33] and, in this sense, there could be every reason to expect that at least these arguments were adjusted to reality.

Apart from the question of whether preambles can be awarded legal value, it cannot be denied that this part of the law is requested to reflect the intentions of the legislator and the reasons that have led to drive the legislative proposal, no matter how questionable they may be. For the purposes of the analysis to take place over the next few pages, relating to the principles that should inform the law and the objectives that it aims to achieve, the discourse reflected in the explanatory memorandum and the parliamentary debates are very important. Thus, in the words of Cerdeira, the preambles would have the function of both report on the *occasio legis* (description of reality) and expose the *ratio legis* (motivation related to principles).[34]

Having described the contents, context and details of the successive reforms that have modified the law that regulates the criminal liability of minors, a critical study of the legislator's discourse will be now carried out. The focus will be on the laws 15/2003 and 8/2006, although the two previous laws (7/2000 and 9/2000) certainly also mark a tendency of higher punitive severity.

Regarding the legislator's discourse reflected in the preamble of the OL 8/2006, when compared to the arguments included in OL 5/2000, it is noteworthy that new value criteria directly related to the principle of legitimate objectives of the penalty have entered the discourse. The original text of the law made an express reference to the "formally punitive but materially corrective-educational nature" of the intervention, as well as to the best interests of the child, and the prohibition of a private prosecution in the process. However, as it has been highlighted previously, the OL 8/2006 incorporated the objectives of general prevention and retribution, and recognised the victim as a part of the process.

---

[31]Cerdeira Bravo De Mansilla (2015), pp. 129 and ff.

[32]Article 114.2 of the Regulations of the Congress of Deputies mentions that the Commission can agree or disagree with the incorporation of the explanatory memorandum as a preamble of the law. Similarly, the Constitutional Court ruling 49/2008 (9 April), which, in its legal basis no.5, expresses that: "the legislator is not constitutionally obliged to justify their legislative options in the explanatory memorandum or preambles of the law." It recognizes, however, "their possible role in the interpretation of the provisions that they present."

[33]Rodríguez-Toubes Muñiz (2013), p. 616.

[34]Cerdeira Bravo De Mansilla ob. cit. (2015), p. 63.

**Table 1** References to the law-and-order model during both 2003 and 2006 law-making processes

| Arguments | OL 15/2003 | OL 8/2006 |
|---|---|---|
| 1) Insecurity | 1# | 8#–4* |
| 2) Victims | 1# | 6#–2* |
| 3) Punitive populism | 1#–3* | 10#–5* |
| 4) More severity | 1# | 3#–4* |
| 5) Accountability | 1# | 7#–6* |

With regard to parliamentary debates, the interventions of deputies and senators will be classified according to diverse categories that directly relate to the characteristics of the law-and-order model. Moreover, the aim is to test if the punitive discourse is similar whether it comes from the socialist party (PSOE) or the conservative party (PP). The analysis of the reforms carried out within the ruling period of each of these two majority parties will give an idea of how they act depending on whether they are in the Government or in the opposition. However, it must be noted that the reform of 2003 was carried out during the process of amendments in the Senate (and in a cursory manner), so the references to the reform of 2006 will be much more abundant, with PSOE in the government and PP in the opposition.[35]

The categories of classification of the legislator's discourse, in accordance with the features of the model described for the legislative phase, are the following:

1. Generalised feeling of insecurity. This category covers references to social alarm and the feeling of impunity.
2. Victims. This category includes any reference made to victims and people damaged by crimes with a great deal of media impact.
3. Indicators of punitive populism. This category includes propaganda messages, reference to the media, the mention of electoral programmes, and immediate reactions to high-profile events.
4. Severity of the criminal penalty. This category includes references to the need to increase punitive severity, in any of its manifestations (extension of the possibility of imposing custodial measures, tougher ways of serving the sanctions, reduction of the possibilities of decreasing the sentence, etc.)
5. Disregard of the social-economic causes of crime. This category includes references to the need to incorporate the proportionality component and/or retribution purpose, independently from the education or other needs of the minor.

Once all the parliamentary interventions have been analysed, Table 1 has included the number of direct references to some of the characteristics of the law-and-order model. In particular, the arguments put forward by deputies and senators can be organised as it follows:

1) Juvenile delinquency is emerging with great force and provokes a great deal of social alarm; not all minors are well-behaved and angelic, since some of them are

[35]Regarding the dates of the legal reforms and the governments of PP and PSOE, see note 8.

dangerous; a breakdown of confidence of the citizens in the law is taking place; the phenomenon of organised crime which worries citizens has emerged; it is hard to understand why some people question the existence of social alarm.
2) The inclusion of the victim in the process does not seek revenge; the Public Prosecutor will ensure that vindictive interests do not enter the criminal proceedings; the incorporation of the victim in the process is required by supranational organisations such as the European Council.
3) It is hard to understand why the legislative proposal has been called populist; this is about adapting the answer to the social reality without making demagogy; this has always been in the electoral programme; there is media pressure.
4) For general prevention reasons, a greater criminal reproach is necessary; the increase in the severity of sanctions for some serious conducts is justified.
5) They are not children, they are youngsters; the law should also be applied to minors under 14 years old; the dividing line between individuals under and over 18 years old must be made very clear (in order to avoid applying the law to adults, even though they are young); for those between 18 and 21 years old an adult's response must be given.

Depending on the sense of the argument, different signs are used to identify those references that criticise the law-and-order model (*) and those that justify it (#). It can be observed that, generally, there is a greater number of references that support the punitive discourse than those that criticise it.

Moreover, some specific expressions and considerations stand out that deserve to be quoted (see footnotes for original in Spanish), in order to give examples of what has been highlighted in this paper:

"The dignity of the victim requires the introduction of the private prosecution in the law" (deputy of a right-wing independence party).[36]

"Nowadays society and young people are convinced that committing crimes comes for free" (deputy of the major conservative party).[37]

"Minors, victims and security: we are all represented in this parliamentary meeting" (deputy of the socialist party).[38]

"The PP included this commitment in its electoral programme…" (deputy of the major conservative party).[39]

"…without giving way to demagoguery" (senator of the socialist party).[40]

---

[36]"La dignidad de la víctima requiere la introducción de la acusación particular en la ley" (Silva Sánchez, CIU, Congress' Session's Records, 6 November 2003, p. 15,423).

[37]"Ahora mismo en la sociedad y en la gente joven existe esa conciencia, que delinquir les sale gratis" (Matador de Matas, PP, Session's Record, Congress, group vote, 23 November 2003, p. 10,962).

[38]"Menor, víctima y seguridad, en este encuentro parlamentario estamos todos" (Barrero López, PSOE, Congress Plenary session, 23 March 2006, Session's Records, p. 8,161).

[39]"El Partido Popular incluyó en su programa electoral este compromiso de ese acuerdo…" (Matador de Matas, PP, Congress Plenary session, 23 March 2006, p. 8,158).

[40]"…sin ceder a ninguna demagogia" (López Aguilar, PSOE, Senate Plenary session, 18 October 2006, p. 5849).

"This morning in news headlines you could read some absolutely unbelievable things (...)" (senator of the socialist party).[41]

"A feeling of victimisation of society has arisen" (deputy of the socialist party).[42]

## 5 Conclusions and Proposals

This paper is limited to the analysis of the legislator's discourse and, thus, leaves out subsequent phases of the juvenile penal system. Another study has been done regarding the possible influence that the reforms could be having on a tougher application of the law.[43] Although the data is not conclusive, a slight tendency towards the excessive use of custodial measures can be noted, especially in the years following the reforms. It is evident that the correct evaluation of the law will contribute to the improvement of criminal law-making policy processes and will have repercussions on its posterior application.

Revision of the empirical research on the efficacy of the measures and treatments imposed in the juvenile justice system highlights that there are certain protective factors with respect to the law-and-order model. The legal practitioners of the system show an undeniable tendency towards models focused on the education and social insertion of the minor, which suggests a resistance towards the change of model promoted from the legislative level. It would be interesting to carry out a thorough study that includes disaggregated data regarding specific crimes affected by the reforms, in order to test the scope of the slight and possibly insignificant tendency towards an excessive use of custodial measures. To do this, it would be necessary to carry out studies of jurisprudence and minors' records. This would allow the analysis of the true effects of recidivism on the judges' decisions in those cases where there is still a margin of discretion. Similarly, it is essential to study the data of implementation of the strictest measures in the case of crimes committed by a group, or being a member of a gang or criminal organisation. Only on the basis of the evaluation of the application of the law will it be possible to address new reforms that improve the scope of the juvenile justice system to resist against the punitive drift that appears to be present at least on a legislative level.

[41] "Esta mañana en titulares de prensa se podían leer cosas absolutamente increíbles (...)" (Martínez García, PSOE, Justice Committee Session's Records, Senate, 10 October 2006, p. 8).

[42] "Se ha dado un sentimiento de victimización de la sociedad" (López Aguilar, PSOE, Congress Plenary session, 23 November 2006, p. 8,145).

[43] García Magna (2018a), op.cit.

# References

Andrés Pueyo A (2006) Violencia juvenil: realidad actual y factores psicológicos implicados. Revista de Enfermería ROL 29(01):38–44

Atienza Rodríguez M (1997) Contribución a una teoría de la legislación. Cuadernos Cívitas

Basanta Dopico JL (2009) La mediación en el ámbito penal juvenil

Becerra Muñoz J (2013) La toma de decisiones en política criminal, Tirant lo Blanch

Bravo Arteaga A, Sierra MJ, Fernández Del Valle J (2009) Evaluación de resultados de la ley de responsabilidad penal de menores. Reincidencia y factores asociados. Psicothema 21 (4):615–621

Capdevila M, Ferrer M, Blanch M (2011) La reincidencia en el programa de mediación y reparación. Generalidad de Cataluña, Departamento de Justicia. Centro de Estudios Jurídicos y Formación Especializada, Barcelona

Cerdeira Bravo De Mansilla G (2015) Principio, realidad y norma: El valor de las exposiciones de motivos (y de los preámbulos). Editorial Reus, Madrid

Díez Ripollés JL (2003) La racionalidad de las leyes penales. Práctica y teoría. Editorial Trotta, Madrid

Díez Ripollés JL (2004) El nuevo modelo penal de la seguridad ciudadana. Revista Electrónica de Ciencia Penal y Criminología (6)

Díez Ripollés JL (2013) Rigorismo y reforma penal. Cuatro legislaturas homogéneas (1996-2011), partes I y II. Boletín Criminológico, articles 2 and 3

Fernández Molina E, Bernuz Beneítez MJ, Bartolomé Gutiérrez R (2017) Juvenile offenders, laws, and rights. In: Decker SH, Marteache N (eds) International handbook of juvenile justice. Springer, Berlin

García Magna D (2018a) La lógica de la seguridad en la gestión de la delincuencia. Marcial Pons, Madrid

García Magna D (2018b) Un ejemplo más de política legislativa securitaria: análisis del discurso del legislador español en el ámbito del Derecho penal juvenil. Revista Brasileira de Ciências Criminais (147)

García Magna D, González Cruz E (2017) "10 años después de la LO 8/2006: el cambio hacia el modelo de la seguridad ciudadana en el ámbito de la justicia juvenil", III Criminology Symposium SEIC

García Pérez O (2005) La introducción del modelo de la seguridad ciudadana en la justicia de menores. Cuadernos de Derecho Judicial (25)

García Pérez O (2010) La práctica de los juzgados de menores en la aplicación de las sanciones, su evolución y eficacia. Revista Electrónica de Ciencia Penal y Criminología (12)

García J, Zaldívar F, Ortega E, De La Fuente L, Sainz-Cantero B (2012) Diez años de funcionamiento de la Ley Orgánica de responsabilidad penal del menor. Consejería de Justicia e Interior, Junta de Andalucía

Garland D (2001) The culture of control. Crime and social order in contemporary society. University of Chicago Press, Chicago

Loeber R, Farrington D, Redondo S (2011) La transición desde la delincuencia juvenil a la delincuencia adulta. Revista Española de Investigación Criminológica 9

Manuel C, Ferrer M, Luque E (2005) La reincidencia en el delito en la justicia de menores. Generalidad de Cataluña. Departamento de Justicia. Centro de Estudios Jurídicos y Formación Especializada, Barcelona

Martín E, García MD, Torbay Á (2013) Evaluación de la efectividad de las medidas educativas en la ley de responsabilidad penal de menores desde la perspectiva de los infractores. Cultura y Educación 25(3):389–398

Montero Hernanz T (2011) La evolución de la delincuencia juvenil en España, Partes 1ª y 2ª. La Ley penal, Revista de Derecho penal, procesal y penitenciario (78):6

Pantoja F (2006) La Ley de Responsabilidad Penal del Menor: situación actual. Cuadernos de Derecho Judicial

Pozuelo Pérez L (2013) La política criminal mediática. Génesis, desarrollo y costes. Marcial Pons, Madrid
Rando Casermeiro P (2010) La distinción entre el Derecho penal y el Derecho administrativo sancionador. Un análisis de política jurídica. Tirant Lo Blanch
Redondo Illescas S, Martínez Catena A, Andrés Pueyo A (2011) Factores de éxito asociados a los programas de intervención con menores infractores, Informes, estudios e investigación. Observatorio de la Infancia, Ministerio de Sanidad, Política Social e Igualdad
Ríos Martín J (2005) La protección de la víctima como coartada legal para el incremento punitivo en la legislación de menores infractores. Cuadernos de Derecho Judicial (25)
Rodríguez Ferrández S (2016) La evaluación de las normas penales. Dykinson, Madrid
Rodríguez-Toubes Muñiz J (2013) El criterio histórico en la interpretación jurídica. Dereito 22
Serrano Tárraga MD (2009) Evolución de la delincuencia juvenil en España (2000-2007). Revista de Derecho penal y Criminología (2)
Toharía Cortés JJ (2003) La imagen ciudadana de la Justicia. Fundación BBVA, Bilbao

# Instrumental Rationality of the Legislator and Social Stereotypes About Crime: Models of Punitive Argumentation

**José Manuel Paredes**

**Abstract** The analysis of the discourses elaborated by legislators to justify the proposals of legislative reform that intend to extend the penal intervention (creating or expanding offences, or aggravating penalties) allows the identification of what the conceptual presuppositions and the arguments used to defend the benefits of the punitive expansion are. The paper considers four punitive reforms of the Spanish Criminal Code and reveals the underpinning stereotypes and prejudices of legislators' (of all ideologies) when it comes to conceiving the role of Criminal Law and its effects on the phenomena of social deviation. It is concluded that the penal discourses of legislators usually lack rigor, only reflecting the prejudices of legislators and lobbies, and usually lacking any solid empirical support.

**Keywords** Rationality · Penal populism · Prevention · Role of sanctions · Critical discourse analysis

## 1 Legislative Discourses As a Subject of Study

Every contemporary legislator claims to propose and adopt rational decisions. What is more, they also assume that their decisions are not only rational, but also reasonable from the point of view of public reason.[1] Thus, at least in public discourses, and especially in those public speeches issued in the most intensely institutional situations (as is the case, for example, with the public statements of government representatives or parliamentary groups when they introduce a bill, with

[1]Public reason (as an intermediate form of justification—intermediate, in comparison with the purely moral judgment—of collective moral decisions and political decisions) is to be understood as the requirement that the rules of practical rationality that we propose and apply be justifiable or, at least, rationally acceptable, to all subjects concerned by the application of such rules (Quong 2017).

J. M. Paredes (✉)
Departamento de Ciencias Jurídicas Básicas, Universidad de Oviedo, Oviedo, Spain
e-mail: paredesmanuel@uniovi.es



J. Becerra (ed.), *Criminal Law-Making*, Legisprudence Library 7,
https://doi.org/10.1007/978-3-030-71348-5_8

the explanatory statements of such bills and with the interventions and debates in Parliament), it seems almost impossible—beyond some anecdotal case—to find examples of politically relevant leaders who claim to propose or support a new bill or the reform of a pre-existing law only for purely selfish, expressive or emotional reasons. Indeed, what happens, at least in Western political culture, is that rationality is conceived as a virtue, but also (and, paradoxically, at the same time) as a presupposition (a transcendental condition, in the Kantian sense), essential for a practical discourse -around taking action- can make sense. Furthermore, in Western political culture, intersubjective reasonability is also considered to be a first-rate political virtue.

Of course, it could well be that this pretension of rationality is simply mendacious: it could well be that it is only a case of hypocrisy, that—in the words of La Rochefoucauld—"*tribute that vice pays to virtue*"; i.e., that legislators, being aware of the value attributed in our culture to the virtue of rationality, hid, behind their claims of acting rationally, pure interests, pure emotions or pure prejudices. Moreover, of course, there is always something in that: knowing how the real political dynamics unfolds, not even the most disinterested and calm of political leaders can or should completely disregard the emotional, symbolic and electoral implications of the political decisions they make. So, yes, it is true: to a certain extent (limited, at least), there is always, when a legislative change is proposed, a certain hypocrisy in the claims that it is made for (pure) rationality, for "*public interest*".

However, since this is true, it appears that it is also true that it is not the whole truth, but only part of it. On the contrary, it is also true that, as a general rule, and within certain limits, legislators also intend, when proposing legal reforms, to obtain through them certain results (at least, according to the framework of beliefs they have) associated to the "*public interest*". Such an intention is, very often (although certainly not always), sincere. That means, as a general rule, that legislative action is not, nor can it ever be, purely rational, but neither is it purely irrational: it is (like any human action and, particularly, like any political action) the fruit of decisions adopted from an inextricable combination of rational egoistic motives, altruistic rational motives (pro-social, for the sake of a collective interest) and "irrational" motives (emotional and/or expressive).[2]

In this paper I would like to concentrate exclusively on the second kind of motives referred to: that part of the legislator's motivation to act that can be valued as (a set of) pro-social motives; those that depend on the intention to obtain, through legislative action, a beneficial result (according to their point of view) for the "*public interest*" (equally defined according to their own framework of beliefs). As indicated above, the pro-social motivation of the legislator is that which normally appears most explicitly, in the form of reasons to take action, in the public speeches that they deliver -particularly in those with a more institutional profile- and that are aimed at justifying legislative action.

[2]I am not including here an additional characteristic: that it (to take action) is a decision taken collectively. On this last feature, see Waldron (2005), pp. 29 ff.

Among these reasons, some will refer to arguments of a moral nature and others, instead, to arguments of an instrumental nature. Thus, in the specific case—the one we are interested in here—of penal reforms for which either offences are created or expanded, or penalties are created or aggravated, the moral reasons given by legislators to justify them usually have to do with: (1) the moral assessment that, according to certain moral principles, which it is claimed are universally accepted, should be given to prohibited and punishable conduct; and (2) the moral feelings that the majority of citizens would harbour (whether this is true or not) in relation to such conduct.

Much can and must be said about these two kinds of moral arguments, in order to critically determine what their true strength is.[3] However, here I would like to concentrate rather on the other kind of reasons that the legislator usually gives, trying to justify the rationality of their endeavour: the instrumental reasons. The instrumental rationality of an action refers to its suitability, in view of the results that it is intended to achieve. In this regard, an action (a legislative action, for example) is all the more rational, from the merely instrumental perspective, because of the increasingly greater coherence between its causal consequences that are foreseeable and the states of things that are intended to take place.[4]

## 2 Instrumental Rationality and Motivating Role of the Criminal Policy

In the specific case of Criminal Law, the instrumental reasons given to justify the legislative action creating or expanding offences, or creating or aggravating penalties, usually concern the role that the criminal law intended to be enacted should fulfil at the commination stage (the moment in which, by means of speech acts, the prescriptive content of the law is communicated to its target audience). On the contrary, it is unusual that, during the legislative discussion on substantive criminal law, reference is made to the impact of the laws and policies at the stages of prosecution or criminal enforcement. Not, at least, to bring up the main arguments of the debate, which tend to have more to do with the moment of the commination.[5]

[3]I have already dealt with some of them in previous papers: concerning the first class (crime as immoral conduct and punishment as a response to mass), see Paredes Castañón (2013); and in relation to the second class (crime as a moral scandal against majority beliefs), see Paredes Castañón (2016).

[4]Kolodny and Brunero (2013).

[5]There are, however, exceptions: mainly in the case of reforms that affect penalties, when it is bitterly discussed whether a particular penalty is (by its nature or its magnitude) morally justified, additional arguments may emerge—in any case, always of secondary importance—related to the instrumental rationality of the process of determining the penalty or the sentence enforcement. This has been the case, for example, recently in Spain, in relation to the reviewable permanent imprisonment (introduced by the Spanish legislator in the reform of the Criminal Code of 2015),

Thus, in the legislator's discourses, along with moral reasons, instrumental reasons that are often invoked to justify a legal reform that creates or expands a crime, or that establishes or aggravates a penalty, usually concern the motivating role that criminal rules should fulfil at the time of the commination. In fact, what is usually argued is that the creation of a crime (either because the crime did not previously exist, or because the conduct in question was not previously subsumable in it, or was so in a less serious crime) or the aggravation of its penalty constitute suitable practices to generate (or, if it is an aggravation, to increase) the motivational effect that the criminal policy is suitable to cause in its target audience. This is an effect that does not occur as long as the legislative reform does not take place. Therefore, it is argued that there would be a serious risk that the public policy (of not intervening by prohibiting and sanctioning or sanctioning more) would have effects that would encourage crime, incentivising through omission practices deviated from the norms of desirable social behaviour.

The following is the causal sequence model that seems to be implicit in this type of discourse:

- The commination through criminal law (through its creation and subsequent repeated communication) is an act of speech by means of which the legislator-sender (acting as a messenger of the State) intends to transmit a message to the target of the policy-receiver. A message whose meaning is a combination of prescription and threat: prescription (act of directive speech), since performing a certain class of actions is prohibited; and threat (act of commissive speech),[6] insofar as it promises to cause harm to the recipient, in the event that they do not comply with the prohibition.
- Under the right conditions, the message transmitted introduces one or several additional reasons (to those that previously existed) in the motivation process of the target of the policy determining their actions.
- Under such ideal conditions, the more serious the action the issuer promises to take (the greater the entity of the threat), the more intense the motivational effect of the legislative commination on the target of the policy. Thus, the motivational effect of the enactment of an offence would always be, *ceteris paribus*, superior to that of other prescriptions. Similarly, the motivational effect of a heavier penalty would always be—under the same conditions—more intense than that of a lighter penalty.

---

when the rationality of its review regime is discussed. Something similar has been happening in the international debate regarding the death penalty, in which it is sometimes argued that the process of applying the death penalty is inefficient (in terms of slowness and cost). It should be noted, however, that in both cases the arguments referring to the moments of the imposition or execution of the sentence are always secondary. And, even more so, are those relating to the instrumental rationality of such processes, given that the debate concentrates mainly on questions of moral justification.

[6]On the concepts of the theory of the acts of speech involved here, see Searle (1991), pp. 459–466.

Again, there are many critical observations that could be made about the simplicity of this model of the causal sequence operating at the time of the criminal commination. Simplicity, on the one hand, in terms of the underpinning model of communication between the legislator and the target of the policy, which seems to ignore the difficulties introduced in the communicative process by both the existence of environmental noise (of a socio-cultural nature), interfering with the understanding of the normative message by its receivers, and how idiosyncratic the decoding processes by these receivers always turn out to be[7]. However, there is also simplicity when it comes to conceiving the process of psychic motivation of the individuals, which is understood on the basis of a naïve behaviourism, in which characteristics of this process are ignored (its nature as a complex system and the non-linear nature of its dynamics) that today are completely proven[8] and that make doubtful, at the very least, the hypothesis that an increase in the gravity of the threat is directly correlated with the intensity of the motivation provided by it.[9]

## 3 The Target of Criminal Law: Case Studies

### *3.1 Four Models of Targets*

In any case, my objective here is not to contrast the model of motivation by means of prescriptive norms handled by the legislator with the evidence provided by the empirical sciences, but rather to examine the contents of said model. In this regard, in addition to the aforementioned simplicity of the model from the causal point of view, the most striking thing about it is its ambiguity when it comes to describing the characteristics of the ideal type of subject that would be the recipient of the normative message, the one who would have to be motivated.

In fact, the analysis of the public discourses made by legislators (especially, as I indicated, those that possess a more markedly institutional character) shows that, in reality, although the starting point of practically every discourse, to justify the instrumental rationality, is a single causal sequence model (in which there would be a straight line and no deviations from the commination by the legislator to the motivational effect on the receiver, and in which the intensity of one and the other would be correlated), the subject to be motivated is not conceived in the same way in all cases. On the contrary, it would rather seem that contemporary legislators use, depending on the areas of regulation involved, different models of the subject to

[7]Cuesta (2000), pp. 95 ff., 155 ff. In fact, the starting point of many criminological theories (such as that of anomie or that of criminal subcultures) are such communication difficulties to try to provide more convincing explanations of the social dynamics that lead to the realisation of criminal behaviours: vid. Downes and Rock (2011), pp. 151 ff.

[8]Carver and Scheier (1998), pp. 250–262.

[9]Nagin (2013).

whom the criminal law is targeted. So, at the end of the day, the motivational process that would justify the legislative action would turn out to be remarkably different, depending on the case.

I propose, in this regard, that, in order to examine this difference in treatment in the legislative discourses of the subject at whom the criminal policy is aimed and to whom it is intended to motivate, we then carry out an extensive follow-up of the discourses of the legislators (of those with a maximum institutional profile): of the explanatory statements and parliamentary debates—especially, in the latter case, the interventions of parliamentarians from the "government parties") in four exemplary cases of reforms of Spanish Criminal Law: in the areas of terrorism, "*gender violence*" (violence against a partner or a former partner) or family violence, road safety and property crimes. Thus, it is possible to compare the very different operations of conceptualisation and categorisation that have been introduced in each of these discourses, when trying to justify the reforms from the point of view of instrumental rationality.

## *3.2 Case 1 (Terrorism)*

In 2003 (7th Legislature), the Spanish Government (Spanish People's Party, *Partido Popular*) introduced in the Spanish Parliament a draft reform of the Criminal Code that, among other things, proposed to modify the penalties for terrorist offences and petty thefts without violence or the use of force.

Note what was said in relation to the first of the topics. In the Bill's explanatory memorandum:

> But, in addition to ensuring this right, the law pursues a clear objective, in accordance with its own criminal nature: fighting crime more effectively. As the authoritative criminal doctrine has pointed out, the greatest deterrent on crime is not the harshness of the penalties, but their infallibility, so that the certainty of a punishment, even if it is moderate, will have more effect than the fear of a more severe punishment coupled with the hope of impunity or non-compliance.
>
> (...)
>
> **Society demands more effective protection against the** most serious forms of crime, in particular terrorist offences, offences related to organised crime and offences that are highly dangerous, a protection which the rule of law not only can but has an obligation to provide. Flexibility in the serving of sentences and prison benefits has its raison d'être in the constitutionally enshrined goal of the offender's rehabilitation and re-education. However, precisely for this reason, legislation **must prevent them from becoming mere instruments at the disposal of terrorists** and the most serious offenders to achieve a very different goal.[10]

[10]Explanatory Memorandum for Basic Law 7/2003, of 30th June, on reform measures for the full and effective enforcement of sentences (Official State Gazette, No. 156, of 1st July 2003). https://www.boe.es/buscar/doc.php?id=BOE-A-2003-13022. Accessed 30 Apr 2018. Emphasis added.

And then in the parliamentary debates in the Justice Committee of the Congress of Deputies:

> (...) my parliamentary group, even though we know what has been the impact of that instrument of previous legislation on the remission of penalty by work, can **share the concern that some citizens have felt** when they have seen people sentenced to many years in prison, in some cases to more than 200 years in prison, because of the upper limit of serving sentences, of the remission of penalty by work and of some practices of certain judges responsible for the enforcement of sentences, have been out on the street -so to speak-, a few years after their conviction -a few years compared to these 200-, 10 or 17 years later.[11]

> **Society has a right to have guarantees** that when someone who offended it terribly with a multiple crime, with a multiple murder, with a car bomb killing four people in one go and preparing to kill four others as soon as he has the slightest opportunity (...) has his sentence reduced from 120 years to 32, 22 or 23 years of effective serving, that is in exchange for that person no longer being offensive and a threat to society as a whole. But even more, not only has that individual person has ceased to be offensive and a threat to society as a whole, but he or she has launched a message of commitment to constitutional democracy and freedoms sufficiently dissuasive in the environment from which he or she comes from.[12]

> The Popular Party has acted, acts and will always act within the rule of law and the reform introduces a series of legal mechanisms that are fully compatible with the Constitution and are aimed at strengthening the principle of legal certainty, perfecting the criminal legal system in order to increase penalties for especially serious offences, as has been made clear in the bill and in the amendments incorporated, and **avoiding possible cases of impunity in practice**.[13]

## 3.3 *Case 2 (Theft)*

Note below how, on the other hand, there was discussion (same time, same bill, same political situation) about the reform of the offence of theft. The explanatory memorandum of the Project read as follows:

> The social reality has shown that one of the main problems to which the criminal justice system has to respond to is that of the delinquency that repeatedly commits its actions, or what is the same, **professionalized crime**. There are numerous examples of those who

[11]Intervention by the MP Manuel Silva Sánchez (CiU) in the session of the Justice and Home Office Committee of the Congress of Deputies on 13/5/2003 (Diario de Sesiones C núm. VII-761). http://www.congreso.es/public_oficiales/L7/CONG/DS/CO/CO_761.PDF. Accessed 30 Apr 2018. Emphasis added.

[12]Intervention by the MP Juan Francisco López Aguilar (PSOE) in the session of the Commission of Justice and Interior of the Congress of Deputies of 13/5/2003 (Diario de Sesiones C núm. VII-761). http://www.congreso.es/public_oficiales/L7/CONG/DS/CO/CO_761.PDF. Accessed 30 Apr 2018. Emphasis added.

[13]Speech by Leocadio Bueso Zaera (PP) in the session of the Justice and Home Affairs Commission of the Spanish Parliament on 13/5/2003 (Diary of Sessions C núm. VII-761). http://www.congreso.es/public_oficiales/L7/CONG/DS/CO/CO_761.PDF. Accessed 30 Apr 2018. Emphasis added.

commit minor offences on a large number of occasions, **offences that due to their individualized amount do not obtain an adequate criminal response**.

(. . .)

This text establishes, in the first place, measures aimed at providing **an adequate response to those cases** in which the perpetrators have already been convicted of criminal activities, through the application of the aggravating factor of recidivism, in this case qualified by the number of offences committed, following a criterion already established in our doctrine and in our legal texts.[14]

And then, in the debates of the Justice Committee of the Congress of Deputies, things like the following were said:

(...) **whoever is not alarmed by some situations of habitual delinquency or of multi-recidivism**, in the technical sense, of some criminals who, surely due to operational difficulties of lack of means, of judges, etc., **are in the street, when they should have a penal sanction** motivated by the transgression of norms to the coexistence that we have given ourselves.[15]

Our democratic state demands that the penalties imposed on repeat offenders should **not be determined with their backs turned to the social transcendence that the irritation of citizens gives to these crime situations**.[16]

(...) this allows us, with greater dogmatic correction, to **distinguish the person who regularly and professionally dedicates himself/herself to committing thefts** from the youngster who should not have done so, but does so one day when he enters a department store and takes with him/her a compact disc. This is what we all her are trying to distinguish, the primary offender, who in this case can perfectly have a misdemeanour penalty, from the regular offender, the professional offender, the recidivist, who should have a higher penalty.[17]

## 3.4 *Case 3 (Road Safety)*

In 2006 (8$^{th}$ Legislature), a Non-Standing Committee on Road Safety and Prevention of Traffic Accidents took action in the Congress of Deputies. The result of this would

[14]Explanatory Memorandum for Basic Law 7/2003, of 30$^{th}$ June, on reform measures for the full and effective enforcement of penalties. Emphasis added.

[15]Intervention by the MP Jaime Javier Barrero López (PSOE) in the session of the Commission of Justice and Interior of the Congress of Deputies of 17/6/2003 (Diario de Sesiones C núm. VII-776). http://www.congreso.es/public_oficiales/L7/CONG/DS/CO/CO_776.PDF. Accessed 30 Apr 2018. Emphasis added.

[16]Intervention by the MP Ana María Torme Pardo (PP) in the session of the Commission of Justice and Interior of the Congress of Deputies of 17/6/2003 (Diary of Sessions C núm. VII-776). http://www.congreso.es/public_oficiales/L7/CONG/DS/CO/CO_776.PDF. Accessed 30 Apr 2018. Emphasis added.

[17]Intervention by the MP Manuel Silva Sánchez (CiU) in the session of the Commission of Justice and Interior of the Congress of Deputies of 17/6/2003 (Diary of Sessions C núm. VII-776). http://www.congreso.es/public_oficiales/L7/CONG/DS/CO/CO_776.PDF. Accessed 30 Apr 2018. Emphasis added.

be the subsequent reform of "offences against road safety", promoted by the Government (PSOE) and introduced in the Criminal Code by Basic Law 15/2007. This Committee discussed—among other things—the role that criminal law could play in suppressing reckless behaviour in car traffic. Note in what terms:

> (...) what we are exploring here today is a **better breeding ground, as I will also try to set out, for prevention and even for education**. (...) Education yes, prevention too, but there will not be a serious policy without also granting its territory, in this field, to criminal law.
>
> (...)
>
> **In line with the classic concept of general prevention, the probability of being sanctioned and its associated cost should be sufficient and suitable to supress this type of conduct** whose most tragic facet is, in many cases, its exclusively capricious or arbitrary origin, which is evident in the simple and conscious adoption by the road user of irresponsible attitudes due to the lack of a sufficient risk assessment or the inadequate weighing of his/her consequences. It is therefore a question of intervening on this list of consequences, putting those that are the result of the final materialisation of the danger before others that make it possible to avoid its realization. To put it more clearly, it is a **matter of conveying to the user the message that his/her reckless or irresponsible behaviour may in fact cause an incident that generates irreparable personal and material damage to other persons or to himself/herself, but even before that irreparable effect, the very fact of behaving in a careless or reckless manner must lead to other serious harm for him/her**.[18]

> (...) consideration should be given to what criminal legislation can do to reinforce the value of road safety; among others (...) **that of fulfilling the objective that is conceptually called general prevention and special prevention, that is, the preventive effect, insofar as the criminal law, precisely because of the entity of the reproach, its importance, is called upon to exercise a special deterrence in the incursion in the conducts that deserve that classification**. This would intentionally have as its objective to reduce the frequency of those conducts and, at the same time, to signify social intolerance with respect to those conducts in view of the damage that they entail and the effects that they produce. (...) I do want to confirm (...) that road safety will be present in this draft reform of the Penal Code, and we will do so (...) especially to express that the road traffic regulations must be taken very seriously, that are many and very important values that are involved in the attitude of drivers in road safety.
>
> (...)
>
> Nor can this be immediately associated with miraculous effects or impact on the reduction of the accident rate, but it will undoubtedly be **sending a very powerful message of commitment and in the course of time it is called upon to reduce that accident rate** and the balance of human pain and losses that this entails.[19]

[18] Appearance of Cándido Conde-Pumpido Tourón, Attorney General of the State, in the session of the Non-Permanent Commission on Road Safety and Prevention of Traffic Accidents of the Congress of Deputies of 23/11/2005 (Diary of Sessions C núm. VIII-437. Available at: http://www.congreso.es/public_oficiales/L8/CONG/DS/CO/CO_437.PDF. Accessed 30 Apr 2018. Emphasis added.

[19] Appearance of Juan Francisco López Aguilar, Minister of Justice, in the session of the Non-Permanent Commission on Road Safety and Prevention of Traffic Accidents of the Congress of Deputies of 20/6/2006 (Diary of Sessions C núm. VIII-610. http://www.congreso.es/public_oficiales/L8/CONG/DS/CO/CO_610.PDF. Accessed 30 Apr 2018. Emphasis added.

Subsequently, the Explanatory Memorandum of Basic Law 15/2007 read as follows:

> The resolutions passed as a result of the debate on the State of the Nation in 2006 is include resolution number nineteen, which states, among other issues, that the Congress of Deputies considers it appropriate to boost the amendment of the Penal Code, taking into account the various proposals being considered in the Committee on Road Safety of the Congress of Deputies, with the aim of **more rigorously defining all offences against traffic safety and those related to road safety, avoiding that certain conducts classified as road violence can go unpunished**.
>
> (...)
>
> We present this Draft Basic Law to amend the Criminal Law on the issue of traffic safety. The basic content of this proposal seeks, on the one hand, to **increase control over the tolerable risk** through the express provision of speeding that must be considered dangerous or levels of alcohol intake that must merit the same consideration. From this estimation of the source of danger, different degrees of unfair conduct are regulated, ranging from abstract danger to perceptible contempt for the lives of others, as the Code had already done. **The penalties and consequences are greatly increased** (...)[20]

## 3.5 *Case 4 (Violence Against Women)*

Finally, in 2004 (8th Legislature) the Government (PSOE, Spanish Socialist Workers' Party) submitted to Parliament a bill on comprehensive protection measures against gender-based violence. It contained, among many others, proposals for the reform of the Criminal Code. In the parliamentary debate of this Bill, in the Committee on Employment and Social Affairs of the Congress of the Deputies, things like the following were argued:

> If **we understand the law as linked to the concept of general prevention**, which is an interesting concept, **not that of negative general prevention**, i.e., not that people are frightened by the fear of punishment, which is what the theories of negative general prevention supposed, **but positive general prevention, (...), bearing in mind that the category of offences and judicial action can serve as a positive pedagogy for citizens to understand that such behaviour**, (...) **i.e., general positive prevention can be favoured**, and I would not criticise the excess of either judicial protection or the excess - in inverted commas - of criminal action in this area.
>
> (...)
>
> It is clear that the increase in penalties (...) does not guarantee or resolve anything at all in relation to the decrease in the crimes. However, general positive prevention (...) What does this doctrine, this approach to the meaning of criminal law, intend to achieve? **It seeks to prevent the commission of crimes by the public, shaping the legal consciousness of citizens to promote their adherence to law and recognition of the values it embodies, its**

[20]Explanatory memorandum to Basic Law 15/2007, of 30 November, amending Basic Law 10/1995, of 23 November, of the Criminal Code on road safety (Official State Gazette no. 288, of 1st December 2007). https://www.boe.es/buscar/doc.php?id=BOE-A-2007-20636. Accessed 30 Apr 2018. Emphasis added.

**mandates and prohibitions, and so it would not be fear but the communicative role of legal values that would lead to this justification**.[21]

(...) it was alleged by those of us who have extensively demanded this law in the past **that it should clearly make explicit zero tolerance of violence**. It is an objective that has been proposed by the feminist movement and you have spoken very well from your position as a feminist. Zero tolerance can be derived from the articles of the bill, but there are some aspects that make it more visible with respect to violence. One of them is undoubtedly the aggravation of penalties. You have said that feminism did not agree very much with this approach and I ask you what would you do to make really visible, taking as a starting point the very articles of the bill, the zero tolerance against violence in a broad sense, socially, culturally, so that society understands that a process has indeed been undertaken in which society as a whole and the State in particular, by means of their instruments, are not going to tolerate violence against women.[22]

This means - and this is a very simple explanation - that the legislative reforms that have been passed in this Parliament **have resulted in women having greater confidence in the administration**. Now we have better legal texts, we have a law on the protective order that is working properly in the judicial bodies and in that sense we can see that **women feel much more protected**.[23]

Accordingly, the Explanatory memorandum of the Law stated that:

Title IV of the Act introduces provisions of a criminal nature, by means of which it is intended to include, among the aggravated types of injuries, a specific one that increases the criminal penalty when the injury occurs against anyone who is or has been the wife of the perpetrator, or a woman who is or has been linked to him by an analogous relationship of affectivity, even without cohabitation. Light coercion and light threats of any kind committed against the above-mentioned women shall also be punishable as a criminal offence.

**To citizens, to women's organizations and specifically to those who suffer this type of assaults, the Law wants to give a strong and robust response and show firmness** by translating them into specific types of criminal offences.[24]

[21]Appearance of Gregorio Peces-Barba Martínez in the session of the Committee on Labour and Social Affairs of the Congress of Deputies on 19/7/2004 (Journal of Sessions C No. VIII-64). http://www.congreso.es/public_oficiales/L8/CONG/DS/CO/CO_064.PDF. Accessed 30 Apr 2018. Emphasis added.

[22]Intervention by María Virtudes Monteserín Rodríguez (PSOE) in the session of the Employment and Social Affairs Committee of the Spanish Parliament on 22/7/2004 (Journal of Sessions C No. VIII-67). http://www.congreso.es/public_oficiales/L8/CONG/DS/CO/CO_067.PDF. Accessed 30 Apr 2018. Emphasis added.

[23]Appearance of Vicente Magro Servet in the session of the Committee on Employment and Social Affairs of the Congress of Deputies of 8/9/2004 (Diary of Sessions C núm. VIII-70). http://www.congreso.es/public_oficiales/L8/CONG/DS/CO/CO_070.PDF. Accessed 30 Apr 2018. Emphasis added.

[24]Explanatory memorandum to Basic Law 1/2004, of 28 December, on Comprehensive Protection Measures against Gender Violence (Official State Gazette, No. 313, of 29th December 2004). https://www.boe.es/buscar/doc.php?id=BOE-A-2004-21760 Accessed 30 Apr 2018. Emphasis added.

### 3.6 Comparative Table

The following comparative table compiles the central pieces of each of the four discourses, to facilitate the appreciation of the differences among them (Table 1).

## 4 Semantics of the Legislative Discourse on the Targets of the Policies

### 4.1 Introduction

Of course, the selected expressions are nothing more than the most prominent samples of the respective discourses that legislators have constructed in order to justify the instrumental rationality of each of the punitive expansion proposals (and that I have selected, in order to give them greater visibility and make it possible to compare them). It is therefore necessary to now reconstruct the semantic structures underlying each of these discourses.

In fact, as always when a discourse is constructed, the tools used to enhance the production of the desired communicative effect are very diverse. In this case, it is a matter of carrying out, by means of the discourse, several acts of speech at the same time: in addition, of course, to the locative act of saying itself, it is also intended to carry out at the same time an act of illocutionary speech of (self-)justification (an expressive act, then); another directive illocutionary act, to motivate listeners to take action (to vote in favour, in the case of the other MPs, and to approve the speaker's performance, in the case of the rest of the audience); and, finally, a fourth speech-act, this one of a perlocutionary nature, consisting of the listeners feeling convinced by the points of view put forward[25].

In order to be successful in the development of all these communicative activities that are intended to be carried out through discourse, all sorts of linguistic and paralinguistic tools are used: syntactic, lexical, rhetorical, etc.[26] In our case, the aspect we are particularly interested in highlighting is the semantic one: i.e., the conceptual structures that are brought into play, by means of their linguistic expression, when trying to develop supporting discourses of this nature.[27]

[25]On the theoretical basis of the concepts and classification of the acts of speech that are used in the text, see Searle (1991, 1994) and Austin (1996).

[26]Casalmiglia and Tusón (2012), pp. 315 ff.

[27]Obviously, in practice, the semantic elements brought into play in legislative discourses do not operate in an isolated way, but are integrated with the rest of the elements: most notably, with pragmatic resources (the parliamentary situation in which they take place, the echo in the media, etc.). See Casalmiglia and Tusón (2012), pp. 91 ff. However, I believe that the critical analysis of semantic contents—which is the subject of this study—is in itself sufficiently significant.

**Table 1** Comparative table: four models of offender

| | Case 1 (Terrorism) | Case 2 (Theft) | Case 3 (Road Safety) | Case 4 (Gender-based Violence) |
|---|---|---|---|---|
| Explanatory Memorandum | *"Society demands more effective protection (...) must prevent them from becoming mere instruments in the service of terrorists (...)"* | *"(...) professionalized crime. (. . .) offences which, due to their individualized amount, do not receive an adequate criminal response. (. . .) an adequate response to those cases (...)"* | *"(...) more rigorously defining all offences against traffic safety (...) avoiding that certain conducts classified as road violence can go unpunished. (. . .) increase control over the tolerable risk (. . .) The penalties and consequences are greatly increased (...)"* | *"(...) To citizens, to women's organizations and specifically to those who suffer this type of assault, the Law wants to give a strong and robust response and to show firmness (...)"* |
| Parliamentary debate | *"(...) share the concern that some citizens have felt (...)" "Society has the right to have guarantees (...)" "(...) avoid possible cases of impunity"* | *"(...) whoever is not alarmed by certain situations of habitual delinquency or multirecidivism, (...) are in the street, when they should have a penal sanction (...)" "(...) not be determined with their backs turn their backs turned to the social transcendence that the irritation of citizens gives to these crime situations." "(...) distinguish the person who regularly and professionally dedicates himself/herself to committing thefts (...)"* | *"(...) better breeding-ground, as I will also try to set out, for prevention and even for education. (. . .) In line with the classic concept of general prevention, the probability of being sanctioned and its associated cost should be sufficient and suitable to supress this type of behaviour. (. . .) of conveying to the user the message that his/her reckless or irresponsible behaviour may in fact cause an incident that generates irreparable personal and material damage to other persons or to himself/* | *"If we understand the law as linked to the concept of general prevention, (...) not that of negative general prevention (...) but positive general prevention, (...) bearing in mind that the category of offences and judicial action can serve as a positive pedagogy for citizens to understand that such behaviour, (...) i.e., general positive prevention can be favoured, (. . .) It seeks to prevent the commission of crimes by the public, shaping the legal consciousness of citizens to promote* |

(continued)

**Table 1** (continued)

| | Case 1 (Terrorism) | Case 2 (Theft) | Case 3 (Road Safety) | Case 4 (Gender-based Violence) |
|---|---|---|---|---|
| | | | *herself, but even before that irreparable effect, the very fact of behaving in a careless or reckless manner must lead to other serious harm for him/her.*" "(...) *that of fulfilling the objective that is conceptually called general prevention and special prevention, i.e. the preventive effect, insofar as the criminal law, precisely because of the entity of the reproach, by its importance, is called upon to exercise a special deterrence.* (. . .) *sending a very powerful message of commitment and in the course of time is called upon to reduce that accident rate* (...)" | *their adherence to law and recognition of the values* (...)". "(...) *that it should clearly make explicit zero tolerance of violence.* (. . .)" "(...) *have resulted in women having greater confidence in the administration.* (. . .) *women feel much more protected.*" |

In this sense, the semantic analysis of the discourses above shows that, in their elaboration, the three classes of semantic operations have been carried out that are usual when it is a matter of (as always, in the context of discourses and essentially discussed concepts, as is usually the case of those that are used in the political debate)[28] developing a conceptual structure that, when it is expressed linguistically, must provide a new way of perceiving the reality: here, not only more convincing, from the theoretical point of view, of its truthfulness, but also more adequate in

[28]Connolly (1993).

practical terms, in terms of the rationality of the human action (state: legislative) on said reality.

The first of the semantic operations developed is one of *categorisation*: it consists of the grouping of different meanings of a linguistic unit under a single category, characterised by some distinctive properties. The second operation that has taken place is one of *configuration of the semantic space*: the networking in relation of some meanings with others, in a common mental space. Finally, thirdly, a *conceptualisation* operation has also been carried out: using different concepts, a certain form of representation of the reality which is intended to be discussed is created.[29]

## 4.2 Semantic Space Configuration: Predominant Conceptual Domains

However, in order to more clearly illuminate how the mental space evoked in each of the four discourses examined is structured, I will present the expression of these semantic operations carried out precisely in the opposite order, starting with those of conceptualisation and ending with those of categorisation.

**Case 1** Firstly, it can be observed, thus, that, in the case of the speeches supporting the reform of terrorist offences, the prominence within the speech is given first and foremost to "*society*" and "*citizens*". It seems, in fact, that it is both terms (and the concepts they represent) that must constitute the central element of the argumentative text that is developed.

**Case 2** On the other hand, when it comes to justifying the reform of the offence of theft, the prominence within the discourse seems to be given rather to "*the offenders*" (the professional, regular offenders).

**Case 3** In the case of the reform of road safety offences, the emphasis is on the term "*prevention*".

---

[29]On all these concepts, typical of cognitive semantics (in which I am inspired here), see Evans and Grenn (2006), pp. 206 ff; Croft and Alan (2008), pp. 25 ff; Hamawand (2016), pp. 121 ff. From the perspective adopted here, therefore, it is not so much a question (as it occurs in the most traditional conception -the veritative-functional- of Semantics: see, for example, Kearns (2011), pp. 24 ff.) of finding an exact definition of the meaning of the terms, propositions and discourses, as to be able to analyse the processes of constitution of such meanings. Precisely, this special attention to the historical processes of configuration of meanings, characteristic of the cognitive approach, is what makes it a useful tool for the critical analysis of discourse (see Fairclough and Wodak (2000), pp. 367 ff.): since it is not limited to carrying out an ideal reconstruction of the meanings in the language-system (the *langue* that Ferdinand de Saussure talked about: Saussure (2006), pp. 33–35, 40–42, 45–47), but, in trying to show how these meanings have come to be created, it pays special attention to the interactions (conceptual and social) that take place in this process.

**Case 4** Finally, in attempting to justify the reform of "*gender-based violence*" crimes, legislators highlight "*confidence*" and "*show firmness*" as the most prominent terms.

It should therefore be noted, that, in each of the four cases, the discourses issued by the legislators propose connections with very different conceptual domains[30]:

- In **Case 1**, the meaning of the discourse focuses on society and citizenship: on how they perceive the phenomenon of terrorism. Thus, the corresponding conceptual domain is limited by terms such as "*feelings*", "*public opinion*", "*indignation*", "*beliefs*", "*justice*", "*deserved*", etc.
- In **Case 2**, on the other hand, the most prominent meaning in the discourse concerns the offenders, with the perpetrators of thefts; more precisely, with certain perpetrators of thefts (professional, regular...). Thus, the conceptual domain to which access is provided is limited by terms such as "*offender*", "*dangerous*", "*recidivist*", "*non-compliant*", "*thief*", "*professional offender*", "*public safety problem*", etc.
- In **Case 3**, the issue of the effect of the criminal commination on the target audience of the policy, potential offenders, is given prominence. The conceptual domain thus evoked is established taking as a starting point terms such as "*intimidation*", "*prevention*", "*taking seriously*", "*costs and benefits*", "*rationality*", "*rational decision*"...
- Finally, in **Case 4**, the most prominent meaning is that of trust. The conceptual domain is then delimited by terms such as "*reassurance*", "*trust*", "*security*", "*fear*", "*authority*", "*consensus*", etc.

### 4.3 Conceptualisation: Prominent Themes in Each Discourse

What is striking is, above all, the diversity of the conceptual domains evoked, when it is a matter of achieving the same objective in all cases: justifying, from the point of view of instrumental rationality, legislative reform proposals with a punitive sense (creation of new criminal offences and/or aggravation of their penalties). That is to say, practically the same legislators (the same parties, sometimes even the same people, in very close legislatures, and with no significant changes in the respective political election manifestoes), pursuing similar ends, however, significantly alter the semantic contents of the discourses they utter to justify their policies, depending on the subject matter in question.

[30]Evans and Grenn (2006), pp. 230–231. From the point of view that interests us here (that of the impact of the semantic operations on legislative discourses -and praxis-), the moment of the configuration of the semantic space proves decisive: it is in this moment when meanings that in principle come from radically different fields are connected and when, by means of a blending process (*blending*: Evans and Grenn (2006), pp. 407–418), terms that, in principle, are distant are associated: "*justice*" and "*indignation*", for example; or "*thief*" and "*recidivist*".

- Thus, in the case of the reform of terrorist offences, the legislators of the Spanish government parties in all cases give discursive pre-eminence to the question of the "*justice*" of the penalty; that is, the retribution, through the magnitude of the penalty imposed, of the wrong and of the infringement of legal rights specific to terrorist offences. The most relevant thing seems to be to determine for the crime the penalty that is considered (that "*the society considers*") as fair. And, on the other hand, they seem quite unconcerned about the empirical effects of the penalty: whether or not it is intimidating, whether or not it is suitable for resocialising, etc.
- In the case of the proposed reform of the theft offence, the type of arguments put forward are of a completely different nature. In this case, in fact, it seems that what is decisive, what gives rise to the justification of the reform, is danger: the extraordinary and specific criminal danger of certain categories of people, with a propensity, practically unstoppable (by professionalisation and regularity), to the commission of offences against property. Petty crimes because of their individual entity, but worrying because of their large number, as well as the fact that the feeling of insecurity they create in the general public stems from a small minority of offenders. It would therefore be a question of getting the right treatment by means of legal-criminal means for this small minority, the only truly worrying minority among those who tend to commit theft offences. And, in this sense, "*getting it right*" is equivalent to finding a punitive reaction effective enough to neutralise (or minimise) the specific criminal danger of that group of offenders.
- In the case of road crime, the legislator's approach to justifying the expansion of criminal intervention is very different: here, it would be more a question of carrying out a motivational operation on potential road safety offenders, in order, in the best case scenario, to convince them of the value of prudence in car traffic ("*educating*" *them*). Or at least, even in the worst case, make them understand that there is no point in infringing such regulations: that the costs of doing so (including the costs of bearing the criminal penalty) always outweigh the possible benefits of recklessness.
- Finally, the legislative justification for increasing criminal intervention in cases of "*gender-based violence*" (physical or psychological violence against a partner or former partner) emphasises the objective of inducing certain feelings and beliefs in victims and potential victims (women): to reassure them, to make them trust the State and the law, etc. Therefore, the punitive legislative reform would primarily focus on promoting and reinforcing that reassuring message.

In short, the main instrumental objectives that legislators claim to pursue with their punitive expansion proposals are, respectively:

- *"Doing justice"*, in the case of punishing terrorist offences: compensating the wrong caused by the offenders with a penalty that takes into account the magnitude of said wrong, as perceived by the majority of society (at least by those to whom legislators attribute the condition of majority).
- In the case of theft, neutralise the (extraordinary) criminal danger of a specific class of offenders of this law: prevent recidivism in the infringement of that subset

that, within the set of perpetrators of theft, are characteriaed by their professionaliaation in crime and their usual dedication to the commission of such acts.
- In the case of road crime, intimidate potential offenders by making them understand the risk of their behaviour, and even trying to change their attitude towards the risk derived from car traffic.
- Finally, in the case of violence against women, to reassure victims and potential victims, assuring them of effective State protection and increasing their confidence in such protection.

So, compensation (terrorism); special prevention, mainly to make it harmless (theft); general prevention, mainly intimidating (road crime); and general positive prevention (violence against women). Four different objectives that are proposed for prohibitions and comminations contained in the criminal law rules, depending on the nature of the infringement and the characteristics that are presupposed to the offender. And all this, I insist, without the change of discourse being justified by any significant alteration either in the social reality or in the parties' political election manifestoes.

## 5 Categorisation: Typology of Model Offender

With this, we arrive at the key idea that I would like to highlight, and that seems to me to be the only one that allows us to explain this striking diversity in the argumentative strategies used in each of the cases. In my opinion, it is evident that, when developing their discourses supporting the punitive measures proposed, Spanish legislators in the cases discussed take as their starting point some very specific categorisations (although they do not do it in a completely explicit way) concerning (criminological) the social dynamics underpinning each of the four different crime phenomena that they try to address by means of their reforms. And also, therefore, concerning the specific characteristics of the category of offenders and victims to whom the criminal commination seeks to address; and concerning the specific way in which the motivation that the prescriptive message of the legal policy is capable of can behave on a case-by-case basis.

- Thus, in the case of terrorism, it seems that the legislator assumes that the terrorist offender is an individual who has been subject to an exotic socialisation process: at least, because of the idiosyncratic political, moral or religious ideas they have acquired, if not because of their entire socialisation process. Due to this exoticism, the motivating messages of the policy could hardly work with them, as they won't reach out to them. So, the only thing that could rationally be aspired to is to neutralise them and then punish them as society thinks they deserve. Without hope, then, of a change in their behaviour; first and foremost, to "do justice", to satisfy the social demands for a just resolution of the conflict between the terrorist and the community.

- Moreover, in the case of the regular (and, very often, also professional) offender of theft crimes, we would find ourselves—according to the legislator—before an individual who is difficult to motivate because of the penal norm. For, as in the previous case, exotic socialisation (in this case, one can imagine, because of their marginal social origin, or even foreign—poor foreigner) would hinder, even make it very often impossible, the effectiveness of normative motivation. Thus, the only solution rationally available to the legislator would consist in devising normative tools that would allow the identification of this category of dangerous individuals and proceed to neutralise them insofar as possible (based on what is compatible with the constitutional and moral limits that exist in the legal system to the increase of penalties).
- Things change, however, when it comes to justifying the repressive intervention in the face of offenders of road safety regulations. In this case, the legislator presupposes that such offenders are fundamentally rational individuals and that, for that reason, it is necessary to try to motivate them, and to achieve it, by means of the intimidation inherent to the penal commination; or, even, to convince them to change their system of values and to respect, convinced, the car traffic safety regulations. The road offender would therefore be a citizen with a "normal" socialisation. And, because of that, criminal commination could indeed operate with them in the way that is considered "normal": motivating, intimidating, convincing...
- Finally, in the case of violence against women at the hands of their partners or former partners, the emphasis is not on the characteristics of the perpetrators, but of the victims. Thus, the increase in punitive intervention would not be justified, from an instrumental point of view, mainly by its preventive effectiveness; nor even by the retributive effect. The main aim would therefore be to reduce the fear and insecurity of the social group (women) who are potential victims of these offences. Reaffirming the State's commitment to its duty to protect them.

## 6 Critique: Legislative Stereotypes, Punitive Ideology and Empirical Reality

Thus, it should be noted that in reality, according to the discourses of the legislators themselves, the reason for expanding punitive intervention in these four areas in two cases (theft and road safety) has to do mainly with preventive needs perceived as real, while in the other two it is based rather on the desire to convey a message to the rest of society (in the case of terrorism), or to a relevant part of it (women, in the case of "*gender-based violence*"). In these other two cases, therefore, the assumption is that what is important is the symbolic effect of the reform, not so much its real effect (on individuals and groups subject to police investigation, prosecution, conviction, enforcement of sentences), which would rather appear to have been conceived as a "collateral damage" of policies with a primarily symbolic purpose.

Moreover, even in the two cases in which it is claimed to be dealing with real criminal problems, in need of a more forceful repressive intervention, only in one of them (road safety) is it assumed that the criminal commination is capable of modifying the behaviour of potential offenders, by rationally motivating them to respect the legal rules of conduct. In the other case, on the other hand (theft), the explicit objective of the legislator seems rather to be the pure neutralisation of the danger of a group of individuals who are not essentially conceived as rational (endowed with a human rationality common to ours) and as fellow citizens, but as mere sources of dangers, with whom seeking to establish any rational communication is absurd. In other words, there is a commitment to penal regulation aimed at (in Günther Jakobs' terminology) "*enemies*", not "*citizens*".[31]

Finally, it is worth drawing attention to the fact that each and every one of the conceptual starting points assumed by the legislator, when constructing their supporting discourses, are more the fruit of stereotypes and prejudices than of demonstrable empirical knowledge.[32] In Semantics, the stereotypes of a predicate are those features that are considered typical of the entities to which the predicate can be applied.[33] The existence of stereotypes is an unavoidable characteristic of natural languages and the conceptual frameworks on which their expressions are based, since it is facilitated by the principle of linguistic economy. However, the critical use of language (which must be demanded when it is a question, as is the case, of justifying high-cost state actions, both in human and economic terms) demands that the stereotypes on which public policy decisions are based that affect - as usually happens with public policies—entire categories of people be subjected to scientific criticism, in order to separate what is based on them from what is due more to prejudice or ideologisation.[34]

[31]Jakobs (2006), pp. 34–44.

[32]Of course, the question that immediately arises is what is the origin of these stereotypes and prejudices. For, even if their assumption by legislators is particularly worrying, it seems obvious that the primary cause of their appearance is not due to them, but that legislators are limited to gathering (uncritically, yes) ideas that exist in the culture that surrounds them. Although, obviously, giving a well-founded answer to the question would require an independent investigation, I would like to point out two ideas in this regard which—although they require empirical verification—could shed some light on the matter. The first one is that the stereotypes referred to about crime arise in the institutional environment of legislators, in those organisations and institutions that surround them: their parties, the ministries and public institutions (police, most notably), the pressure groups with which they interact, the media that listen to them and influence them, the think-tanks with greater political influence... In other words, they are stereotypes shared by (at least a good part) of a certain political elite (see Mumby and Clair (2000), pp. 263 ff., on the deformations provoked in discourses by the existence of organisations that seize them); but not necessarily—at least not to the same extent—by the rest of society. The second idea has to do with the way in which these stereotypes are received, as "established know-how" and, consequently, unquestionable. In other words: the way in which stereotypes and prejudices enter the legislative discourse has much to do with the limitations of political participation procedures, especially in criminal matters (I have referred to this question in Paredes Castañón (2016), pp. 170–178).

[33]Hurford and Heasley (1997), pp. 108–109.

[34]Zunda (1999), pp. 313 ff.

Indeed, as I have studied elsewhere in greater detail, the social construction of the concepts of risk on which the justifications for prohibitions and criminal sanctions are intended to be based is by no means an innocent process, but rather, like any social cognition process, is subject to abundant biases, which must be detected and combated: ethnocentric biases (assigning characteristics based on maintaining the coherence of one's own discourse), ideologising biases (assigning characteristics that hide part of reality) and representativeness biases (assigning characteristics without taking into consideration how others see it).[35]

In the specific case of the justification of criminal policies (and, in particular, punitive legislative actions), this warning seems to me to be particularly relevant: to assume, as the Spanish legislator does in the cases that have been studied (and almost always), that the vast majority of offenders or potential offenders to whom the prescriptive message inherent in the criminal commination is addressed lack the necessary level of rationality and, consequently, the ability to be motivated by Criminal Law, constitutes not only a huge mistake from the theoretical point of view (as empirical evidence shows just the opposite), but a clear demonstration of reactionary political-criminal orientation (shared, unfortunately, to the right and left), which must be denounced and combated.

Said combat must be conducted on two different levels. On a theoretical level, demanding that criminal legislation stops being the result of (class-related, racist, nationalist) prejudices and the expressive (and demagogic) obsessions of political parties and pressure groups, and start to be based on solid empirical studies (criminological, sociological, etc.) on criminal danger, the possibilities of motivation and prevention, the effects of penalties, etc.

However, it must also be substantiated on a moral and political level: denouncing the apathy of some legislators who publicly acknowledge in their discourses (even if they do not dare to say it openly) that most of the offenders targeted by criminal repression "*are not like us*" (the good citizens, it is understood), so that with them only the harshest coercion can be used (taking advantage, incidentally, of the effort to also send reassuring messages to the "decent citizens"). This is not only false, but is the starting point that allows the justification, with good conscience (in legislators and the public), of all the abuses and nonsense of the punitive approach.

In my opinion, therefore, although it is true that arguments of instrumental rationality can sometimes lead to abuse, there is an ongoing previous battle, which is to ensure that criminal legislators take the problems of instrumental rationality of legislation seriously, so that they rely on a theory of the rationality of criminal law worthy of the name, and not on the usual catalogue of unfounded prejudices and empty platitudes. Because discussing—seriously, I mean—the effects of criminal prohibitions and penalties, the real characteristics of offenders and the possibility of influencing them effectively, would already (despite the risks) be a very significant advance on the regrettable state of irrationality in the current legislative discussion.

---

[35]Paredes Castañón (2003), pp. 18–24.

# References

Austin JL (1996) Cómo hacer cosas con palabras. Paidós, Barcelona
Carver CS, Scheier MF (1998) On the self-regulation of behavior. Cambridge University Press, Cambridge
Casalmiglia H, Tusón A (2012) Las cosas del decir. Manual de análisis del discurso. Ariel, Barcelona
Connolly WE (1993) The terms of political discourse. Princeton University Press, Princeton
Croft W, Alan CD (2008) Lingüística cognitiva. Akal, Madrid
Cuesta U (2000) Psicología social de la comunicación. Cátedra, Madrid
Downes D, Rock P (2011) Sociología de la desviación. Gedisa, Barcelona
Evans V, Grenn M (2006) Cognitive Linguistics. An Introduction. Edimburgh University Press, Edimburgh
Fairclough N, Wodak R (2000) Análisis crítico del discurso. In: Van Dijk TA (ed) El discurso como interacción social. Gedisa, Barcelona, pp 367–404
Hamawand Z (2016) Semantics. Equinox, Sheffield
Hurford JR, Heasley B (1997) Curso de Semántica. Visor, Madrid
Jakobs G (2006) Derecho penal del ciudadano y Derecho penal del enemigo. In: Jakobs G, Canció Meliá M (eds) Derecho penal del enemigo. Thompson Civitas, Madrid, pp 21–56
Kearns K (2011) Semantics. Palgrave McMillan, Houndmills
Kolodny N, Brunero J (2013) Instrumental rationality. Stanford Encyclopedia of Philosophy. https://plato.stanford.edu/entries/rationality-instrumental/. Accessed 26 Apr 2018
Mumby DK, Clair RP (2000) El discurso en las organizaciones. In: Van Dijk TA (ed) El discurso como interacción social. Gedisa, Barcelona, pp 263–296
Nagin DS (2013) Deterrence in the twenty-first century. Crime Justice 42:199–263
Paredes Castañón JM (2003) El riesgo como construcción conceptual: sobre el uso y el abuso de las ciencias sociales en el discurso político-criminal del Derecho Penal del riesgo. Revista Catalana de Seguretat Pública 13:11–29
Paredes Castañón JM (2013) La justificación de las leyes penales. Tirant lo Blanch, Valencia
Paredes Castañón JM (2016) Punitivismo y democracia: las "necesidades sociales" y la "voluntad popular" como argumentos político-criminales. Libertas, Madrid 4:153–202
Quong J (2017) Public reason. Stanford Encyclopedia of Philosophy. https://plato.stanford.edu/entries/public-reason/. Accessed 26 Apr 2018
Saussure F (2006) Curso de lingüística general. Akal, Madrid
Searle JR (1991) Una taxonomía de los actos ilocucionarios. In: Valdés Villanueva LM (ed) The Search for Meaning. Lecturas de filosofía del lenguaje. Tecnos, Madrid, pp 449–476
Searle JR (1994) Actos de habla. Cátedra, Madrid
Waldron J (2005) Derecho y desacuerdos. Marcial Pons, Madrid
Zunda Z (1999) Social Cognition. MIT Press, Cambridge

# Part III
# The Post-Legislative Stage: Implementation and Result Analysis

# The Victim As a Client of the Penal System

**Claudio González**

**Abstract** This paper explores one of the most palpable managerial manifestations of contemporary criminal policy, we refer to the process of introducing the client-user paradigm in the penal system. To do this, we review the process of how the victim acquired prominence, reaching the point of being treated as the client of a service provider company (service and product criminal justice). We also observe the complex debate about what should be understood by "client" in public administration, and how that discussion impacts on criminal policy. To concretize that, we will focus on the Chilean reality, exposing our analysis on the called Models of Attention to Users of the criminal justice system, especially those implemented by the Public Ministry of Chile. Based on this observation, we conclude that this managerial manifestation corresponds to an ongoing process, which has a positive side related to improving access to "the justice service". However, on the other hand, there could also be unwanted political and criminal consequences, such as the risk that many customer service policies become only a "symbolic or substitute" offer to resolve the criminal conflict. We conclude that the origin of this danger is that some of these measures are inspired to improve the image of the institutions of justice among the citizens, and not aimed at profound changes in the criminal justice system.

**Keywords** Criminal-policy · Client-user · Victims · Management · Managerialism

Phd, in Law and Social Science University of Málaga, with specializations in Criminal Law and Criminal Policy. This article corresponds to a project financed by the National Research and Development Agency of Chile (ANID). The name of the project is: "Analysis of the Concept and Use of the Efficiency in the Chilean Penal System: the Quantitative-Managerial Factor" Fondecyt/N° 3180458.

C. González (✉)
Institute for Public Affairs, Center for Studies in Citizen Security, University of Chile, Santiago of Chile, Chile

 
J. Becerra (ed.), *Criminal Law-Making*, Legisprudence Library 7,
https://doi.org/10.1007/978-3-030-71348-5_9

# 1 Introduction

Historically, criminal law, criminal policy and criminology have focused on the undisputed protagonist of the criminal conflict, the offender. Stablishing various procedural and criminal guarantees around the accused has been the axis of almost all liberal criminal law. However, in the last decades this state of affairs has mutated, thus, both the criminal sciences and the criminal legislation itself, have turned their gaze towards other actors in the criminal scene. The literature explains this change due to the increasing prominence of the victim in the criminal process. The disciplinary earthquake has been such that it has given rise to new criminological aspects, such as victimology (Bustos-Ramírez and Larrauri-Piojan 1993; Tamarit-Sumalla 2006; Cerezo-Domínguez 2010) and, to a lesser extent, victim-dogmatics (Cancio-Meliá 2001).

The truth is that the "rediscovery of the victim" is an uncomfortable and controversial issue for criminal policy. Undoubtedly, there are serious reasons to restrict the victim's participation in the formulation of criminal legislation (Shapiro 1997), especially because of its dangerous connection with the so-called "punitive populism" phenomenon (Díez-Ripollés 2004; Bottoms 1995; Garland 2001). However, despite the obvious problems generated by a hyper-valued victim in the configuration of criminal policy, the pro-victim discourse has ended up penetrating deeply into the current criminal system (Díez-Ripollés 2007).

In any event, beyond the privileged role of the victim in criminal policy, there is a set of areas where its consideration seems sensible. A first context corresponds to everything related to criminal mediation and restorative justice, notwithstanding criticism of its limited range of applicability to address the hard core of criminal law, its validity is incontestable (Highton et al. 1998). Another field, where the relevance of the victim also seems of importance, has to do with the protection and defense of their rights in criminal proceedings, of this type are the rights to be heard or even to take legal action if necessary, among others (Maier 1991).[1]

A third possible context, no longer comes from the purely criminal field but arises from certain organizational and managerial needs of the criminal system. This occurs

[1]Victim status is normatively collected by the Chilean Criminal Procedure Code, the most relevant norms are art. 6th, which establishes protection for the victim, art. 12 that recognizes its quality as intervening in the criminal process. In addition, articles 108 and 109, referring to the procedural subjects, establish the essential rights of the victim (defined as the one offended by the crime), among others: :*"a) Request protection measures against probable harassment, threats or attacks in against you or your family; b) File a complaint; c) Exercise against the accused actions aimed at prosecuting civil responsibilities arising from the punishable act; d) Be heard, if requested, by the prosecutor before the latter requests or resolves the suspension of the procedure or its early termination; e) Be heard, if requested, by the court before ruling on the temporary or final dismissal or other resolution that terminates the case; and f) Challenge the temporary or final dismissal or the acquittal, even if it had not intervened in the case process...").* (Writer's traslation and interpretation, from spanish original) National Congress Library: https://www.leychile.cl/Navegar?idNorma=176595&idParte=0.

when the victim is conceptualized and treated as a mere client of the criminal system, with all the implications that this may produce. In other words, once the victim is installed in the criminal field, the victim has begun to colonize another point of change in modern criminal models, namely, the organizational dimension of the system.

This last point is related to one of the most relevant changes in contemporary criminal policy, which is the intense and massive incorporation of new management tools from the New Public Management, also known as managerialism. This transformation is not only having effects of an administrative nature but also has brought about changes in the configuration of the purposes of the criminal system.

Thus, one of the iconic transformations of the management model are the proposals about the customer concept that the so-called modern public management has developed. This client-user paradigm has been strongly driven by one of the most current management trends, the so-called Public Management for Results (PMR). This current synthetically proclaims that the ultimate goal of the company (institution or organization) is its results, in this way, it is possible to align the business model, the final product and the performance of the organization, which for this trend is none other than "Customer satisfaction".[2]

Without a doubt, the transfer of managerial thinking that nests the client-user paradigm to the criminal system is not an easy task. First of all, because there is still a lot of debate within the public sector itself about the relevance of this organizational model, and second, because in our disciplinary context relevant questions arise such as: What do we understand as a client within the criminal system? Is it the same customer as user or as beneficiary? How is a client concept compatible with the classical structure of liberal criminal law? How do the concept of criminal efficiency with the client-user paradigm complement? Among others.

## 2 New Organizational Tools in Criminal Systems

As of today, there is profuse literature and international studies that account for the transformational phenomenon of the criminal system, this mutation would be taking place through organizational changes by introducing a broad spectrum of new management tools in the criminal system (Garland 2001; Simon 2012; Harcourt 2013; Harcourt 2007; Brandariz 2014; Vigour 2006). This literature, either of critical or descriptive approach to the phenomenon, whether of Anglo-Saxon origin (where it was initially developed), from continental Europe or from other contexts such as Latin America, agrees that this is a complex and current phenomenon, which is

[2]An example of how this management model based on the results and the preeminence of the client over any other consideration is found in the idea of Osborne and Plastrik (1998, p. 226), they argue that the "user approach" can help reduce the bureaucracy, they indicate, "when public bodies become accountable to their clients, their behavior changes. It is an effective tool for change. " (Cornejo 2012, p. 3).

penetrating beyond the mere organizational dimension of the criminal system, materializing in the long run in political and criminal consequences of the first order (González 2018).[3]

One of the most suggestive theoretical approaches of contemporary criminology that addresses the organizational issue has been, without a doubt, the so-called actuarial paradigm. Historically, the works of Feeley and Simon were pioneers in delimiting this theme, especially in *The new penology* (1992) and in *Actuarial justice: The emerging of a new criminal law* (Simon and Feeley 1994). Thus they opened the way to what has been called *the new penology*, a critical tendency that would be characterized by describing a scenario where: (a). The collective or category of subjects is prioritized over the individuals over whom criminal power is exercised. (b). Individuals are understood as subjects that need to be managed, and (c). The rules of evaluation and decision are adapted to the technocratic forms of knowledge, focused on the idea of probability and risk.[4] However, it would be Harcourt (2007, p. 1) who defined punitive actuarialism as a tendency characterized by the use of statistical methods, instead of clinical ones, based on large databases, with the objective of determining the different levels of criminal action from one or more group features, for the purpose (1) of predicting (determining) past, present or future criminal conduct, and (2) of administering a criminal political solution.

However, we believe that the explanation via actuarial paradigm does not cover all the organizational-criminal phenomena, therefore, we believe that the perspective of the managerial analysis of the criminal system can offer better scientific performance. Perhaps the greatest flaw of actuarialism is that it focuses, which is certainly reasonable, almost exclusively in the control of the dangerous subject for the criminal system. But we set the new criminal political object in the emergence of the client-user paradigm, which is based on the idea that victims (and probably other users) have become one of the axes on which a large part of contemporary criminal policy.

Nevertheless, it is clear that the extreme implementation of the "service delivery model", the executing arm of the client-user paradigm, can cause the empowerment

---

[3]In the Spanish language context, analyzes in this line are still scarce. In Latin America, some reasons could be the late entry into the accusatory model and the low preponderance of organizational techniques in the justice system. The latter is the effect of the lack of a critical authors and regional literature in the field of administration and complex political processes covered by the national security model.

[4]The actuarial denomination derives from the way in which insurance companies act when they proceed to classify their insured in different groups according to the probability of risk assigned to them. The category development process continues until the moment that the costs of developing a new category outweigh the benefits expected from it. Typically, the categorization will not descend to the individual level (Ortiz de Urbina 2003, p. 49). If the empirical and theoretical development of actuarialism has an Anglo-Saxon wedge, in the opinion of some, a similar phenomenon would have occurred in the field of European continental criminal tradition through the German doctrine of criminal law oriented to efficacy / efficiency (oriented to the consequences), especially through the work of the Frankfurt school (Ortiz de Urbina 2003, p. 51). (Writer's traslation and interpretation, from spanish original).

of certain users and this in turn create a chain effect in order to increase punitive demands. That is, by a more remote way (to accommodate the criminal system to what the client wants: "the client is always right"), the same conclusions of actuarialism can be reached, that is, intense punitivism and massive criminal management of dangerous subjects.

Therefore, what is really "problematic" of this new phenomenon are not the organizational transformations in themselves, but, as indicated by the critical currents, that these are organizational reforms carried out by specifically managerial public policies. Understanding by these, those that essentially look at the efficiency and results of the criminal system, and that will not necessarily be positive for the organization in terms of quality of the justice system or in better safeguards of citizens' rights. A very lucid reference to this point is found in Brandariz (2014), p. 120:

> In sum, the managerial rationality of the NPM, imported from the operating modes of private entities of a business nature, has been introduced in recent decades in a field of public policies that at first seemed distant from that operational logic, such as the criminal and prison system. At this point the managerial logic has managed to overcome certain obstacles, derived from the particular sovereign and legal-constitutional position of the courts, the centrality of the fight against crime in the field of state policies, or the traditional refractoriness of public activity to cost control.[5] (writer's traslation and interpretation, from spanish original)

Some political-criminal consequences of this transformation are related to criminalization processes, with the speed that the incorporation of new management tools can contribute to criminal prosecution models or even with the way and priorities in which the criminal legislative agenda can be developed. However, not all consequences can be categorized as negative, in fact, there are a number of management elements that we could hardly refuse to be inserted into the criminal system. For example, the necessary introduction of organizational tools to handle and control the management of criminal institutions, the use of computer science in order to optimize the resources of the State, or to adapt the access to criminal justice via the improvement of its management, among others. In this last point, is probably incorporated the improvement of the models of attention to "clients" and users, and their satisfaction.

Regarding the Latin American context, organizational transformations to the criminal system have gone hand in hand with the criminal justice reforms of the last 30 years. What began as code changes and the demolition of the old criminal inquisitive model has resulted in modifications to the system's own operability

[5]Due to its extension, in this article we cannot refer in detail to this Organizational-Criminal Dilemma, that is, how to introduce technology and management without affecting criminal guarantees, and at the same time, how to incorporate them without becoming criminogenic catalysts. The same applies to the incorporation of the customer service model, how to add, for example, concepts such as customization or marketing without transforming the criminal system into a simple provider of "managerial" services without content. We will deal with these matters in successive work.

(Maier et al. 2000; Binder 2000; Duce 2009; Riego and Duce 2007; Vargas and Dezhazo 2005). Likewise, these changes initiated in the context of criminal justice quickly permeated the discipline, being visible today in other contexts, such as civil, labor, etc. (Valdivia 2006).

In some countries the organizational transformations began in the specific management of their Courts, Appeals or Supreme,[6] but quickly extended to the offices and organization of the lower instance courts, such as guarantee, flagrancy or oral courts (Vargas 2014). As for the section of the criminal system where these changes were made, they initially had their first reception in the criminal justice system, but then they have become visible in other contexts, namely, the field of police organization, the scope of the organization of crime prevention activities, the prison system (outsourcing of services). In short, there is practically no area of the criminal system, which to a greater or lesser extent, has not been touched by this wave of organizational transformations.

This diversity of areas in the process of transformation is congruent with what international literature, especially Anglo-Saxon, mentions as aspects of the criminal system that have also changed in their own contexts, some of them are: the increase in public/private collaboration in matters of citizen security and the fight against crime; implementation of outsourcing models towards private security, and outsourcing of criminal defense and the prison field; the use of strategic plans in justice organizations; the tendency to standardize processes in the various agencies of the criminal system, among others.

If it were possible to summarize these changes in two great contexts, these would be: (a). The incorporation of novel management tools into the criminal justice system, which has resulted in new management models and, (b). The entry into the system of new professionals trained in the world of economics, engineering or administrative sciences, who have generally brought with them an important experience in the field of private management.

The client-user paradigm somehow emerges from both aspects, but in more detail we could connect it with six areas or indicators of the managerial model in the criminal system:

1. The orientation of the system towards service delivery models with the objective of increasing productivity.
2. In relation to the previous point, the tendency of certain agencies of the system to incorporate the customer-user service model from private services.

[6]For example, Costa Rica, after the implementation of the Organic Law of the Judiciary Power, with the reforms of the Law of Judicial Reorganization (N°: 7728 of December 15, 1997) introduced a series of organizational reforms. The High Court was the first to experience the benefits of a better organization of the firm. The Constitutional Chamber served as a "guinea pig" to test case follow-up systems to implement support mechanisms to increase the production of judicial decisions (Rivera-Cira 2001).

3. The massive incorporation, to improve efficiency, of the use of performance and management indicators and, correspondingly, of the use of management control models.
4. The extended use of audits and external evaluations of the criminal justice system agencies.
5. The incorporation, especially at the police level, of large statistical bases and tools to measure the quality of service, such as ISO standards or similar.
6. The integration to the different criminal justice organizations of professionals trained in the areas of economics, engineering, administrative sciences.

Each of these six elements has contributed in one way or another to allow the subject to whom the criminal system is dedicated to have been reconfigured. It is no longer a criminal system that pivots on the idea of protection of the accused citizen against the power of the State, but it is a system with multiple missions, including that of satisfying various users of the justice system with different interests and most of the times contradictory interests.

## 3 The Emergence of the Client-User Paradigm in Criminal Policy

As we have said before, the "acclimatization" of management concepts from the private sector to the context of the public sector is quite controversial, a much more controversial situation in the context of criminal law due to the nature of the "service" provided, or rather, the social values at stake. In the case of the topic of the user in international literature there is no agreement, so it is possible to observe the use of concepts such as "customer", "consumer", "buyer", "user", "citizen" and some Anglo-Saxon terminologies such as "stakeholder" and "taxpayer" (Cornejo 2006; Alford 2002).[7] The truth is that in general the reflections made in the public

[7]In principle, none of the RAE dictionary meanings of the word client is directly acceptable to characterize a service provided by an institution such as the Prosecutor's Office. The only near meaning would be "*person who buys in a store, or who regularly uses the services of a professional or company*". Etymologically it comes from the Latin cliens, clientis, who was the one under the protection or guardianship of another, whom he listened to, followed and obeyed. "*This sense has changed in modern Spanish: the merchant, the banker, the university professional do not see in the client someone who humbly obeys them, but a person who favors them because they pay for their merchandise or services. However, the ancient Latin denotation is still maintained today in political science, in whose framework are called clients the citizens who turn to politicians for favors, and clientelistic politics, which is based on that type of corrupt relationship, in which the politician lends favors - jobs, promotions, pensions - in exchange for votes.*" On the other hand, the word "user" has three possible meanings (1). That it uses something. (2). Said of a person: That has the right to use something foreign with a certain limitation. (3). Said of a person: That, by governmental concession or by another legitimate title, enjoys a use of water derived from public current. (DRAE 2018; http://etimologias.dechile.net/?cliente; http://www.elcastellano.org/palabra/cliente). (Writer's traslation and interpretation, from spanish original).

sector (Subirats 1994; Fiorentini 1990; Barzelay 1992, 1998) Chias (1995, pp. 32–34), tend to be quite critical of the use of the client concept, user or managed, preferring that of citizen.

For example, Barzelay (1992), argues not to recommend the use of the word client in the public sector, which in many situations "client" is more than pure rhetoric, since it is a concept that structures arguments to achieve objectives and lines of action. The author indicates that the use of the term client promotes a high level of confusion and pseudo-interpretations, since it invokes very diverse concepts such as user, beneficiary, fundraiser, co-producer and, citizen-owner.

If we assume the concept of customer-user as a consumer, it leads us to the idea of the interaction between the subject and the companies through the use of price markets. Even considering how debatable the consumer assimilation might seem, it could serve as an explanation for the introduction of the concept of "customer satisfaction". On this, Cornejo (2006), citing Kelly (2005) and Moore (1998) points out:

> "In the public sector, the ability to satisfy the user has important differences. Moore (1998) points out that the emphasis on public sector users presents the problem of identification. Obviously, the users of public bodies are citizens. While observing institutions oriented to the provision of services and benefits of citizens, it is possible to carry out the exercise of identification, segmentation and evaluation, however, public bodies also impose obligations on citizens based on the public interest and not the private interest of the obliged citizens. In this case, it is not possible to use the criteria of user satisfaction. This situation has been called the *dissatisfied consumer dilemma* in a market model for public administration. (Cornejo 2006, p. 7)." (writer's traslation and interpretation, from spanish original)

In summary, as indicated by Chias (1995, p. 33), citing Fiorentini (1990), the concept "citizen-client" is related to a citizen with a high discretionary and substitute power when choosing a service, in a context of free and competitive exchange. That is, a situation in which the citizen can choose between public and private options. But in the criminal sphere, said "high capacity for choice" is non-existent, simply because there is no market as in the private sphere, despite the economically focused efforts to give a market shape to something that clearly cannot have it.

The truth is that in practice the term is used with some lightness, and neither the uses of international organizations as the OECD, nor the language used in organizations to spread the principle of the quality of service to the user, finish clearing up the doubts. In any case, the nomenclature that is preferred over others is that of "client-user".

In sum; Is it acceptable to assume, in order to understand the word client or user, that the criminal system is a market and that the Prosecution conceptually is "a company"? Be that as it may, the word client is inevitably linked to the world and the vision of private business. Perhaps, the concept of client makes some sense in the field of the defense, as a legal benefit of being defended in a lawsuit, but not in the Office of the Prosecutor, which does not defend particular interests but social interests through public criminal action, as mandated by law and the Constitution.[8] On the other hand, the concept of "beneficiary" is only understandable under a very broad conceptualization of "provision" of services, which obviously does not help to clarify this issue either.

As indicated earlier, perhaps all of the above could be understood as another expression of the prominence that the victims, in this case their empowerment as "consumers" of a product, have assumed in contemporary criminal systems. The truth is that the literature on this subject usually refers to the victims as a pressure group for the configuration of the criminal policy (Garland 2001). But in this case the relevance of the victims would already be given or encouraged by the institutions of the criminal system, through the customer orientation paradigm, without the need for external factors. Thus, the idea of consumer rights through the rights of the victim has been innocently introduced into the criminal system through the use of ambiguous and managerially symbolic language. This incrustation has occurred especially in the organizational dimension of the criminal justice system, and then moved to the substantive and procedural legal-criminal sphere, digging into specific punitive sections. It is, therefore, a way by which victims and other users, under the guise of the client-user idea, have ended up colonizing, without intending to, important sectors of political-criminal discourse.

A possible political-criminal hypothesis is that, under this conceptual arrangement, it really underlies the claim to build a favorable platform to facilitate the entry of various elements of the provision of private services, such as customer loyalty, the privatization of accessory services, customer service models, the "suggestion" to always listen to the customer or consumer, customer portfolios, concepts of complaint and claim management, market segmentation, or outsourcing of organizational operations that aim towards customer satisfaction such as call centers, among others.[9]

The foregoing, in principle, is perfectly subsumable in what is theoretically called the client paradigm in public management. This paradigm, among other things, accounts for the rhetorical power of the concept of client, by introducing the idea of learning in the organization, based on market (customer) requirements. In this way, customer preferences could play a fundamental role in defining the public good, and consequently be relevant in setting organizational objectives (Richards

[8]Article 83.- *An autonomous, hierarchical body, with the name of Public Prosecutor's Office, will exclusively direct the investigation of the facts constituting the crime, those that determine the punishable participation and those that prove the innocence of the accused and, where appropriate, exercise public criminal action in the manner provided by law. Similarly, it will be up to it to adopt measures to protect victims and witnesses. In any case, it may exercise jurisdictional functions."* (Political Constitution of the Republic of Chile). (writer's traslation and interpretation, from spanish original).

[9]A remote case of this is, for example, Law 20,861 referring to the Criminal Analysis Unit of the Chilean Prosecutor's Office. This uses the concept of "criminal market," a clearly managerial reference, which we interpret, linked to diversity and the segmentation of crimes. Nor are references to "client portfolio" concerning users of the criminal system infrequent.

1994). In short, we would not be so distant from a kind of clientelism, personalization or customization of criminal justice, which would be inextricably linked to the idea of productivity and efficiency. Both objectives could be organizationally stimulated and achieved through the search for what the client requires, and how criminal policy should behave.

## 4 Materialization of the Client-User Paradigm in the Criminal System

As previously indicated, the materialization of the client-user paradigm in the criminal system is mostly noticeable in the criminal justice system, the reason for this is because in that place a large number of interfaces between criminal institutions and citizens (customers-users) are generated. It is precisely at the stage of secondary criminalization (implementation of the criminal law) where it is possible to measure citizen satisfaction with criminal policy. Here it is also more obvious to observe the debates regarding cost-benefit feasibility, management modeling, reorganization, statistics, process management, etc., issues, than in the primary criminalization phase (definition of crimes) or in the tertiary criminalization phase (execution of sentences and post-trial periods), although it exists, its presence for now seems less intense.

However, within the criminal justice system, the client-user paradigm is most noticeable in the Prosecutor-Police tandem and in the way in which access to justice is managed in the Judiciary sphere. For the purposes of this article, we will focus on describing how a political-criminal culture focused on the client-user has been installed in the Chilean Public Ministry. Which does not mean that this process is not happening at the level of the police or the Judiciary power, in fact, this last institution is one of those that develops the most avant-garde policies in this regard.[10]

Undoubtedly, one of the factors that has prompted criminal institutions to introduce this new paradigm is the claim to improve their image in front public opinion and, especially, in front of their users. This fact is manifested in their strategic plans, in their stated objectives or even in their public accounts. Thus, for example, the Public Prosecutor's Strategic Plan for the years 2016–2022, establishes as objective “a better relationship and attention with our users”. This was reaffirmed in the public account of the year 2018, textually the National Prosecutor indicated:

> Last year, we executed our second Annual Institutional Plan, based on the lines of work contained in our 2016-2022 Strategic Plan. In that context, today I can report that we reach one hundred percent compliance in the nine initiatives we prioritized for 2017. In this way:. . . 6.- We improve the Information System and the User Service System, with adjustments in the protocols of attention and the implementation of new features of the

---

[10]A current study that addresses the organizational areas of the Judiciary in Chile can be seen at: http://decs.pjud.cl/documentos/descargas/Estudio_Modelo_Orga__nico_Final.pdf.

"My Prosecutor Office" portal, among other advances. [11] (writer's traslation and interpretation, from spanish original)

But the general factor of this process has been the reforms of the State, or it can be said that this general factor is the general plan of modernization of the State of Chile. These reforms initiated since the beginning of democratic governments have tended to a systematic effort to improve the quality of service and user care in public administration. Thus, for example, Supreme Decree No. 680 of 1990, of the Ministry of Interior, approved instructions for the establishment of Information Offices for the public user in the State Administration. Later these offices would evolve into the so-called OIRS (Information, Claim and Suggestions Offices), over time, all of the above, was enhanced with the emphasis placed on the simplification and elimination of procedures taking advantage of the emergence of the technologies of the information and communication (TIC), becoming part of the digital government agenda. (Cornejo 2012).

Although today we can clearly see that the last two strategic plans of the Prosecutor's Office the former (2010–2015), and the one currently in force (2016–2022), highlight the importance of the user within the Public Ministry's plans, the truth is that this was already embedded in the early organizational stages of the Chilean criminal procedure reform and especially in this institution. Although the concept or word "customer" is used less and less regularly, the management aspect of the model persists.

One of the first fully managerial documents where the client-user paradigm is embodied in the Prosecutor's Office, does not emanate from the implementation of a specific model of customer service, but due to the "organizational experiment" of installing the Balanced Scorecard (BSC) in the Public Ministry of Chile.

The Balanced Scorecard or *Cuadro de Mando Equilibrado (CMI)*, as it is also known in Spanish, is inserted into what is called the management control area, and broadly consists of "in the use of a comprehensive performance measure to control and readjust the strategy. In addition to the financial perspective, it incorporates that of the client, that of internal operations and that of innovation and learning"[12] (Durán-Pich 2010, p. 436). To implement this model its creators (Kaplan and Norton 2004, 2013),[13] designed a series of indicators in four areas: (1). Financial perspective; (2). Customer perspective; (3). Perspective of internal operations and (4). Perspective of learning and innovation. In this way, by connecting and linking the indicators of one area with those of the others, it is possible to determine the results

---

[11]http://www.fiscaliadechile.cl/Fiscalia/Cuenta_Publica_Fiscal_Nacional_2018.pdf.

[12]Writer's traslation and interpretation, from spanish original.

[13]The origin of this line of scientific management was the product of an article by Robert S. Kaplan and David P. Norton published in the Harvard Business Review in 1992. In this work, it is related their experience related to a project at Nolan Institute on "measurement of results of the companies of the future". Subsequently, given the success of this publication and its successive expansion, they decided to launch a book called The Balance Scorecard (1996) and to this day it is almost a working manual for many types of organizations, both private and public.

of the organization and see how value is being created towards the future (Durán-Pich 2010, p. 441).

At present, the BSC is applied in multiple areas of the public sector,[14] and at international level there are several criminal justice institutions (prosecutor offices, courts or police) where it is increasingly common to observe it. In the case of the Chilean Public Prosecutor's Office, this institution launched, in the first decade of this century, a pilot program called: "Implementing directive guidelines for the Prosecutor's Office, with correlated indicators under the Balanced Scorecard methodology"[15] (Lillo and Godoy 2006). In this report, the authors, both officials of the Management, Evaluation and Control Unit of the National Prosecutor's Office at that time, discuss the vision, advantages and methodology necessary to apply the BSC in a Prosecutor's Office. According to this document, the orientation that this scorecard should have is towards the user and with results adjusted to the law. In this study, the organizational "positioning" that the institution intends towards direct users is evident, and the inconvenience of not proceeding in this way would be that these users would foreseeably not cooperate in clarifying the criminal acts.

In much more specific terms, this report establishes that the advantages for the Public Prosecutor's Office of applying the BSC would be: "1) .- It allows communicating to all the organization's officials the issues that are important for a regional prosecutor's office (mission, vision, objectives by area) 2) .- It helps to internalize a work culture based on superior objectives, therefore it generates teamwork. 3) .- Balances public management between immediate action and the preparation of the future. 4).- It allows a systemic and comprehensive analysis of the indicators defined by the institution."[16] (Lillo and Godoy 2006, p. 4).

Beyond the managerial rhetoric used in this document, the relevant aspect is that through this methodology the Chilean Prosecutor's Office, even today, with certain nuances, establishes its evaluation band and management indicators. The authors themselves conclude: "We can point out that this management control model is applicable to a public institution whose mission is criminal prosecution, since it is a powerful and modern methodological tool to design and control the objectives in each of the areas of the organization"(Lillo and Godoy 2006, p. 14). Evidently, the use of the BSC provided an explicitly managerial tool for the Prosecutor's Office. This is relevant for our work two reasons: first, it makes clear the customer-user orientation philosophy in this type of organizations,[17] and second, it is a document

[14]Another of the public sectors where this phenomenon is also observed is in the field of public health. A study on the applicability of the BSC in 57 hospitals of high complexity in Chile verified the improvement of their management, at least in costs, goal monitoring and process standardization. (Leyton et al. 2015).

[15]Its use has varied over time, but for example, the Public Prosecutor's Strategic Plan (2010–2015) assumes this language. In the Lillo and Godoy Report (2006) it is understood as a client; "Those direct users, that is, those who participate basically as intervenors in an illicit".

[16]Writer's traslation and interpretation, from spanish original.

[17]The Strategic Plan of the Public Prosecutor's Office –SPPP- (2010–2015, pp. 13 and 34), refers to the citizen user of a prosecution service in the following terms: "Customers, Users and / or

that comes from one of the most important institutions of the criminal system; The institution itself is also a faithful reflection of the administrative criminology set in motion.

As previously stated, over time this paradigm materialized in a model that tends especially towards the evaluation that clients-users-beneficiaries make of the criminal justice system. In order to implement this evaluation model, two organizational tools are currently used, both supervised by the Victim and Witness Attention Division (VWAD). The consecration of these tools is observed in the strategic objectives of the Public Prosecutor's Strategic Plan (PPSP) corresponding to the years 2009–2015 and in the 2016–2022 Strategic Plan. The specific objective indicates: "to improve the perception and satisfaction of the users, through the implementation and consolidation of a model oriented to a timely attention and that generates channels of reciprocal communication between the institution and its users, specifically, the victims and witnesses."

1. The first tool is the so-called OPS Model (Orientation, Protection and Support). "This general model of user care of the Chilean Prosecutor's Office allows the generation of specialized lines of intervention with specific procedures in all the regional prosecutors of the country, for those victims who, due to their condition, nature of the crime, or other situation, require a specialized care and protection, as is the case of victims of domestic violence, minors victims of sexual crimes and complex protection cases. (Public Account VWAD, 2014)". It is not up to us at this point to assess whether this model is effective and efficient, or if it only constitutes a political-criminal substitute. It is enough for now to mention it as another example of the user orientation of this organization.[18]
2. A second tool is the so-called IUSS model or Information and User Service System. As can be assumed, this model does not originate from the Prosecutor's Office or from public institutions in general. It comes from business quality management practices, which seek to increase competitiveness and meet customer expectations. Consequence of the fact that quality is a strategic factor of the company, ISO 9001/2000 quality standards have been developed, which have also been implemented in the prosecution offices and the police. They imply that

Beneficiaries are defined as the group of people, organizations or entities that receive or use the goods and / or services provided by an Institution. Likewise, each Service and / or Strategic Product defined by the agency must be associated with a Client, User and / or Beneficiary." On page 34 it is established that within this nomenclature would be included: complainant, victim, witness, police, auxiliary agencies and the community in general (they are called a priority segment), in the secondary segment we have: superior courts, oral trial courts and guarantee courts, complainant lawyer, public criminal defenders and private defenders and other public bodies.

[18]As with most instruments that seek user satisfaction, this was evaluated by an external company, which concludes that the implementation of this model is satisfactory. In one of its points, it states verbatim "The confidence that the interviewed users have in the Prosecutor's Office stands out, 78.4% of them expressed a favorable disposition to return to declare in the Prosecutor's Office, and 80.4% were favorable to recommend other people to attend to give a statement." (DAVT Cuenta Pública 2014, p. 3).

the product must be measured with different instruments, such as external audits, always seeking customer satisfaction (Pérez 2004). In concrete terms, the UISS of the Prosecutor's Office tries to cover three areas:

2.1. A telephone service area, through an outsourced call center model, which offers, among other services, the information of the cause and its progress. This service is also evaluated, and according to the last evaluation, "71.1% of the respondents managed to solve their requirement by calling the call center of the Prosecutor's Office..." (DAVT 2014).
2.2. A second area refers to face-to-face attention. The evaluation carried out in 2014 by an external audit company[19] once again described this program as very satisfactory. This study of the evaluation of the Public Ministry service (2014), specifically assessed the SIAU-face-to-face model, and among its main points we highlight: "The reasons given to satisfactorily evaluate the SIAU Model correspond to the good care delivered (57%), the speed of attention (23%), the clear information provided (22%), the good service provided (21%), the delivery of response or solution to the problem (13%) and the speed of the solution (12%), among other things".
2.3. The third area of the SIAU Model corresponds to the virtual attention space, which consists of a project that addresses the attention through the Prosecutor's Office website, in what is called "Mi fiscalía en línea" ("My online prosecutor's office"). The model began operating in 2013 and has served to meet the requests that, under the Transparency Law are made to the institution.

Finally, it is important to add that all the architecture that consolidates the User Service Models and the evaluation of user satisfaction in Chile, is indirectly driven by Law 19,553 of 1998. This regulation transformed the structure of the remuneration of Chilean public employees, because before this regulation the wages were fixed, independent of the performance of the officials. The reform includes an "incentive for modernization" composed of three elements: a base component, an increase in institutional performance and an instrument for collective performance. (Cornejo 2012, p. 6).

Institutional performance is granted in relation to the efficient and effective execution by the Services of the Management Improvement Programs. These programs establish specific objectives to be met each year, whose degree of compliance is measured by management indicators or other instruments. Thus, the goals and their indicators must be linked to the definitions of institutional mission, strategic objectives and relevant products of each service. This management improvement

[19]The external auditing company that performs this evaluation is one that deals with market research. We refer to GFK-ADIMARK. http://www.adimark.cl/es/clientes.asp This evaluation refers to one of the CGI (institutional management commitments) between the Prosecutor's Office and the Ministry of Finance within the respective institutional strengthening plan.

program is enforceable by signing a performance agreement between the Ministry of Finance and the respective service or institution.

In the case of the Public Prosecutor's Office, this is regulated by Law No. 20,240 of 2008 that "It perfects the system of incentives for the performance of prosecutors and public prosecutor officials." Without going into further details of the law, it states:[20]

> Article 4.- The institutional management bond will be granted in relation to the execution of an Institutional Management Commitment. The fulfillment of the Institutional Management Commitment of the previous year, will entitle the officials indicated in the first paragraph of Article 2, to a 10.7% bonus, provided that the institution has reached a degree of compliance equal to or greater than 90 % of annual management goals to which it has committed. If said degree of compliance is equal to or greater than 75% and less than 90%, the percentage this bonus will be 5.35%. Any compliance below 75% will not entitle officials to any bonus.[21] (writer's traslation and interpretation, from spanish original)

The way in which this is made operational is that the Prosecutor's Office annually agrees to certain commitments to comply with the Ministry of Finance, and through external audits the fulfillment of said goals is validated.[22] One of these goals corresponds to the field of "user satisfaction", which to date has been validated with 100% of the objectives met. Therefore, user satisfaction not only has criminal political consequences that we have described, but it is directly related to the remuneration component that public employees (civil servants) of the Prosecutor's Office finally receive. This incentive is called an "institutional bond".

## 5 Conclusions

1. As an object of study: The criminal political analysis to be made about the insertion of the client-user paradigm or any of the managerial transformations cannot be based on the idea of all or nothing. At least in the case of Latin American criminal justice, they are complex changes, because we are facing a delicate criminological context and therefore, the risk of such organizational changes becoming criminogenic factors is high.
2. Models and evaluations with content: The need for modern justice is a reality in Latin America, thus, the relationship of the subjects with the organization does not only have to do with issues of good management, but with the very foundations of a democratic state. This requires that evaluations, especially those carried out by external auditing companies, be carried out considering the greatest

[20] https://www.leychile.cl/Navegar?idNorma=268531.

[21] The performance agreement report is available at: http://www.fiscaliadechile.cl/Fiscalia/images/home/decreto_refrenda_informe_cumplimiento_CGI_2017.pdf.

[22] The auditing company that is currently evaluating the agreement is: http://grupopanal.cl.

possible number of dimensions, not only those related to "superficial bureaucratic upgrades" (Vicher 2009).

3. Management by Results (MbR): It is clear that the penetration of managerialism in this field is led by the MbR, but after that, it is possible that politically and criminally underlies a mercantile or marketing idea of the justice system (Garland 2001). For this reason, their transfer must be done in a studied and thoughtful way, the criminal system is complex and errors in their public policies have a cost and damage, most of them irreparable. Badly extrapolated concepts can end up building punitive realities, so you cannot use keywords uncritically when setting up the criminal system.
4. User satisfaction cannot be the ultimate goal of the criminal system: Criminal organizations should undoubtedly consider the concept of "user orientation", but not regard this as their criminal political ethos. Institutions, in a context as sensitive as the criminal system, cannot leave much of their mission delivered to what the legitimate subjective perceptions of citizens require. The truth is that these institutions should tend to behave in a technical way and that their organizational behavior is as close as possible to criminal rationality.

## References


Alford J (2002) Defining the client in the public sector: a social-exchange perspective. Public Admin Rev 62(3):337–346

Barzelay M (1992) Gestión pública estratégica: Concepto, análisis y experiencias. El caso IPIA. Instituto de estudios fiscales, Madrid

Barzelay M (1998) Atravesando la burocracia. Fondo de Cultura Económica, México

Binder AM (2000) Ideas y materiales para la reforma de la justicia penal. Buenos Aires, Editorial Ad-Hoc

Bottoms A (1995) The philosophy and politics of punishment and sentencing. In: Clarkson C, Morgan R (eds) The politics of sentencing reform. Clarendon, Oxford

Brandariz J (2014) El Gobierno de la penalidad. La complejidad de la política criminal contemporánea. Dykinson, España

Bustos-Ramírez J, Larrauri-Piojan E (1993) Victimología presente y futuro. Hacia un sistema de penas alternativas. Ed, PPU, Barcelona

Cancio-Meliá M (2001) Conducta de la víctima e imputación objetiva en Derecho penal. J. M. Bosh Editor, Barcelona

Cerezo-Domínguez AI (2010) El protagonismo de las víctimas en la elaboración de las leyes penales. Tirant lo Blach, Valencia (España)

Chias J (1995) Marketing Público. Por un gobierno y una administración al servicio del público. McGraw-Hill, España

Cornejo M (2006) Coordinación de iniciativas de atención al usuario en la administración pública chilena. Documento de trabajo N° 5. Instituto de Asuntos Públicos (INAP), Santiago

Cornejo M (2012) Calidad de servicio y atención al usuario: la experiencia del Servicio de Registro Civil e Identificación de Chile. XII Congreso internacional del CLAD sobre reforma del Estado y de la administración Pública, Cartagena, Colombia, 30 oct. – 2 nov, 2012

DAVT, Cuenta Pública (2014) Cuenta pública de división de atención a vićtimas y testigos de la fiscaliáde Chile. http://www.fiscalia-dechile.cl/Fiscalia/quienes/docu/division_atencion_victimas_testigos.pdf
Díez-Ripollés JL (2004) El nuevo modelo penal de la seguridad ciudadana. Revista Electrónica de Ciencia Penal y Criminología:06–03
Díez-Ripollés JL (2007) La política criminal en el encrucijada. BdeF, Buenos Aires
Duce M (2009) Reformas a la justicia criminal en América Latina: una visión panorámica y comparada acerca de su gestación, contenidos, resultados y desafíos. In: Dammert L (ed) Crimen e Inseguridad, Políticas, Temas y Problemas en las Américas. Flacso Chile-Catalonia, Santiago de Chile, pp 189–224
Durán-Pich A (2010) El canon del management. Los libros clave. Deusto editorial, Barcelona
Feeley M, Simon J (1992) The new penology. Notes on the emerging strategy of corrections and implications. Criminology 30(4):449–473
Fiorentini G (1990) Amministrazione Pubblica e cittadino: le relazioni di scambio. Editoriale Giuridiche Economiche, Roma
Garland D (2001) La cultura del control. Crimen y orden social en la sociedad contemporánea. Gedisa editorial, Barcelona
González C (2018) Gestión, gerencialismo y sistema penal. Editorial BdeF, Buenos Aires
Harcourt BE (2007) Against prediction. University of Chicago Press, Chicago
Harcourt BE (2013) Política criminal y gestión de riesgos. Editorial Ad-Hoc, Buenos Aires
Highton E, Alvarez G, Gregorio C (1998) Resolución alternative de disputas y sistema penal. La mediación penal y los programas víctima-victimario. Editorial Ad-Hoc, Buenos Aires
Kaplan R, Norton D (2004) Cómo medir el rendimiento en la empresa. En Harvard Bussiness Review. Deusto, España
Kaplan R, Norton D (2013) El cuadro de mando integral/balanced scorcared. Gestión, Barcelona. 2000
Kelly J (2005) The dilema of unsatisfied customer in a market model of public administration. Public Admin Rev 65(1):76–84
Leyton C, Huerta P, Paúl I (2015) Cuadro de mando en salud. Salud Pública Mex 57:234–241
Lillo S, Godoy M (2006) Implementar un cuadro de mando para una fiscalía con indicadores correlacionados bajo la metodología balanced scorecard. Documento recuperado desde: http://www.cejamericas.org/index.php/biblioteca/biblioteca-virtual/doc_view/3171-implementar-un-cuadro-de-mando-para-una-fiscal%C3%ADa-con-indicadores-correlacionados-bajo-la-metodolog%C3%ADa-balanced-scorecard.html
Maier JBJ (1991) Las víctimas y el sistema penal. Revista Jueces Para la Democracia:31–52
Maier JBJ, Ambos K, Woischnik J (2000) Las reformas procesales penales en América Latina. Editorial Ad-Hoc, Buenos Aires
Moore M (1998) Gestión Estratégica y Creación de Valor en el Sector Público. Ed, Paidos, Madrid
Osborne DY, Plastrik P (1998) "La Reducción de la Burocracia", Ed. PAIDOS, Madrid, España
Ortiz de Urbina I (2003) Derecho penal orientado a las consecuencias y ciencias sociales: El análisis económico de la política criminal. Tesis doctoral. Universidad Complutense de Madrid, Madrid
Pérez JA (2004) Gestión por procesos. Cómo utilizar ISO 9001:2000 para mejorar la gestiónde la organización, Agencia Española para la Calidad, ESIC Editorial, Madrid
Richards S (1994) El paradigma del cliente en las gestión pública. Gestión y Análisis de las Políticas Públicas GAPP 1:5–16
Riego CR, Duce M (2007) Manual de derecho procesal penal. Editorial jurídica, Santiago de Chile
Rivera-Cira T (2001) Nuevas tendencias y organización judicial en Costa Rica. In: Fuentes A (ed) Reforma Judicial en América Latina: Una tarea inconclusa. Institute of Latin American Studies, London. Recuperado de: http://www.oas.org/jurídico/spanish/publi2.html
Shapiro B (1997) Victims and vengeance. Why the victims's rights amendment is a bad idea. The Nation 264:11–19
Simon J (2012) Gobernar a través del delito. Gedisa, Barcelona

Simon J, Feeley M (1994) Actuarial justice: The emerging new criminal law. In: Nelken D (ed) The futures of criminology. Sage, London, pp 173–201

Subirats J (1994) Análisis de políticas públicas y eficacia de la administración. Ministerio para las Administraciones Públicas, Madrid

Tamarit-Sumalla JM (2006) La victimología: cuestiones conceptuales y metodológicas. In: Baca, Echeburúa, Tamarit (eds) Manual de Victimología. Tirant lo Blanch, Valencia, pp 17–50

Valdivia C (2006) La reforma judicial como política pública. ¿qué podemos aprender del proceso de reforma procesal penal? In: Silva J, García J, Leturia F (eds) Justicia civil y comercial, una reforma pendiente, bases para el diseño de la reforma procesal civil, 1st edn. Universidad de Talca, Chile, pp 183–218, www.puc.cl

Vargas J (2014) Herramientas para el diseño de despachos judiciales. In: Huachaca D (ed) La reforma procesal penal, cuestiones fundamentales. Ara Editores, Lima

Vargas J, Dezhazo P (2005) Evaluación de La Reforma Judicial en América Latina. CSIS, Center for Strategic and International Studies CEJA, Washington

Vicher D (2009) Reflexiones sobre las reformas neogerenciales ¿hacia una nueva reforma administrativa? Revista Chilena de Administración Pública (13):53–85

Vigour C (2006) Justice: l'introduction d'une rationalité managériale com- me euphémisation des enjeux politiques. In: Droit et société, N°, 6364. Editions Juridiques Associées, Paris

# Punitiveness and Criminal Law-Making Policy. Four Homogeneous Legislative Terms (1996–2011)

**José Luis Díez-Ripollés**

**Abstract** This paper intends to make a contribution to the understanding of contemporary Spanish criminal law-making policy. Between 1996 and 2011, Spain's criminal law experienced numerous reforms, despite the fact that in 1995 a brand-new penal code was enacted. Moreover, this frenetic legislation took place in a time where the two majoritarian political parties, the conservative and the socialist parties, successively ruled the country for a similar period of time. It is worthwhile to question whether the majority of those reforms correspond to some identifiable feature of current criminal justice policy. More precisely, given the widespread European tendency towards punitivism, it is useful to determine to what extent these reforms predominantly matched that trend. The results show a picture of mostly rigorous reforms, regardless of the ruling political party, which focused particularly on a few relevant and illustrative issues.

**Keywords** Criminal law-making policy · Spanish criminal law reforms · Criminal policy · Punitiveness

## 1 Introduction

A new Spanish criminal code came into force in 1995. It substituted an old criminal code that had been modified many times since its introduction in 1848. The new legislation was expected to take into account the new social, juridical and criminological reality concerning crime prevention and prosecution in modern Spain. It was very strongly influenced by comparative criminal law, especially that of Western continental European countries.

J. L. Díez-Ripollés (✉)
Facultad de Derecho, Universidad de Málaga, Málaga, Spain
e-mail: ripolles@uma.es



J. Becerra (ed.), *Criminal Law-Making*, Legisprudence Library 7,
https://doi.org/10.1007/978-3-030-71348-5_10

At the time, punitivism hadn't yet arrived to Western continental Europe. Instead, the expansion of intermediate sanctions and new provisions concerning crimes of the powerful were in fashion. Spain's 1995 penal code, often called the penal code of the new Spanish democracy, met these requirements very closely. A profound renewal of our penalty system took place, notwithstanding the fact that resources for a real implementation of the new penalty system were lacking and some traditional provisions with a high, possibly unnoticed, potential to restrain imprisonment growth were abolished.[1] Besides, brand new provisions to punish criminal behaviour in the socio-economic field came into force.

Nevertheless, just two and a half years after passing the law, a continuous and ever-increasing trend to reform the new penal code took root in Spanish policy makers. Suffice to say that from 1998 to 2010, 24 substantial reforms of the Spanish penal code have been enacted. To those, the brand-new law on juvenile justice, passed in 2000, and its three substantial reforms that came into force later on must be added. This amounts to 28 reforms in total, meaning that, on average, more than two substantial reforms a year, either of the penal code or juvenile justice law, have taken place throughout these 13 years.[2] Some of these reforms have been very ambitious. The reforms carried out by the laws of 15/2003 and 5/2010 contained, respectively, 186 and 169 modifications of a penal code built on 639 legal provisions.

It is relevant to say that throughout this time, the two predominant Spanish political parties have in turn ruled the country. Each of them, the conservative *Partido Popular* (Spanish People's Party or PP) and the socialist *Partido Socialista Obrero Español* (Spanish Socialist Workers' Party or PSOE) held both the government and the majority in parliament for two consecutive legislative terms, the PP ruling from 1996 to 2004 and the PSOE from 2004 to 2011. This sequence of two consecutive legislative terms and government held by the two majoritarian parties has never taken place again since then.[3]

---

[1]That was the case of a quasi-automatic 'good time' credit system, or periodical general pardons.

[2]We do not mention the numerous criminal procedural and penitentiary reforms, which have also taken place throughout these years, because they are not subject to analysis in this paper.

[3]Out of our study period is a following legislative term from 2011 to 2015, when the conservative *Partido Popular* held absolute parliament majority again and ruled the country. We skip also the next three legislative terms, between the end of 2015 and the end of 2019, with a very unstable political situation and four different governments, two of them provisional ones, when four general elections took place. Our intention of comparing two consecutive legislative terms of both majoritarian political parties explains this restriction.

It is worth to mention that Law 7/2012 passed another substantial reform of the penal code in 2012. Moreover, in 2015 three new substantial reforms of the penal code, one of them containing 260 legal modifications, were passed by Laws 1/2015, 2/2015 and 4/2015. In 2019, laws 1/2019 and 2/2019 passed two more limited reforms of the penal code.

## 2 Goals and Methodology

This paper intends to make a modest contribution to the understanding of contemporary Spanish criminal law-making policy. In this sense, it is worthwhile to wonder whether the majority of those reforms correspond to some identifiable feature of the current criminal justice policy. In particular, taking into account the widespread European tendency towards punitivism, it is useful to make estimations as to what extent the reforms of the new Spanish criminal code predominantly match that trend.

In order to achieve this goal, I will estimate the frequency that these legal reforms have created new or increased already existing criminal behaviour provisions, or, on the contrary, have restricted or repealed already existing criminal behaviour provisions. Likewise, I will check the frequency that these same legal reforms have established new or harsher deprivation of liberty penalties, or, on the contrary, have restricted or even substituted deprivation of liberty penalties, both in already existing and new criminal behaviour provisions.

Additionally, it is interesting to make two further estimations. Firstly, whether a remarkably different criminal policy drift on the aforementioned alternatives can be appreciated throughout this 16-year period in accordance with the ruling political party. Secondly, what kinds of criminal issues are repeatedly targeted by this number of legal reforms throughout this period.

Notwithstanding the limited contribution that the contrast between punitiveness and non-punitiveness gives to the understanding of a national criminal justice policy,[4] the confinement of this study to criminal law-making policy provides the opportunity for applying this contrast to a scarcely explored field of research. The consistent results reached in Spanish legislation is worth the effort.

Tables 1 and 2 include all legal reforms from 1996 to 2011, split into two consecutive time periods. The first table coincides with the rule of the conservative party (Table 1) and the second table with that of the socialist party (Table 2).

From left to right, the first column lists every substantial reform of either the Penal Code or the Law on Juvenile Justice throughout the period in chronological order.

The second column disaggregates every criminal law issue that each reform deals with, although very secondary legal modifications are put aside. Garnet red text highlights the issues which embrace modifications of the general provisions of the penal code; black text highlights the reforms on the specific provisions of the penal code; and blue text refers to issues concerning the juvenile justice law reforms.

There is an unavoidable subjective component in the disaggregation which has been carried out. Firstly, reformed provisions have been excluded which are, in the author's opinion, of no significance to this study, since they do not modify the number or extension of criminal behaviour provisions or deprivation of liberty penalties. Secondly, disaggregation, or aggregation, of criminal law issues do not

[4]See Díez-Ripollés (2013), pp. 62–78.

strictly follow a legal systematic pattern; otherwise it would have given rise to very disparate classes in extension and importance; consequently, legal systematic patterns have been supplemented by the author's considerations on the criminal-policy relevance of the corresponding issues. Nonetheless, it has been seriously intended not to depart from consensual criteria.[5]

The third and fourth columns proceed to a double assessment: In the third column, whether the reform implies a new or increased criminalisation of any social behaviour (plus sign), or a restriction, even abrogation, of a so far criminalised social behaviour (minus sign). In the fourth column, whether the reform entails new or harsher prison and arrest penalties for existing or just-introduced crimes (plus sign), or it means a restriction or substitution of the prison and arrest penalties at the corresponding crimes (minus sign). An *equal* sign means no significant change, and an *asterisk* sign means it is irrelevant.

**Table 1** Reforms 1996–2003

| Criminal Law Reforms 1996-2003. | Issue | Enlargement of Criminal Behaviour | New or Harsher Prison or Arrest Penalty. |
|---|---|---|---|
| **LO 2/1998 de 15 junio** | - Illegal rallies or demonstrations.<br>- Menacing demands in public of terrorist actions. | +<br>+ | +<br>+ |
| **LO 7/1998 de 5 octubre** | - Refusal either to military service or to community service. | - | - |
| **LO 11/1999 de 30 abril** | - Rape.<br>- Sexual abuse.<br>- Sexual harassment.<br>- Indecent behaviour and pornography before minors.<br>- Promotion of prostitution.<br>- Corruption, or use for obscene or pornographic purposes, of minors.<br>- Limitation for crimes against minors. | +<br>+<br>+<br>=<br>+<br>+<br>+ | =<br>+<br>+<br>+<br>=<br>+<br>* |
| **LO 14/1999 de 9 junio** | - Domestic violence. | + | + |
| **LO 2/2000 de 7 enero** | - Manufacturing or use of chemical weapons | + | + |
| **LO 3/2000 de 11 enero** | - Bribery in international economic transactions. | + | + |
| **LO 4/2000 de 11 enero** | - Illegal manpower trafficking.<br>- Illegal human trafficking of foreigners.<br>- Criminal association for human trafficking. | =<br>+<br>+ | +<br>+<br>+ |
| **LO 5/2000 de 12 enero.** | - A brand new law on juvenile justice. | = | - |
| **LO 7/2000 de 22 diciembre** | - Terrorist crimes.<br>- Aggressive behaviour towards public authorities.<br>- Crimes through means capable of wreaking havoc.<br>- Serious juvenile delinquency.<br>- Limitation for serious juvenile delinquency. | +<br>+<br>+<br>=<br>+ | +<br>=<br>+<br>+<br>* |
| **LO 8/2000 de 22 diciembre** | - No deportation of foreign human traffickers sentenced to prison. | = | + |
| **LO 3/2002 de 22 mayo** | - Repeal of criminal offences concerning refusal either to do military service or to do community service | - | - |
| **LO 9/2002 de 10 diciembre** | - Parental kidnapping of minors.<br>- Postponement of juvenile justice law enforcement for young adults. | +<br>= | +<br>+ |
| **LO 1/2003 de 10 marzo.** | - Disrespectful or menacing behaviour towards local authorities sheltered by terrorist organizations. | + | + |
| **LO 7/2003 de 30 junio.** | - Extension of maximum prison term up to 40 years.<br>- Restrictions on open prison regime and parole eligibility. | =<br>= | +<br>+ |

(continued)

[5]See a similar way of evaluating criminal law reforms in Lappi-Seppälä (2007), pp. 234, 246–247, 252, 256; Von Hofer and Tham (2013), pp. 46–49.

**Table 1** (continued)

| | | | |
|---|---|---|---|
| | - "Truth in sentencing" provisions on penitentiary regime. | = | + |
| **LO 11/2003 de 29 septiembre.** | - Enhanced punitive effects of aggravating circumstances and multi-recidivism. | = | + |
| | - Compulsory deportation of foreigners either sentenced to prison under 6 years, or having served ¾ of a prison sentence over 6 years. | = | - |
| | - Upgrading to felony of perpetration of certain repeated misdemeanours. | = | + |
| | - Domestic violence. | + | + |
| | - Non-coercive pimping and pandering | + | = |
| | - Illegal human trafficking of foreigners. | + | + |
| | - Criminal association for perpetrating misdemeanours. | + | = |
| **LO 15/2003 de 25 de noviembre.** | - 3 months instead of 6 months as minimum prison term. | = | + |
| | - Substitution for weekend arrest by short-term prison | = | + |
| | - Substitution for weekend arrest by home detention, for misdemeanours. | = | - |
| | - Limited expansion of community service. | = | - |
| | - Re-offender criminal behaviour –delito continuado- | = | + |
| | - Suspended prison sentence. | = | - |
| | - Suspended and substituted prison sentence for domestic violence crimes | = | + |
| | - Default imprisonment. | = | + |
| | - Victim's pardoning | + | * |
| | - Terms for limitation of crimes and penalties. | + | * |
| | - Increase of minimum economic amount, for property and socio-economic felonies and crimes. | = | - |
| | - Menace | = | - |
| | - Menacing demands in public of terrorist actions. | = | + |
| | - Rape and sexual abuse | + | = |
| | - Use of minors for obscene or pornographic purposes. | + | + |
| | - Possession of child pornography. | + | + |
| | - Joyriding. | + | = |
| | - Fraud. | + | - |
| | - Intellectual property. | + | + |
| | - Receiving and money laundering. | + | + |
| | - Crimes against the environment and natural resources. | - | - |
| | - Mistreatment of pets. | + | + |
| | - Drug trafficking | + | - |
| | - Road traffic crimes. | + | = |
| | - Money counterfeiting. | + | = |
| | - Breach. | + | + |
| | - Public disturbances. | + | + |
| | - Manufacturing, keeping and commerce of biological weapons | + | = |
| | - International crimes and related offences. | + | + |
| **LO 20/2003, de 23 diciembre.** | - Call for or promotion of illegal popular elections or polls. | + | + |
| | - Financing of illegal associations with public resources. | + | + |

Source: Díez-Ripollés (2013) Rigorismo y reforma penal. Cuatro legislaturas homogéneas (1996–2011). Boletín Criminológico 2-3(142-143)

The tables contain a lot of information that we are not able to fully analyse now, therefore I will confine myself to some relevant facts. It should be highlighted that my intention is to carry out a personal evaluation, based on a contents analysis of the different legal reforms, of trends in Spanish legislative criminal policy throughout four politically contrasting and recent legislative terms. No quantitative data presented herein intends to draw statistically significant conclusions. Moreover, the qualitative lines of argument expounded are susceptible to further insights and nuances. Nevertheless, I think the study provides a useful overview of recent Spanish criminal legislation.

## 3 Some Quantitative Clues

Let's first proceed to a quantitative approach.

1. A quick glance at column 3 of both tables shows that the vast majority of criminal law-making decisions intend to increase criminalisation: 42 times in Table 1 and 37 times in Table 2, that is to say, 79 times in total. On the contrary, only on very rare occasions does decriminalisation or the restriction of criminalisation take place: 3 times in Table 1 and 4 times in Table 2, amounting to 7 in total.

**Table 2** Reforms 2004–2011

| Criminal Law Reforms 2004-2011. | Issue | Enlargement of Criminal Behaviour | New or Harsher Prison or Arrest Penalty. |
|---|---|---|---|
| **LO 1/2004, de 28 diciembre** | - Suspended and substituted prison sentences in gender violence crimes. | = | + |
| | - Domestic and gender assault. | = | + |
| | - Gender mistreatment, threat or coercion. | = | + |
| | - Breach of domestic or gender sentences. | = | + |
| **LO 2/2005, de 22 junio.** | - Repeal of criminal offences concerning the call for or promotion of illegal popular elections or polls. | - | - |
| | - Repeal of crime concerning financing of illegal associations with public resources. | - | - |
| **LO 4/2005 de 10 octubre.** | - Unsafe manufacturing, keeping and commerce of explosives, or other substances or devices capable of wreaking havoc. | + | + |
| **LO 7/2006, de 21 noviembre.** | - Promotion of doping in sport. | + | + |
| **LO 8/2006, de 4 diciembre.** | - Expansion of delinquent behaviours punished with confinement for juveniles. | = | + |
| | - Extension of maximum confinement term for juveniles in most cases. | = | + |
| | - Hardening of confinement regime for juveniles. | = | + |
| | - Referral of sentenced juvenile delinquents to ordinary prison regime after reaching 18 years. | = | + |
| | - Repeal of juvenile justice law enforcement provisions for young adults. | = | + |
| **LO 13/2007, de 19 noviembre.** | - Illegal manpower trafficking. | + | = |
| | - Illegal human trafficking of foreigners. | + | = |
| **LO 15/2007, de 30 noviembre.** | - Road traffic crimes. | + | + |
| **LO 2/2010 de 3 marzo** | - Abortion | - | - |
| **LO 5/2010 de 22 junio.** | - Corporate criminal liability. | + | * |
| | - Increase of maximum term for home detention. | = | + |
| | - Reinstatement of weekend arrest for re-offenders' petty crimes. | = | + |
| | - Loosening of restrictions on open prison regimes. | = | - |
| | - Substituted prison sentence. | = | + |
| | - Compulsory deportation of convicted foreigners. | = | + - |
| | - Terms for limitation of crimes and penalties. | + | * |
| | - Illegal human organs trafficking or transplantation. | + | + |
| | - Housing and job mobbing. | + | + |
| | - Illegal human trafficking. | + | + |
| | - Rape and sexual abuse. | + | + |
| | - Child grooming. | + | + |
| | - Promotion of prostitution. | + | + |
| | - Use of minors for obscene or pornographic purposes. | + | + |
| | - Software privacy | + | + |
| | - Larceny, burglary, robbery. | + | = |
| | - Misappropriation of real estate. | = | + |
| | - Fraud. | + | = |
| | - Illegal suspension of payments. | + | = |

(continued)

**Table 2** (continued)

| | | | |
|---|---|---|---|
| | - Software damages. | + | + |
| | - Minor offences against intellectual property. | = | - |
| | - Investment and securities fraud. Insider trading. | + | + |
| | - Bribery in private economic transactions. | + | + |
| | - Match fixing. | + | + |
| | - Money laundering. | + | = |
| | - Tax crimes. | - | + |
| | - Urban planning crimes. | + | + |
| | - Crimes against the environment and natural resources. | + | + |
| | - Mistreatment of pets and tamed animals. | + | = |
| | - Illegal possession, manufacturing, manipulation or commerce of radioactive or ionizing substances. | + | + |
| | - Drug trafficking. | = | - + |
| | - Road traffic crimes | = | - |
| | - Counterfeiting of identity or banking cards, trafficking and use. | + | + |
| | - Illegal use of authentic official or commercial documents. | + | = |
| | - Bribery, influence peddling and other crimes in public administration. | + | + |
| | - Bribery in international economic transactions. | + | + |
| | - Concealment. | + | = |
| | - Manufacturing, keeping and commerce of land mines and cluster bombs. | + | = |
| | - Organised crime and criminal groups. | + | + |
| | - Terrorist crimes. | + | + |
| | - International crimes and related offences. | + | = |
| | - Piracy. | + | + |

Source: Díez-Ripollés (2013) Rigorismo y reforma penal. Cuatro legislaturas homogéneas (1996-2011). Boletín Criminológico 2-3(142-143)

Furthermore, 41 times must be added (23 in Table 1 and 18 in Table 2) when the criminal law-making decision has neither supposed an expansion nor a restriction of criminalisation.

In percentage terms, in 62.20% of all cases an expansion of criminalisation occurred, and only in 5.51% of cases did a decriminalisation or restriction of criminalisation take place. In the remaining 32.28% of cases, no change appeared in this field.

The same can be said for column 4, where decisions on restriction or substitution of deprivation of liberty penalties, although more frequent than the decisions for decriminalisation of column 3, are a clear minority (12 in Table 1 and 8 in Table 2) amounting to 20.[6] Still, the establishment of new or harsher prison or arrest penalties more than quadrupled the previous figure, 44 times in Table 1 and 41 times in Table 2, making a combined total of 85. In very few cases did legislators not take advantage of the criminal law-making decisions to introduce modifications on deprivation of liberty penalties (10 times in Table 1 and 11 times in Table 2) amounting to 21 in total, approximately the same number as those cases in which restriction or substitution of deprivation of liberty penalties took place.

Again, in percentage terms, legislative decisions which make possible new or harsher deprivation of liberty penalties constituted 67.5% of all legal modifications,

[6]On the two occasions where a sign + and a sign − coexists, I count each sign as a unit.

whereas only in 15.9% of cases were prison or arrest penalties substituted by other penalties or reduced in their scope. Furthermore, only in 16.6% of cases did the legal modification have no effect on those penalties.

All in all, legislative modifications introducing more punitive provisions clearly go beyond 60% of all criminal law-making decisions, while legislative modifications lessening the rigorousness of existing provisions are firmly in the minority, comprising between 5% and 16% of all cases. In other words, each time a decriminalisation or reduction of criminalisation is adopted, 11 legislative decisions on criminalisation are enacted; and each time one prison or arrest penalty is substituted or reduced, 4 prison or arrest penalties are newly created or enhanced.

2. Any change in power, from a conservative to a socialist party, has had very little, if any, significance.[7] The number of substantial legal modifications scarcely differs (68 under conservative rule, 59 under socialist rule), although the reform laws enacted by the conservative party are more than double those of the socialist party: 19 law reforms as opposed to 9. The amount of legal modifications enhancing the scope of criminal behaviour (42 under conservative rule with 37 under socialist rule) or increasing prison or arrest penalties (44 under conservative rule, 41 under socialist rule) is slightly higher in the initial conservative period than in the later socialist one. Nevertheless, criminal law-making decisions for curtailing the use of deprivation of liberty penalties are also more common during the conservative period (12 for conservatives and 8 for socialists) whereas a similar number of legislative decisions are made for the decriminalisation, or restriction of criminalisation of social behaviours, in both political periods (3 for conservatives and 4 for socialists).

In percentage terms, the similarities between the two political parties are evident: 62% of all legal modifications adopted by conservatives and 63% of those by socialists produced further criminalisation of behaviours. Similarly, the enhancement of the use of prison or arrest penalties took place in 67% of all legislative decisions made by conservatives and 68% by socialists. Despite the low figures and the opposite trends, similarities remain in relation to the decriminalisation of behaviours and the reduction in the use of deprivation of liberty penalties: 4.4% of all cases of decriminalisation of behaviours are to be ascribed to the conservatives versus 6.8% to the socialists. Furthermore, conservatives substituted or reduced deprivation of liberty penalties in 18.2% of cases whereas the socialists did so in 13.3% of cases.

[7] It must be remembered that the studied period comprises of four terms, the first two under conservative rule and the second two under socialist rule.

## 4 A Qualitative Approach

In the following section of the paper, we proceed to a qualitative analysis of the contents of the legal modifications that have been carried out throughout the period. For analytical purposes, the most relevant modifications regarding topic and frequency are included.

1. Firstly, the important reforms that have taken place in the General Section of the penal code are analysed. They have comprised, to a greater or lesser extent, the system of liability and the system of sanctions, together with the sentencing and penitentiary systems, with the outcome being a much more rigorous General Section than the original one.

In the field of criminal liability and sentencing, the most significant reforms are: the introduction of corporate criminal liability; the repeated extension of the limitation period for offenses and penalties; the greater levels of punishment as a result of the concurrence of aggravating circumstances; and the upgrade to felony of certain repeated misdemeanours.

Reforms have been particularly numerous in the penalty and corrections system: the reduction of the minimum prison term from 6 to 3 months; the extension of the maximum period of imprisonment up to 40 years; the introduction of 'truth in sentencing' provisions; the substitution of weekend arrest by short prison terms;[8] easier requirements for suspended prison sentences, notwithstanding the repeated tightening of the conditions of suspension for crimes of domestic and gender violence; the restrictions on eligibility for open prison regime and parole.[9]

2. If we consider now the Special Section of the penal code, its catalogue of crimes, felonies and misdemeanours, it can be noted that there have been significant changes in favour of more stringency. Interestingly, these changes have been focused on only a few kinds of criminal offenses.

Sexual offenses have been the subject of four legal reforms, three of those being extremely comprehensive. All of them have either increased criminal behaviour or increased prison sentences, or both. Rape, sexual abuse (especially of minors), the promotion of prostitution, and the use of minors for obscene or pornographic purposes have undergone three successive reforms, with each more punitive than the last.

Crimes of domestic and gender violence have also undergone four legal reforms, two of which were single-issue reforms of these crimes. All of them have led to either an extension of offenses or to a greater use of imprisonment, or both. The crimes of human trafficking, in all its different variants, have undergone five legal

[8]Although weekend arrest is substituted by home detention in the case of misdemeanours, later reforms increase the maximum term for home arrest and reinstate weekend arrest for re-offenders' petty crimes.

[9]A later reform limitedly loosens restrictions for open prison regime.

reforms with two of them being single-issue reforms. Again, all of these have involved an expansion of criminalisation, a greater use of imprisonment, or both.

There have been two major reforms of terrorist offenses, and three more reforms regarding the issue of incitement of terrorist actions. Without exception, they either increased criminal behaviour or harden prison penalties, or both. Furthermore, two additional reforms have increased offenses and toughened up the punishment of terrorism-related behaviours, such as damage by means capable of wreaking havoc or putting people at risk, or the illegal trade in explosives or other substances or devices capable of wreaking havoc.

Other groups of crimes have also undergone repeated consideration by a strict legislator:

Road traffic crimes have experienced three legal reforms; while the first and a second major reform involves a significant expansion of offenses and strengthening of prison penalties, the latter allows judicial discretion to reduce the prison sentence in less serious cases.

Corruption offenses have been extended to cover private and international transactions through three legal reforms. This has been accompanied by a legal reform that has increased the criminalisation of (and punished with new or harsher prison penalties) the crimes of bribery and other closely related crimes against public administrations.

Non-terrorist organised crime and criminal groups have obtained an autonomous criminal status through a significant reform. This was anticipated through several reforms, which either increased the criminalisation of illicit associations and any cooperative behaviour with them, or, more importantly, repeatedly hardened the prison penalty and the penitentiary regime of those convicted of organised crime.[10]

Another group of legal reforms has been primarily motivated by international obligations: In the first instance, this is the case for four reforms relating to a new or more rigorous prosecution of the illegal trade in chemical or biological weapons, in radioactive or ionising elements and materials, and in landmines and cluster bombs. International obligations have also played a role in two reforms of international crimes and related offenses.[11]

3. I believe that it is instructive that very few legal reforms have had as their paramount or guiding purpose the restriction or abrogation of criminalisation, or the elimination or reduction of prison sentences provided.

Throughout the period, there have only been two legal reforms whose purpose has been to repeal existing criminal offenses: The first refers to offenses of the refusal to complete military service (or an alternative service), which was preceded three and a half years ago by a reduction in the scope of such offenses and their penalties. The second refers to the crimes of calling for, authorisation of or promotion of illegal

[10]Not to mention the repeated expansion and harshening of money laundering crimes.

[11]Notwithstanding that some other reforms, although mainly driven by the domestic criminal policy debate, may also respond to international requirements.

elections or referendums, and of public funding of illegal associations, crimes which were both introduced by the conservative party under intense political scrutiny and whose repeal took place only a year and a half later under the auspices of a socialist parliamentary majority and government.

Apart from these two reforms, it should be noted that a new law notably restricted abortion as a criminal offense insofar as a more generous system of legitimate abortion was introduced. Beyond that, it is worth mentioning an ambivalent reform of drug-related crimes, where a mitigating circumstance for less serious cases was introduced.

## 5 Specific Considerations of Juvenile Criminal Law

A separate view of the legislative changes that have taken place in the field of juvenile criminal law leads us not only to very similar results to those of adult criminal law, but where the increase in punitiveness is actually more evident.

Certainly, it must be stressed that the new Spanish Organic Law *LO* 5/2000 that regulates the criminal responsibility of minors was a milestone in our criminal justice system. It established a modern, rehabilitation-oriented and moderate law for juvenile delinquency. However, subsequent substantive and procedural reforms, some of them passed before the entry into force of the *LO*. 5/2000, have significantly changed their character.

Although those reforms have already been calculated in the preceding section on quantitative references, it should be remembered that after its enactment, the *LO*. 5/2000 has since undergone three further substantive legal reforms. All of them have meant a harshening of the treatment of juvenile offenders, without containing a single legal modification intended to soften the current punitive provisions for minors.

Once again, these unidirectional legislative changes are distributed throughout the period analysed. The new law on juvenile justice was enacted during a legislature with a PP parliamentary majority. However, before giving way to a PSOE parliamentary majority, the PP parliamentary majority passed two substantive reforms that have helped to tighten the law since, with the first one even before the *vacatio legis* term of the brand new *LO*. 5/2000 had ended. The arrival of the PSOE to power did not change things. In 2006, the PSOE passed a third legal reform, which was not only a stand-alone reform but was also ambitious and very rigorous.

If we go more into the detail of the qualitative contents of these three legal reforms, we can see that the first one, *LO*. 7/2000, ensured that juveniles convicted of the crimes of homicide, murder, rape, terrorism or any other crime punished with 15 or more years of imprisonment under the adult criminal code could be confined to a closed facility for up to 8 years (10 in case of accumulation of sentences). In these cases, the terms of limitation were equated with those that apply to adults.

The third of the reforms, *LO*. 8/2006, increased the number of delinquent behaviours that could be punished with confinement to a closed facility, and it extended the maximum closed confinement terms in most cases. In addition, it enabled and even made it mandatory in certain cases to refer juveniles reaching the age of 18 years to adult prisons under the ordinary regime.

Finally, the reforms of 2003 and 2006 initially postponed the enforcement and then definitively repealed the legal provision making possible the application of juvenile justice law to young adults between 18 and 21 years old.

## 6 Conclusions

It has been confirmed that one of the features that best characterises the rampant criminal law-making policy of the studied 16 years is the increasingly marked tendency towards an expansion and hardening of the Spanish penal system. It is noteworthy that the ideological differences between right and left parties on this matter have blurred to the point where it has become difficult to perceive a distinct criminal policy between the PP and the PSOE over the years.

This rigorous legislative policy, although affecting the entire criminal justice system, has some stark issues. Primarily, there has been a major expansion of prison penalty in all its aspects, be it the reduction of minimum and the extension of maximum tariffs, the accumulation of penalties, the hardening of the penitentiary regime, or its application in new or already existing criminal behaviours. Contrary to some appearances, the remaining non-custodial penalties have lost relevance within the system.

Throughout these years, sexual offenses have been shown to be the preferred instrument to catalyse all the fears and concerns raised by a society that increasingly provides fewer concrete certainties. Despite the low rates of sexual crimes in Spain, the sex offender has become the contemporary 'witch' to be vilified at all costs, and whose punishment must enable society to exorcise itself from modern uneasiness and insecurity.

The strong presence of violent domestic and gender crimes in penal reform reflects an excessive and naive relevance that the community is giving to crime control initiatives in establishing social equality between genders. While this is a significant problem, the criminal justice system can only make a modest contribution to its resolution.

These years have also witnessed the appearance of the concept of organised crime and its successive increases. This concept has not only correctly embraced worrying phenomena such as the illegal international trafficking of persons and goods or terrorist acts, but it has also served to confer a new and aggravated criminal status on any cooperative perpetration of traditional criminal behaviours, such as robberies. Over time, the concept has been transformed into a useful catchall where all traditional interests linked to national security are included.

Apart from abortion and an occasional reform aimed at moderating disproportionate punishment in drug-related crimes, any reforms aimed at reducing criminal intervention have been conspicuous by their absence in this period. In addition to this, there has been a clear tendency to progressively approximate the criminal law of minors with adult criminal law.

This study has attempted to characterise criminal legislative policy in recent decades from a very particular dimension. Subsequent studies that use different dimensions, such as the progress made in protecting collective legal interests, especially of a socio-economic nature, or the extent to which the successive reforms affect judicial discretion, may obtain a more complete insight into current criminal legislative policy.

## References

Díez-Ripollés JL (2013) Social inclusion and comparative criminal justice policy. J Scand Stud Criminol Crime Prevent 14(1):62–78

Lappi-Seppälä T (2007) Penal policy in Scandinavia. In: Tonry M (ed) Crime, punishment and politics in comparative perspective. Crime and justice, vol 36. University of Chicago Press, Chicago

Von Hofer H, Tham H (2013) Punishment in Sweden: a changing penal landscape. In: Ruggiero V, Ryan M (eds) Punishment in Europe. Palgrave McMillan, London

**José Luis Díez-Ripollés** Dr. iur., holds the chair for Criminal Law at the University of Malaga and has been head of the Andalusian Institute of Criminology at the University of Malaga for 27 years, until 2017. He is current Vice President of the International Penal and Penitentiary Foundation, as well as President of the Criminal Law-Making Policy Working Group of the European Society of Criminology. His publications on this issue include, among others, Rationality in Criminal Law Making. Rational Decision Making in a Complex Socio-Legislative Process, in Oliver-Lalana, D, ed, Conceptions and misconceptions on legislation, Springer, 2019; La racionalidad de las leyes penales. Práctica y teoría, Trotta, 1st ed. 2003, 2 ed. 2013 (The Rationality of Criminal Law Making. Practice and Theory).

# Brazilian Post-1988 Constitution Criminal Policies: Comparing Law-Making with Impacts on Incarceration

**Carolina Costa Ferreira, Clara Moura Masiero, and Érica Babini Lapa do Amaral Machado**

**Abstract** This article seeks to discuss how criminal reforms in Brazil, occurring in the post-1988 Constitution period, constitute an increasingly expansionist criminal policy, alternating, nevertheless, between legitimate and illegitimate punitive tendencies. The illegitimate criminal expansion is one of the main causes for the unsustainable mass incarceration in progress in Brazil. Based on an empirical survey of the criminal laws passed in Brazil between 1940 and 2017, it was noticed that Brazilian criminal law reacted intensely to the "criminalisation mandates" contained in Constitution, producing criminal and criminal procedural laws in response to the guarantee of a "Citizen-Oriented Constitution". The problem tackled by this paper involves understanding national criminal policy tendencies, particularly their effects and criminological legitimacy, identifying them as couched in punitivism or left realism. In order to assess the complexity underlying Brazilian political movements after the 1988 Constitution, this article is based on quantitative data and a qualitative analysis of the criminal policies guiding the criminal laws intended to tackle crimes committed based on race and gender. This research method has led to the conclusion that law-making does not necessarily result in increased incarceration, contrary to the common theoretical-criminological belief that assumes that all neo-criminalisation equates to incarceration and penal populism, thereby suggesting the need for delimiting another criminal policy tendency for this phenomenon, referred to as left realism.

**Keywords** Criminal policy · 1988 Brazilian Federal Constitution · Legislative process · Criminal reforms · Mass incarceration

C. C. Ferreira
Brasília Public Law Institute (IDP), Brasília, Brasil

C. M. Masiero (✉)
Saint Jude University, Universidade São Judas (SP), São Paulo, Brasil

É. B. L. do Amaral Machado
Catholic University of Pernambuco (UNICAP), Recife, Brasil



J. Becerra (ed.), *Criminal Law-Making*, Legisprudence Library 7,
https://doi.org/10.1007/978-3-030-71348-5_11

# 1 Introduction

This article discusses perspectives of Brazilian criminal policy based on an empirical approach. It aims to examine the effects of legislative choices, especially regarding the demands of civil society for the protection of legal interests reflecting the defence of human rights after the entry into force of the 1988 Constitution. In other words, it seeks to discern, based on specific areas (gender and race), the impact on incarceration from such legislation, thereby questioning whether it is the consequence of a populist criminal policy of a punitive nature, or whether it reflects democratic spaces resulting from social achievements, characteristic of left realism.

This paper is linked to the study entitled "Descarcerização e Sistema Penal: a construção de políticas públicas de racionalização do poder punitivo [Prison Abolition and Penal System: the framing of public policies to rationalise punitive power]" of the "CNJ Acadêmico" project, promoted by the National Council of Justice, in conjunction with the *Coordenação de Aperfeiçoamento de Pessoal do Ensino Superior* [Coordination Office for the Improvement of Higher Education Personnel] (CAPES), and coordinated by the *Grupo de Pesquisa de Políticas Públicas de Segurança e Administração da Justiça Pena*l [Research Group on Public Security Policies and Criminal Justice Administration] (GPESC/PUC/RS), in partnership with the *Grupo Candango de Criminologia* [Candango Criminology Group] (GCCrim/UnB) and *Núcleo de Estudos e Pesquisas em Criminalidade, Violência e Políticas Públicas de Segurança* [Crime, Violence and Public Security Policies Studies and Research Center] (NEPS/UFPE). This study, carried out between 2012 and 2016, had as one of its objectives the mapping of all legislation in the form of criminal provisions enacted between 1940 (date of Penal Code, Decree-Law No. 2.848, of 7 December 1940) and 2015 (last year of the study) and respective justifications.

By updating with law-making up to December 2017, the mapping pointed to a total of 321 (three hundred and twenty-one) criminal laws passed in Brazil between 1940 and 2017. The material was prepared by researching all laws produced in Brazil during the period, using the "Portal da Legislação [Legislation Portal]" website fed and maintained by the *Centro de Estudos Jurídicos da Presidência da República* [Centre for Legal Studies of the Presidency of the Republic], linked to the Sub-Office for Legal Affairs of the President's Chief of Staff (http://www4.planalto.gov.br/legislacao). For each law, a search for the terms "crime" and "punishment" was carried out, in addition to skimming to verify the existence or otherwise of a criminal or criminal procedure subject matter.

After this mapping, the research team discussed the elements that the database should consist of: firstly, a spreadsheet containing all the laws found on the Legislation Portal, separated by year, number, subject matter, existence of a justification and full/compiled text.[1] The justifications for the legal amendments were taken from the Chamber of Deputies website (http://www2.camara.leg.br/), for subsequent qualitative analysis of the reasoning that led to the proposed changes in criminal laws.

For an analysis of the political and criminal movements embodied by the approved laws, the last step was to verify the impact on incarceration of these perspectives, by analysing the official data on the prison system,[2] under which, based on the enactment of the analysed laws, we sought to identify incarceration resulting therefrom and compare whether there was an increase in the prison population in the years following the entry into force of the law in question.

In this article, we chose to limit the qualitative analysis to laws aimed at penalising crimes committed on the grounds of gender and race, in order to verify their criminal and political trends as well as their legitimacy. To this end, it is divided into three parts. The first part explains the basic concepts in the field of criminal policy, defining this concept as it currently stands as part of the field of criminal sciences and linking it to legislative policy, the subject of this study. The second topic presents the results of the quantitative research and the focus of the qualitative research, in order to reflect on law-making with regards to race and gender in Brazil, after the 1988 Constitution, and the impacts on incarceration that these laws have produced—or not. The last topic of discussion presents the political and criminal tendencies guiding the qualitative analysis of the research data: on the one hand, penal populism, consisting of the merely expansionist criminal policy movements giving rise to mass incarceration; and, on the other hand, so-called "left realism", consisting of criminalisation reflecting the protection of legal interests in the context of the defence of human rights. Lastly, the study's conclusions are presented, pointing to the fact that not all law-making in the criminal field involves an increase in the prison population and that Brazilian criminal policies ambiguously combine penal populism with left realism practices.

[1]The "Portal da Legislação" publishes two kinds of legal text: "full text" and "compiled text". The former indicates all the changes that the law has undergone, striking out any text expressly repealed by the new law. The—sets out the "clean" text, according to its most updated version.

[2]Despite all the criticism regarding the forms of collection by Brazilian States and the lack of an obligation on them to submit data, the *Levantamento Nacional de Informações Penitenciárias* [National Survey of Penitentiary Information] - InfoPen - remains the main public database for information on prison population in Brazil.

## 2 Delimitation of the Field of Criminal Policy

One cannot deny the countless difficulties surrounding and underlying the concept of Criminal Policy.[3] Its central importance in the field of criminal sciences, the lack of a clear definition of its scope of knowledge and, consequently, the way it "serves" the varied ranges of conceptions and interests requires casting a questioning and critical look at its nature and function.[4]

The definition of Criminal Policy is not uniform. The effort to conceptualise it necessarily requires determining the most general and essential features drawn from the universe of varying doctrinal contributions on the subject. Here it is enough to refer to two classifications: Criminal Policy in a broad, strict sense and Criminal Policy in a theoretical, practical sense.

The former denotes the scope and breadth of actions in the field of Criminal Policy. Thus, in the strict or absolute sense of the term, it is the set of "principles or recommendations for the reform or transformation of criminal law and bodies entrusted with enforcement, encompassing public security policy, judicial policy and penitentiary policy".[5]

Broadly speaking, Criminal Policy is not limited specifically to penal problems of controlling infringement (criminal law, criminal procedural law, penitentiary law), but comprises reflections, developments and enforcement of broader social action policies. As such, here we discuss general social policies to tackle the causes of the criminal phenomena, with intervention being essentially for punishment (criminal policy in a strict sense), its ultimate and most burdensome element.

Thus, criminal policy in a broad sense and criminal policy in a strict sense share a species/genus relation, as noted in Freitas' explanation:

> By incorporating all social and economic policies of social control, criminal policy in a broad sense is analogous in terms of species/genus, the latter only dealing with the penal means of limiting crime. While penal policy consists of a response to criminal issues bound by the fulfilment of the punitive function of the state, criminal policy in a broad sense is a policy for social transformation.[6]

The second classification places the existence or otherwise of a theoretical, and therefore scientific, statute on Criminal Policy at the core of the discussion. In a practical sense, criminal policy constitutes the universe of activities aimed at the rational tackling of crime ("the set of procedures by which society organises responses to criminal phenomena"[7]). The theoretical sense denotes the study and development of theoretical principles intended to guide and rationalise the practical

---

[3]Criminal Policy is often defined as "obtaining and fulfilling management criteria in the field of criminal justice". Zipf (1979), p. 4.

[4]Freitas (2008).

[5]Batista (2007).

[6]Freitas (2008), p. 53.

[7]Delmas-Marty (2004), p. 42.

activities of combating crime. In the former case, criminal policy is considered eminently practical and thus devoid of a scientific nature.

In the latter sense, criminal policy is defined as a theoretical activity for practical purposes and for this reason may be considered as criminal science. It should be noted that there is an intersection between the two classifications: the object of criminal policy as theoretical knowledge is both criminal policy in a broad sense and criminal policy in a strict sense.

The fact is that, despite theoretical ambiguities, this article takes as a starting point the conception of the integrated model of criminal sciences, based on the paradigm of societal reaction, according to which—primary, secondary and tertiary—criminalisation processes are of fundamental interest, along the lines of that pointed out by Alessandro Baratta[8] regarding the functions of criminal policy in a new integrated model of criminal sciences; for the author, criminal policy must be the limit of actions in order to enforce "Criminal Law pursuant to the Constitution, from the perspective of an comprehensive policy for the protection of rights".[9] Thus, the idea of criminal policy as a promoter of fundamental rights is combined with the need to consider such criteria in order to analyse criminal reforms and, as part of them, to analyse respective criminal policy reasoning/tendencies.

According to Santiago Mir Puig, "all Criminal Law corresponds to a particular criminal policy, and all criminal policy depends on the general policy of the State to which it corresponds[10]". In other words, Criminal Policy—or at least its meaning—must be derived from the constitution; therefore the 1988 Brazilian Federal Constitution is the starting point of our research.

In Brazil, since the 1988 Constitution, there has been a rise in law-making, includinglaws with penal repercussions in particular. The fact is that Article 5 of the Constitution, upon establishing provisions on fundamental rights and guarantees, also provides for "criminalisation mandates".[11] This rise can be seen in the following chart (Fig. 1):

[8]Baratta (2000), pp. 27–52.

[9]Baratta (2000), p. 48.

[10]Mir Puig y Bidasolo (2007), p. 4.

[11]"XXXIX - there can be no crime without a prior law defining it, or punishment without prior sentencing*; XL - criminal law shall not be retroactive except to benefit the defendant; XLI - the law shall punish any discrimination in violation of fundamental rights and freedoms; XLII - acts of racism constitute an unbailable and imprescriptible offense, subject to the punishment of imprisonment pursuant to the terms of the law; XLIII - the law considers act of torture, unlawful trafficking of narcotics and related drugs, terrorism and acts defined as heinous crimes as unbailable crimes not eligible for pardon or amnesty, with instigators, perpetrators and those acting omissively, when having the power to prevent, being held liable; XLIV - the acts of armed, civil or military groups against constitutional order and the rule of law constitute an unbailable and imprescriptible crime; XLV - no one may be punished for the acts of another. Pursuant to the law, the obligation to repair the damage and the order to forfeit property may be extended to the successors and enforced against them, up to the limit of the value of the transferred assets; XLVI - the law shall govern sentencing and shall adopt the following punishments, among others: a) deprivation or restriction of liberty; b) loss of property; c) fine; d) alternative community service; e) suspension or annulment of

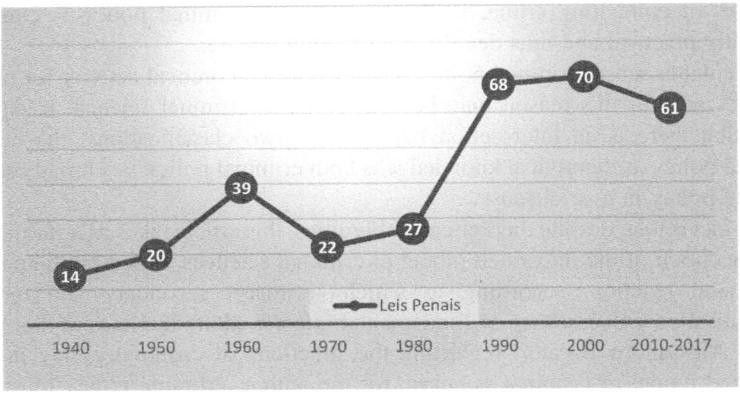


**Fig. 1** Approved Criminal Laws vs. Decade. Source: Prepared by the authors from data obtained from the survey, "CAPES and CNJ Acadêmico Research Project: Descarcerização e Sistema Penal — A construção de políticas públicas de racionalização do poder punitivo" (2011)

It should be noted that in Brazil, especially in the years following the 1988 Constitution, there has been significant increase in criminal law-making. This phenomenon is not unique to criminal laws; there has also been an increase in other branches of law. Furthermore, it is not an exclusively Brazilian phenomenon, as Mireille Delmas-Marty[12] notes that, although the contemporary phenomenon of a rise in law-making is not specific to criminal law, it has been uniquely affected.

The fact is that, as pointed out by Garland[13] and Díez Ripollés,[14] as well as in Brazilian criminal policy research discussed below, Criminal Law is in motion and, among the change processes, there are different criminal policy tendencies in existence.

Garland's theory is that denial responses (which deny the inadequacy of the penal system and seek to endow it with more punitive powers) and symbolic responses (which are instrumental, put into effect to symbolise that something is being done when, in fact, its effectiveness in achieving its intended purpose is quite doubtful) are the most common and recurring not only in the United States and Great Britain, but in all Western countries, making penal populism a Western tendency.

José Luis Díez Ripollés disputes this conclusion that there is a widespread tendency towards penal populism in the Western world and proposes another model of criminal policy analysis. This model abandons the aspects of "punitivism"

rights; XLVII - the following punishments shall not be permitted: a) death penalty, except in the event of declared war, pursuant to art. 84, XIX; b) life punishment; and c) forced labour; [...]" (Brazil. Constitution of the Federative Republic of Brazil 1988. http://www.planalto.gov.br/ccivil_03/constituicao/ConstituicaoCompilado.htm. Accessed 30 Apr 2018.

[12]Delmas-Marty (2004).

[13]Garland (2008).

[14]Díez Ripollés (2015).

and "moderation" and creates others: a "socially inclusive" and "socially exclusive" criminal policy. According to the author, these categories work best because what ultimately matters is the social effect generated by a particular criminal policy.

Brazilian research, as detailed below, diverges somewhat as to the post-1988 Brazilian criminal policy trends, but coincides with the diagnosis regarding the expansion of criminal laws, especially after the enactment of the 1988 Constitution. These laws, which are fundamentally ambiguous in terms of their content and interpretations, despite the criminalisation mandates, tend to produce more pain.[15]

On the other hand, the situation of mass incarceration in Brazil must be highlighted. Brazil is home to the third largest prison population in the world (in 2016, there were 726,712 inmates[16]), according to the ranking organised by *International for Criminal Policy Research*[17] and also boasts the third highest incarceration rate—342 inmates per 100,000 inhabitants, according to data published in the Penitentiary Information Survey.[18] Considering the proportion of people imprisoned for every 100,000 inhabitants—a criterion used by the United Nations to discuss the treatment of imprisoned persons—Máximo Sozzo[19] found that Brazil is in first place, in punitiveness, in Latin America, far ahead of Peru, Colombia, Mexico, Argentina, Ecuador, Bolivia and Guatemala.

The scenario is even worse when one considers that the data does not represent all inmates, as the report points out: "the states of Acre, Espirito Santo, Pernambuco, Piaui, Rondônia and Tocantins did not report the total number of people in custody in jails at police stations in June 2016[20]"; moreover, it is not the most up-to-date number as references date from December 2015 to June 2016.

In any case, it is undisputed that the number of inmates is growing rapidly (157%, if we consider the data produced between 2000 and 2016), without necessarily having consequences on the country's overall crime situation. Note: the main crimes leading to incarceration[21] are primarily crimes against property (278,809 people imprisoned) and drug trafficking (176,691 people imprisoned), while the number of crimes against persons (84,686 people imprisoned) is much less.[22] On the other

[15]Here we adopt the idea defined by Nils Christie that the enforcement of criminal law is a "process of delivering pain". If we do not name criminal punishment, as it is enforced in Brazil, as the production and reproduction of pain, we cannot seriously discuss proposals to limit mass incarceration (Christie 2016).

[16]Brasil. Departamento Penitenciário Nacional (2016). Accessed 25 April 2018.

[17]Institute for Criminal Policy Research. Highest to Lowest: Prison Population Total. Available at: http://www.prisonstudies.org/highest-to-lowest/prison-population-total?field_region_taxonomy_tid=All. Accessed 25 April 2018.

[18]Brasil. Departamento Penitenciário Nacional (2016). Accessed 25 April 2018.

[19]Sozzo (2017), p. 6.

[20]Brasil. Departamento Penitenciário Nacional (2016), p. 10. Accessed 25 April 2018.

[21]An alert is that 66% of the prisons that make up the national data reported receiving, whether or not regularly, confirmation of punishment to be served by persons deprived of liberty in the establishment, thereby showing another deficit in the data.

[22]Brasil. Departamento Penitenciário Nacional (2016). Accessed 25 April 2018.

hand, according to data from the Anuário do Fórum Brasileiro de Segurança Pública [Brazilian Public Security Forum Yearbook], in 2016, 61,283 people were intentionally killed involving violence, representing a rate of 29.7 per 100,000 inhabitants.[23] In these cases, the rate at which they are handled is certainly not effective,[24] varying across the range of States with a low margin of 10%. In other words, "the higher the difference (in percentage terms) between the bottom and the top [Police inquiries and judgments by the judiciary], the greater the idea of impunity, since this may indicate that a large number of violations of rights are not duly examined by the courts".[25] As a matter of fact, the reflux of the prison system's incapacity is demonstrated by the fact that 40% of the prison population is made up of temporary inmates.[26]

In light of the foregoing, what is questioned here is whether the legislative processes of law-making on criminalisation are actually the cause of the mass incarceration process in Brazil. Yes, because this paper questions to what extent the expansion of criminal laws involves punitive practices and is a reflection of a penal populism movement, since it is hypothesised that this legislative movement may be an interesting reflection of the Federal Constitution in Brazil in the sense of encouraging social participation and the demand for enforcing the rights recognised therein.

Based on the agreement and disagreement with the theories described below, we point out the distinction between "penal populism" and "left realism". The former is characterised, as David Garland[27] suggests, as being illegitimate and probably irrational; the latter is supposedly legitimate and rational, even though it represents the expansion of penal action, because it derives from a real social problem and stems from the discourse produced by the people involved in the conflict. In the latter case, it is possible to find a defensible effect beyond symbolism, in that it can be handled by society in its daily uses of the legal grammar.

Like Garland, Díez Ripollés[28] also identifies a significant politicisation of national criminal policies. In this regard, he highlights three phenomena in this direction. The first phenomenon involves the fact that criminal policy no longer reflects ideological differences, for example, between right and left. According to the author, "only evidence of old distinctive markers remains, such as increased resistance to stigmatization of the offender on the left, or the occasional reluctance of the right with respect to punitive action that is excessively invasive of the personal

[23]Fórum Brasileiro De Segurança Pública (2017).

[24]There are no national surveys on case flow*, because the data is compiled by States and Municipalities. See discussion in Cano (2006).

[25]Ribeiro and Silva (2010), p. 16.

[26]Brasil. Departamento Penitenciário Nacional (2016). Accessed 25 April 2018.

[27]Garland (1999).

[28]Díez Ripollés (2015).

sphere".[29] In other words, it is possible to find considerable differences between right-wing and left-wing criminal policy, especially in terms of the social sphere in which each side advocates for penal action.

The second phenomenon is linked to the demonstration that the criminal policy agenda is determined and shaped predominantly by political parties and not by authentic social demands or, mainly, by social problems to be dealt with. This situation corroborates the author's conclusion that value-based or ideological decisions are more of a factor in criminal policy frameworks than utilitarian or efficacy considerations.

The third phenomenon points to the fact that foreign criminal policy practices, or international obligations, are increasingly influencing national decisions on crime prevention or reduction, that is, on national criminal policy:

> The most prestigious foreign models, among which the United States stands out for many countries, penetrate the criminal policy decision-making centers in a widespread manner; this interaction is positive, and justifies studies of comparative criminal policy.[30]

As such, Díez Ripollés warns of the need to create an analytical model that enables rigorous analysis of national criminal policies in order to be able to compare them. To this end, he lists three theoretical assumptions that must be taken into consideration in relation to criminal policy: (1) criminal policy is part of public policies as a whole; (2) the purpose of all criminal policy is to prevent delinquency within socially acceptable parameters; (3) the implementation of any criminal policy requires the selection, design and implementation of specific objectives that are consistent with that purpose.[31]

In order to carry out this analysis, our starting point will be empirical research on Brazilian penal reforms in order to put forward a relationship between criminal policy—especially penal legislative policy—and mass incarceration in Brazil, by cross-referencing the results of this research with incarceration rates. In this way, our intention is to develop and differentiate, through questioning, the two criminal policy trends that currently co-exist and are sometimes blended together: left realism and penal populism.

## 3 Criminal Policies in Brazil: Current Situation

It is quite true that there is a significant lack of research on current penal legislation, from its production and, especially, with regards to its effects.

---

[29]"sólo restan indicios de antiguos signos distintivos, como una mayor resistencia a la estigmatización del delincuente en la izquierda, o las ocasionales reticencias de la derecha hacia intervenciones punitivas en exceso invasivas de la esfera personal" (Díez Ripollés 2015, p. 146).

[30]Díez Ripollés (2015), p. 149.

[31]Díez Ripollés (2015).

In any case, here we would like to highlight five studies on Brazilian criminal policy: Marcelo da Silveira Campos' thesis;[32] Luis Wanderley Gazoto's dissertation;[33] Ana Claudia Cifali's thesis,[34] Carolina Costa Ferreira's dissertation[35] and Clara Moura Masiero's dissertation.[36]

Gazoto's research consisted of analysing criminal laws (regarding common crimes[37]) enacted after the 1940 Criminal Code until the first half of 2009. In the analysed period, 122 laws were identified. Out of said laws, the author identified that 80.3% were more burdensome.[38] 12.3% were more beneficial[39] and 7.4% had mixed content[40] or were indifferent.[41] Gazoto also analysed the bills that were pending in the 53rd Parliamentary Term of the Chamber of Deputies (period from 1st January 2007 until 30th June 2009), of which 308 bills dealing with criminal law were identified, and "about 95% are to increase punishment and impact on crime rates[42]". Moreover, he analysed the bills of the 52nd and 53rd Federal Senate Parliamentary Terms (1st January 2003 until 30th June 2009), of which 172 bills dealing with criminal law were identified, of which "about 97% are to increase punishment and impact on crime rates".[43]

It should be noted that, although he analyses the recitals existing in bills,[44] his classification as burdensome or beneficial takes into account only the extent of punishment and the increase/decrease in criminalisation of conduct. In this sense, he regards all burdensome laws as falling under penal populism, which he characterises as irrational and disproportionate penal severity.

---

[32]Campos (2010).

[33]Gazoto (2010).

[34]Cifali (2015).

[35]Ferreira (2017).

[36]Masiero (2018).

[37]As such, election and military offenses are excluded.

[38]"Laws defining new offenses, increasing punishment or restricting criminal rights, such as provisional release, change in sentence applied, etc., were considered as burdensome."

[39]"Beneficial laws include those promoting the revocation of crimes, the reduction of punishment, or the establishment of benefits, such as new reasons for excluding punishability" (Gazoto 2010, p. 211).

[40]"The group of mixed laws includes those, at the same time, giving rise to a greater burden for offenders and, in other situations, establishing benefits." (Gazoto 2010, p. 211).

[41]"Thereby considering those only particularizing crimes, relating to already existing sentence and conduct of the same sort" (Gazoto 2010, p. 210).

[42]Gazoto (2010), p. 280.

[43]Gazoto (2010), p. 280.

[44]Based on this, he concluded: "the recitals of bills almost always argue for the need for repression, without, however, presenting empirical data able to support their positions; purely rhetorical exaggerated appeal to the ethical and moral value of state protection for the interest in question is common, but without reference to proportionality criteria; not infrequently, parliamentarians express that their concerns stem from newspaper readings and media influence in general." (Gazoto 2010).

As such, he identifies tendencies toward penal severity among all major political parties to the same degree of intensity. It turns out that, as will be explained below, the expansionary tendency may even remain the same over time, but attention must be paid to the scope of action on which criminal justice intends to act.

For example, Gazoto identified that "the subject of 'minorities, racism, children, women, the elderly, etc.' gained relevance, especially in the Governments of Fernando Collor, Sarney and, more recently, under the Lula Government".[45] In other words, it is coincidentally a demand from the post-1988 Constitution or post-democracy era. Furthermore, he states that "most of these laws were the suggestion of the Workers' Party: by the Government of President Lula, or by Deputies Paulo Paim (PT/RS) and Iara Bernardi (PT/SP)".[46] Lastly, he concludes that the Workers' Party is responsible by far for Brazilian penal populism "as to its intensification, chiefly as to anti-racism and gender violation criminal legislation."[47]

In fact, as Cifali pointed out in his research on the Lula administration's criminal policy, the defence of vulnerable sections of the population emerged starting from the election manifesto, which affirmed "the party's concern about physical and symbolic violence, such as the discrimination suffered by women, young people, the elderly and migrants".[48] As such, it would be difficult to speak about the irrationality of these penal reforms, which is a fundamental feature of populism. This is not to say that there was no populism in this government. On the contrary, Cifali pointed to penal populism laws during the period. The truth is that ambivalence is a main point of criminal policies, not only in Brazil.[49]

Campos'[50] research brings more nuances to the discussion of criminal policy tendencies in Brazil. He also surveyed federal laws passed in Brazil that addressed the issue of public security and criminal justice, with the research period focusing on the post-1988 Constitution era. Thus, in the period between 1989 and 2006, 84 laws were selected, the qualitative analysis of which revealed six criminal policy trends to the researcher: (1) more punitive laws, (2) laws that are linked to an alternative penal policy, (3) laws which turn to new institutional arrangements, (4) laws that seek to criminalise new conduct, (5) laws that establish privileges for a particular population group, and (6) laws that combine more than one of these trends in their contents.

In other words, the researcher developed his own definitions and highlighted the complexity of arising criminal policy movements, going beyond analyses focusing on the intensification of criminal policy and differentiating punitivism from new

---

[45]Gazoto (2010), p. 210.

[46]Gazoto (2010), p. 238.

[47]Gazoto (2010), p. 294.

[48]Cifali (2015).

[49]"For David Garland, the ambiguity that marks the functioning of crime control mechanisms in the contemporary context is related to two distinct reasons, one instrumental, focused on risk management, and another symbolic, focused on the social demand for punishment and revenge against the accused".

[50]Campos (2010).

criminalisation. Among the conclusions reached by Marcelo Campos, we highlight here the co-existence, in the analysed period, of laws that sought to extend rights and guarantees with more punitive laws, sometimes combined in criminalising laws that sought to "guarantee" rights through criminalisation of conduct.

Ferreira's[51] and Masiero's[52] dissertations are included in the research project "Descarcerização e Sistema Penal: a construção de políticas públicas de racionalização do poder punitivo", as previously described.

Based on this database, both dissertations chose to focus their analysis on criminal policy by scope of action. The need for criminal policy analysis by subject focus is due to the perception of this research that the same law can feature different criminal policy strategies/trends, depending on the subject it is dealing with.

Ferreira's thesis focused her analysis on Brazilian criminal policy in the field of punishment enforcement, thereby examining the 17 bills that amended Law No. 7.210, from 1984 to 2016. The analysis of the Bills' justifications and the debates in the Committees and Plenary Session of the Chamber of Deputies and the Federal Senate showed that the Legislature does not have an adequate instrument to verify viability and foresee the consequences of a legislative change, thereby being guided by the influence of the media to construct facts that could possibly result in more criminal laws. To improve the quality of criminal laws passed in Brazil, she advocates the adoption of a Legislative Impact Study[53] as a condition for the enactment of a criminal law. After all, as the researcher pointed out, the Penal Enforcement Law itself provides for a National Council for Criminal and Penitentiary Policy (CNPCP), with the power to "propose criminal policy guidelines on crime prevention, Criminal Justice administration, and the enforcement of sentences and security measures" (LEP [Penal Enforcement Law], Art. 62, item I). To this end, it is necessary to engage and restructure the CNPCP for this very important task of keeping the legislative criminal debates informed and significant.

---

[51]Ferreira (2017).

[52]Masiero (2018).

[53]The author proposes a model Prison Impact Study, consisting of 15 questions: (1) what is the problem?; (2) does the problem exist nationwide?; (3) is the subject matter relevant to the Penal Enforcement Act (LEP)?; (4) should the problem change the LEP?; (5) does the proposal affect the principles of criminal enforcement? (6) what are the objectives of the legislative proposal? (7) what are the options for achieving the objectives of the legislative proposal? (8) how can the different problem-solving options be compared in terms of effectiveness and efficacy (costs and benefits)? (9) was the legislative proposal drafted following objective criteria from a particular criminal policy? Can the criminal policy guiding the proposal be identified?; (10) will the legislative proposal cause economic, social and environmental impacts? Who will be affected? How can such effects be evaluated? (11) will the objective of the legislative proposal be evaluated? How? By whom?; (12) will the application of the object of the legislative proposal be monitored? How? By whom?; (13) were the proposed changes based on data on the Brazilian prison population?; (14) will the proposed changes affect the structure of the criminal justice system or the Brazilian prison system? (15) were stakeholders/affected parties consulted during the discussion of legislative proposals? What were their contributions to the analysis of the proposal? (Ferreira, 2017).

In turn, Masiero's[54] dissertation focused on the scope of action regarding discrimination-related crimes, justified by prejudice, or also referred to as hate crimes. Her focus was further limited to laws aimed at addressing sexist, racist and anti-LGBTQ violence. Thus, the criminal laws concerning "sex", "gender", "women", "sexual orientation",[55] "gender identity"[56] and "race" were analysed (totalling 29 laws, that is, around 10% of the criminal laws enacted between 1940 and 2015). Among these, only "gender identity" is not featured in any criminal law. The empirical research also involved interviews with activists from these social movements. The field confirmed that there is some permeability between the actions of social movements and Brazilian criminal policy. In fact, laws that are closest to the discourse of the social movement involved result in greater effectiveness (what the author referred to as a "left realism" tendency); while laws that did not stem from an actual empirical problem or did not absorb the discourse produced within social movements end up lacking in effectiveness and shaping an unnecessary measure (what the author referred to as "penal populism").

Masiero's dissertation therefore concluded that not every expansion of criminal law consists of "penal populism" (irrational and unnecessary criminal policy) and that legitimate criminal expansion with acceptable effectiveness is also possible, which the author classified as "left realism", in the event of meeting the following variables: (1) arising from an actual social problem; (2) involving harm to a relevant legal interest; and (3) incorporating the discourse produced by the social actors involved/affected by this problem.

In view of the discussion presented, this article aims to take a closer look at the definition and contrast between "penal populism" and "left realism", thereby involving one more variable in the debate: the effect of a given criminal law on incarceration.

Before proceeding with this plan, it is also essential to mention the discussion put forward by Díez Ripollés[57] regarding the analysis of criminal policy. This is because this author is also opposed to analyses that focus only on the severity or moderation of a given criminal law, by focusing his analysis on the effects of criminal laws.

---

[54]Masiero (2018).

[55]Sexual orientation is, in the words of Raupp Rios (2001, p. 49), "the identity attributed to individuals based on where they direct their desires and/or sexual conduct, whether at others of the same gender (homosexuality), of the opposite sex (heterosexuality) or of both genders (bisexuality)".

[56]Gender identity "refers to the subjective perception of falling under a specific gender. Despite social norms that seek to divide the world between men and women, there is a wide range of individuals who are not included under such norms. Gender identities are multiple and varied. In fact, the very nomenclature used in the definition of non-normative genders is multiple and varied, and may even depend on the cultural context. Examples include the following categories: trans women*, transgender, transsexual, multigender, cisgender, non-gender, transeuntes de gênero*, transvestite, gender outlaw, queer gender, drag queens*, crossdressers and intersexuals" (Masiero 2018).

[57]Díez Ripollés (2015), pp. 158–159.

## 4 Analysis of Criminal Policy: Going Beyond Severity/Moderation

The analytical model proposed by Díez Ripollés refers to the capacity of the corresponding national penal system to minimise the social exclusion of those coming into conflict with criminal law. This means assessing criminal policies according to their ability to allow "adoption, recovery, consolidation or at least not worsening of an acceptable level of social inclusion with respect to suspects and criminals".[58]

In this way, Díez Ripollés creates two new categories for criminal policy analysis: an inclusive approach and an exclusionary approach, which reflect opposing courses of action with the goal of preventing delinquency among people prone to coming into conflict with criminal law:

> El enfoque inclusivo pretende asegurar que el sospechoso o delincuente se encuentre, tras su contacto con los órganos de control penal, en iguales o mejores condiciones individuales y sociales para desarrollar voluntariamente una vida conforme con la ley. El enfoque exclusivo quiere garantizar que el sospechoso o delincuente se encuentre, tras su contacto con los órganos de control penal, en unas condiciones individuales y sociales en las que le resulte más difícil infringir la ley o evitar ser descubierto[59]

This proposal is based on two essential and correlated assumptions: (1) that maintaining a certain level of social inclusion for suspects, convicts and ex-convicts is one of the most effective crime prevention strategies; and (2) that bringing about or deepening the social exclusion of suspects, convicts and ex-convicts through correctional institutions gives rise to higher crime rates in the medium and long term. These hypotheses are undoubtedly pending definitive confirmation, as the Spanish professor himself warns. However, they could be put to the test by this analytical model.

It can be assumed that an inclusive criminal policy would necessarily correspond to a moderate criminal policy, while an exclusionary one would always be more punitive; however, the author refutes this hypothesis as they do not necessarily exist in the same societies. The fact is that Societies closer to the side of inclusion than to social exclusion, for example, despite being more sensitive to social equality and the condemnation of property crimes, tend to develop processes of law-making on criminalisation regarding behaviours of the most powerful social sectors to a greater extent than the specific criminal policies of the most exclusionary societies. Thus, in

[58] Adquisición, recuperación, consolidación o al menos no empeoramiento de un aceptable nivel de inclusión social de los sospechosos y los delincuentes". Díez Ripollés (2015), pp. 158–159.

[59] "The inclusive approach aims to ensure that the suspect or offender is, after contact with correctional authorities, in the same or better individual and social condition to live life voluntarily in accordance with the law. The exclusionary approach seeks to ensure that the suspect or offender is, after contact with correctional authorities, in an individual and social condition in which it is more difficult to break the law or avoid being discovered". Díez Ripollés (2015), p. 159.

this area of penal action, they are more punitive than more socially exclusive societies. In this regard,

> Sociedades consideradas muy incluyentes pueden diseñar programas de criminalización primaria muy extensivos, con la finalidad de prevenir procesos de desorganización social que pudieran amenazar su capacidad integradora. Es, sin duda, el caso de los países nórdicos respecto a su política de persecución del tráfico y consumo de drogas, y quizás esté siendo ya respecto a la persecución de la prostitución y la pornografía infantil; ello es compatible con una práctica moderada y bienestarista a la hora de aplicar las correspondientes reacciones penales.[60]

The idea of the Spanish author is to establish a comparative line of reasoning under which, at one end of the spectrum, there are States with the most socially inclusive criminal policy and, on the other, States with the most socially exclusionary criminal policy, while other countries would be placed further to one side or another, depending on their proximity to one side or another.

To determine the level at which the different criminal justice systems are placed, Díez Ripollés[61] highlights that one has to identify punitive rules and practices and, on this basis, unveil what effects are produced on the people involved, that is, whether they give rise to social inclusion or exclusion. However, for a rigorous comparative analysis, the author goes further and suggests the transformation of these rules and practices into indicators, thereby making it possible, finally, to carry out comparisons.

To establish this line of reasoning, Díez Ripollés takes two hypotheses as a starting point: the first concerns indicators and the second includes the countries that will serve as a paradigm for one end of the spectrum and the other.

As for the indicators, the author suggests nine key indicators, under which other indicators are grouped, making a total of 25. According to the author, these indicators have the qualities necessary to reveal the socially inclusive or exclusionary effects of a criminal system, as well as to characterise its system comparatively along the respective spectrum.

The author's second hypothesis proposes that the two paradigmatic criminal policy models at either end of the spectrum regarding their effects of social inclusion or exclusion may be represented, at the beginning of the twenty-first century, among western countries, by the United States of America (federal system and the system of most of its federated states), on the one hand, and by European Nordic countries (Denmark, Finland, Norway and Sweden), on the other.

[60]"Societies considered as very inclusive can draw up very extensive primary criminalisation* programmes, with the purpose of preventing social disorganisation processes that could threaten their capacity for integration. This is, without a doubt, the case of the Nordic countries regarding their policy of persecuting drug trafficking and use, and perhaps it already applies with respect to the persecution of prostitution and child pornography; this is compatible with a moderate and welfare-oriented practice when applying the corresponding penal responses". Díez Ripollés (2015), pp. 167–168.

[61]Díez Ripollés (2015).

In this regard, for the author, the American criminal justice system constitutes the Western criminal policy model most strongly inspired by the social exclusion of suspects or convicts. On the other hand, European Nordic countries have a criminal policy model that is more decidedly focused on the social inclusion of those brought under the fold of the criminal justice system.[62]

What is interesting to note in this regard is that, despite currently being on opposite sides of the spectrum, both countries shared, for several decades of the second half of the twentieth century, the same model of penal action: re-socialisation. It was not until the 1980s that this progressive divergence began to emerge.

Hence the relevance of carrying out a comparative study, because it allows us to realise with empirical clarity that the penal action choices are not natural and inevitable, but rather political choices with specific purposes. Lastly, Díez Ripollés[63] intends to provide a comparative study proposal, in order to make it possible, based on parallel investigations of the application of the proposed analytical and typological model, to measure the level of social inclusion or social exclusion brought about by countries' criminal policies.

## 5 Criminal Policy Trends: Left Realism vs. Penal Populism

Following the line of reasoning defended by Masiero,[64] it is understood that, in order to analyse criminal policies and, more importantly, their legitimacy, the analysis must be directed at their justifications. Not only must there be an analysis of official justifications, which appear in the Recitals of a Bill, but also of unofficial ones, which are possibly the real or actual reasons. As part of this analysis, four aspects should be verified: (1) whether the proposal stems from an actual social problem, (2) with harm to a relevant legal interest (especially a violation of human rights), (3) whether other branches of law cannot cope and, above all, (4) whether it results from mobilisation by social actors involved/affected by this problem.[65]

In addition to these indicators, this article analyses the impact of incarceration in order to identify whether law-making resulted in an impact—increase or decrease—on the Brazilian national prison population. Notwithstanding the data shortcomings, as previously explained, the numbers provided by the national system, INFOPEN, will be the verification criterion. The objective is to identify, starting from the

---

[62]Díez Ripollés (2015).

[63]Díez Ripollés (2015).

[64]Masiero (2018).

[65]Masiero (2018).

enactment of the law, whether it resulted in incarceration and to compare, in the years following the entry into force of the law and, in case of positive response, whether (or not) there was a punitive increase.

If it is not possible to verify these aspects, it is understood that the respective legislation is the result of a "penal populism" criminal policy, as Garland[66] or Gazoto[67] understands it, or an "exclusionary" policy, according to Díez Ripollés. In other words, it is legislation that gives rise to norms with an intensification of penalisation, without an empirical justification or social support legitimising it, therefore being due to irrationality. Most likely, its effect will also be innocuous, except that it will lead to an unnecessary expansion of the penal system.

On the other hand, if the above aspects are present based on the analysis of a criminal law, it is argued that this law, even if it intensifies penalisation, is not populist, but rather falls under "left realism". This category includes legislation that, while creating new crime definitions, does so based on the justification of tacking real social problems, involving human rights violations, which previously were not one of the concerns of criminal legislators. This does not necessarily mean the intensification of incarceration, since the law can create a crime definition and endow it with punishment alternative to prison sentences, for example. In any case, this paper's assumption is that "left realism" laws have a much greater potential for efficacy and[68] effectiveness,[69]—including of a symbolic nature—than laws falling under "penal populism".

Let's look with a focus on race and gender issues; it is important to point out that the category termed as "(women)" refers to laws that do not expressly relate to the category of "women", but whose legislation came about to protect women from discriminatory practices.

Another interesting fact of this first analysis comes from understanding how criminalised social categories have changed over time, except for race, which has remained the same from the 1950s until today. For example, the attention paid to women and the female gender is a phenomenon that dates back to the 2000s, although concerns about marital status and gender in general were concerns held by women (appearing in the 1960s). In this case, the database consists of 31 laws (Fig. 2; Table 1).

[66]Garland (1999).

[67]Gazoto (2010).

[68]"The effectiveness of the law, encompassing the most varied situations - observance, enforcement, application and use of law - can be understood generically as statutory implementation of the legal text" (Neves 2011, p. 46).

[69]Effectiveness refers to the achievement of the purpose of the law and the fulfilment of the "aim" that guided the law-making, that is, the implementation of the means and end deriving abstractly from the legal text (Neves 2011).

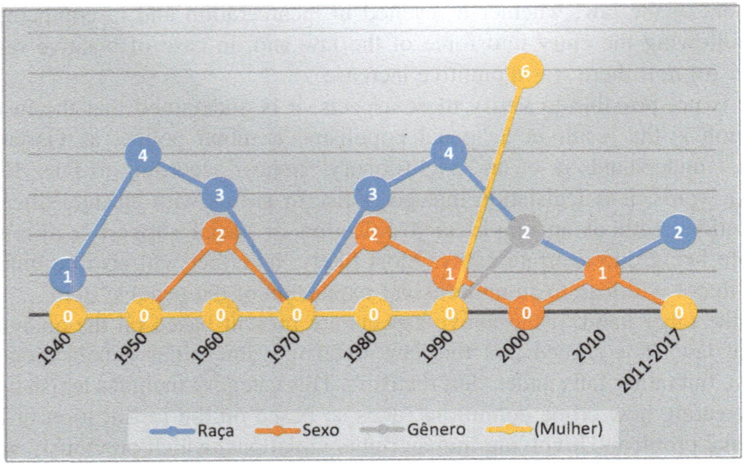


**Fig. 2** Decade x social category contained in Brazilian criminal law. Source: Masiero, Clara Moura. Lutas sociais e polÚtica criminal: os movimentos feminista, negro e LGBTQ e a criminalização das violências machista, racista e LGBTQfóbica no Brasil. Tese (doutorado). Universidade do Vale do Rio dos Sinos (UNISINOS). Direito. 2018

The laws from the period are broken down as follows:

The production of criminal statistics is a separate debate that deserves further discussion, especially because the ways in which data is collected, timeframes, information gathering, etc., have always been the subject of much disagreement. In fact, the issue adjusts to the political environment of each era, so much so that it is possible to identify that "race" as a concept only appears in a statistical survey in 1872 in the General Census of Brazil, but "was only taken as a parameter of population classification by police in the 20th century".[70]

The fact is that only in the 1990s were there professional, technical aspects, such as a democracy consolidation strategy. Thus, the discussion of human rights, transparency and government control have become the requirements of new times, such that in 2004 the process of centralising information commenced starting from data collection carried out through forms completed by the managers of all the prison establishments in the country.

In 2014, a major methodological change was implemented in the process with "the reformulation of the collection instrument, the aggregation of information quality analysis components and the publication of a detailed analytical report and the complete survey database in an open format[71]". However, the changes are still insufficient in terms of maximisation, such that the version of the latest data until

[70]Lima (2011), p. 107.

[71]Brasil. Departamento Penitenciário Nacional (2016, p. 5). Accessed 25 April 2018.

**Table 1** Database: criminal legislation

| | Legislation | Bill | Headnote | Social Category |
|---|---|---|---|---|
| 1. | 1947 Constitution | Historical Records of the Constituent Assembly | Constitution of the United States of Brazil | Race |
| 2. | Law no. 1.390/ 1951 Afonso Arinos Law | Bill 562/1950 | It includes among criminal offences the commission of acts resulting from racial or skin colour prejudice | Race |
| 3. | Law no. 1.802/ 1953 | Bill 1451/1949 | It defines crimes against the State and the Political and Social Order, among other measures | Race |
| 4. | Law no. 2.083/ 1953 | Bill 403/1948 | It governs Press Freedom | Race |
| 5. | Law no. 2.889/ 1956 | Bill 249/195 | It defines and punishes the crime of genocide | Race |
| 6. | Law no. 4.117/ 1962 | Senate Bill 36/1953 | Brazilian Telecommunications Code | Race |
| 7. | 1967 Constitution | Institutional Act 4/1966 | 1967 Constitution of the Federative Republic of Brazil | Race |
| 8. | Law 5.250/ 1967 | National Congress Bill 23/1966 | Press Law | Race and gender |
| 9. | Law no. 5.473/ 1968 | Bill 3232/1965 | It governs the granting of positions among other measures | Gender |
| 10. | Law no. 7.170/ 1983 | National Congress Bill 17/1983 | It defines crimes against national security, political and social order and establishes respective prosecution and trials, among other measures | Race |
| 11. | Law no. 7.437/ 1985 | Bill 5328/1985 | It includes, among criminal offences, the commission of acts resulting from prejudice based on race, skin colour, gender or marital status, providing new wording for Law No. 1390 of 3rd July 1951—Afonso Arinos Law | Gender |
| 12. | 1988 Constitution | Historical Records of the Constituent Assembly | Constitution of the Federative Republic of Brazil—1988 | Race Gender |
| 13. | Law no. 7.716/ 1989 Caó Law | Bill 668/1988 | It defines crimes resulting from prejudice based on race or skin colour | Race |
| 14. | Law no. 8.081/ 1990 | Bill 5249/1990 | It establishes the crimes and punishment applicable to acts of discrimination or prejudice based on race, skin colour, religion, ethnicity or national origin, | Race |

(continued)

**Table 1** (continued)

| | Legislation | Bill | Headnote | Social Category |
|---|---|---|---|---|
| | | | committed by the media or by a publication of any kind | |
| 15. | Law no. 8.882/ 1994 | Bill 3261/1992 | It adds a paragraph to Art. 20 of Law No. 7.716, of 5th January 1989, which "defines the crimes resulting from prejudice based on race or skin colour." | (Nazism) |
| 16. | Law no. 9.029/ 1995 | Bill 229/1991 | It prohibits requiring pregnancy and sterilisation certificates, and other discriminatory practices, for hiring purposes or to retain employment legally, among other measures | Gender |
| 17. | Law no. 9.459/ 1997 | Bill 1240/1995 | It amends Arts. 1 and 20 of Law No. 7.716, of 5th January 1989, which defines crimes resulting from prejudice based on race or skin colour, and adds a paragraph to Art. 140 of Decree-Law No. 2,848 of 7th December 1940 | Race |
| 18. | Law no. 9.455/ 1997 Torture Crimes Law | Bill 4716/1994 | It defines torture crimes, among other measures | Race |
| 19. | Law no. 10.224/ 2001 | Bill 61/1999 | It amends Decree-Law No. 2.848, of 7th December 1940—Criminal Code, to establish provisions on the crime of sexual harassment, among other measures | (Women) |
| 20. | Law no. 10.741/ 2003 | Bill 3561/1997 | Provides for the Elderly Statute and other measures | Race |
| 21. | Law no. 10.803/ 2003 | Bill 7429/2002 | It amends Art. 149 of Decree-Law No. 2,848, of 7th December 1940—Criminal Code, to establish the punishment for the crime defined therein and state the elements to be met to establish conditions analogous to slavery | Race |
| 22. | Law no. 10.778/ 2003 | Bill 4493/2001 | It establishes the compulsory notification, in Brazilian territory, of cases of violence against women assisted by public or private health care services | Gender |
| 23. | Law no. 10.886/ 2004 | Bill 3/2003 | It adds paragraphs to Art. 129 of Decree-Law No. 2.848, of 7th December 1940 - Criminal Code, creating the special crime referred to "Domestic Violence" | (Women) |
| 24. | Law no. 11.106/ 2005 | Bill 117/2003 | It amends Arts. 148, 215, 216, 226, 227, 231 and adds Art. 231-A to Decree-Law No. 2,848 of 7th December 1940—Criminal Code, among other measures | (Women) |
| 25. | Law no. 11.340/ 2006 | Bill 4559/2004 | It creates mechanisms to curb domestic and family violence against women, pursuant to § 8 of Art. 226 of the Federal | Women Gender |

(continued)

**Table 1** (continued)

| | Legislation | Bill | Headnote | Social Category |
|---|---|---|---|---|
| | Maria da Penha Law | | Constitution, the Convention on the Elimination of All Forms of Discrimination against Women and the Inter-American Convention on the Prevention, Punishment, and Eradication of Violence against Women; it establishes provisions for the establishment of Courts for Domestic and Family Violence against Women; it amends the Code of Criminal Procedure, the Criminal Code and the Criminal Enforcement Law; among other measures | |
| 26. | Law no. 12.015/ 2009 | Bill 4850/2005 | It amends Title VI of the Special Part of Decree-Law No. 2.848 of 7th December 1940—Criminal Code, and Art. 1 of Law No. 8.072, of 25th July 1990, which establishes provisions on heinous crimes, pursuant to item XLIII of Art. 5 of the Federal Constitution and repeals Law No. 2,252, of 1st July 1954, dealing with criminal solicitation of a minor | (Women) |
| 27. | Law no. 12.033/ 2009 | Bill 36/2009 | It amends the wording of the sole paragraph of Art. 145 of Decree-Law No. 2.848, of 7th December 1940—Criminal Code, making criminal prosecution condition on a complaint by the victim based on the specified defamation | Race |
| 28. | Law no. 12.288/ 2010 Racial Equality Statute | Bill 6262/2005 | It establishes the Racial Equality Statute; it amends Laws no. 7.716 of 5th January 1989, Law no 9.029, of 13th April 1995, Law no7.347, of 24th July 1985, and Law no 10.778, of 24th November 2003 | Race |
| 29. | Law no. 13.104/ 2015 Femicide Law | Bill 8305/2014 | It amends Art. 121 of Decree-Law No. 2.848, of 7th December 1940—Criminal Code, to establish femicide as a qualifying circumstance for the crime of homicide, and Art. 1 of Law No. 8.072, of 25th July 1990, to include femicide in the list of heinous crimes | Female gender |
| 30. | Law 13.160/ 2016 | | Law regulates the provisions of item XLIII of Art. 5 of the Federal Constitution, governing terrorism, dealing with investigative and procedural provisions and reformulating the concept of terrorist organisation | Race |
| 31. | Law. 13.497/ 2017 | | It amends Law 8.072 of 1990 to include genocide as a heinous crime | Race |

Source: Compiled by the Authors

June 2016 benefited from the specialised technical support of the *Fórum Brasileiro de Segurança Pública* [Brazilian Public Security Forum].

Moreover, although the database indicates criminal laws relating to the scope of "gender and race" dating to 1946, it will only be possible to verify any impact on incarceration from 2004, from when national data on the issue began to be produced.

Based on these issues, it is important to point out that, in order to verify the impact on incarceration, it was necessary to have a new focus, especially since some of said legislation did not necessarily involve criminalisation. In this regard, according to the table, the laws referred to in items 1, 8, 12, 22 and 27 deal with either the recognition of the legal value of the subject or refer to procedural issues, which led to them being ruled out.

In this case, 25 laws remained. Among these, some statutes are legislative modifications of the original statute, for which reason, for the purposes of understanding this text, the decision was made to group them. In this case, the laws referring to items 13, 15, 17 and 28 relating to the original wording of Law No. 7.716/1899 (Law defining crimes based on race or skin colour) were reduced to the latter, such that the analysis as a whole reverted to 22 pieces of legislation. It is worth noting that we chose not to perform a similar procedure in relation to the Criminal Offences Law (items 2 and 11) because different issues are addressed in each piece of legislation, as seen in the table. The incarceration breakdown[72] can be seen in the following graph (Fig. 3):

The impact on incarceration of the areas of action is viewed as follows (Fig. 4):

As can be seen, the impact on incarceration is incredibly small. In fact, the impact is even smaller, given that the crimes of genocide and torture involve multiple forms that are not reduced only to the areas of action investigated here. In other words, as it is not possible, with a quantitative approach, to ascertain the criminal acts, the data here may be overestimated, and in this case the impact on incarceration is even smaller.

Upon discussing new crime control strategies, which derive from the new collective consciousness formed in modern times, Zedner questions as follows:

[72]Some methodological clarifications are needed: (a) The data between December 2005–December 2008, regarding rape offences refer only to cases in which the perpetrator is a man. It is interesting to note that the modification in the original named crimes against customs of the Criminal Code only took place in 2009, but since the Dec/2008 data, mention is already made of a subject man or woman as perpetrator. Nevertheless, for this issue the decision was made to use only data with a male perpetrator. The same happened with offence of indecent assault (Art. 214 of the Criminal Code), regarding which, despite the phenomenon of statutory definition continuity and the repeal of the crime definition of Art. 214, in 2009, the data alludes to the crime definition up until June/2016. (b) Regarding crimes relating to domestic violence, the data only indicates its existence as "domestic violence" starting from December 2008and only from June 2014 is reference made to art. 129, §9 of the Criminal Code. Moreover, the data provided here refers to a male or female perpetrator.

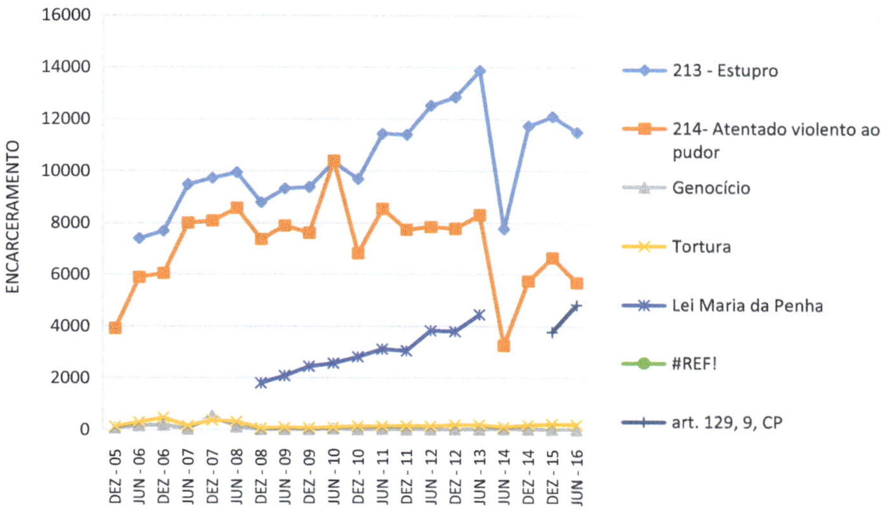


**Fig. 3** Source: produced by authors

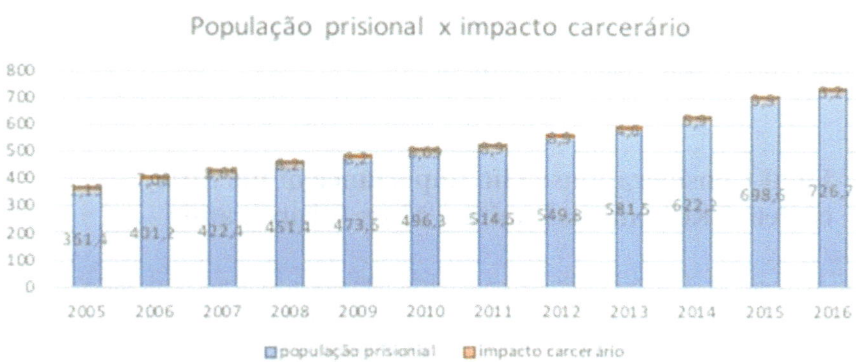


**Fig. 4** Impact on incarceration vs. prison population (From a methodological point of view, it is also important to point out that some years there are only reports for a half-year period, which implies there being a huge decrease in the impact on incarceration, although there is no reduction in prison population. This is the case for the 2005, 2013, 2015 and 2016 reports). Source: produced by authors

"however is collective consciousness reactionary or are the punitive policies of crime control the direct product of the populist mandate".[73]

The author questions this approach because she understands that the use of the concept of populism is carried out in a weak manner, as a result of emotional feeling,

[73]"pero es la conciencia colectiva reaccionaria, o las políticas punitivas del controle del delito son el produto directo del mandato populista?" (Zedner 2018).

punitiveness and conservative morals.[74] However, she presents research in which popular action can prevent arbitrary attitudes, thereby resisting populism.

The challenge raised by Zedner converges with the questioning put forward by Matthews,[75] with the query of what punitivism really means, since she understands that there is no precise conceptual definition and they are based on the common constructs of criminology.

Matthews (2005, p. 179) develops his argument by presenting several situations involving retribution, with elements of disproportionality and excess. In this regard, he argues that in recent years what has been outlined as an example of punitivism is actually an expression of symbolism.[76]

The results obtained in this research, with the comparison of criminal laws approved from 1988 to 2017 on "race" and "gender" with data on incarceration in Brazil indicate, at first, the need for separation of what is referred to as penal populism from the demands for recognition, in the (albeit restricted) field of Criminal Law, of legal interests reflecting the struggle for Human Rights. The results obtained here deserve a closer analysis on the role of Criminal Law from the perspective of the protection of Human Rights, as already discussed by Alessandro Baratta and reviewed by Roberto Galvão Faleiros Júnior[77] and Raquel da Cruz Lima.[78] They consist of the start of the discussion on the limits of penal punitivism. A follow-up of the research undertaken thus far should address the limits of left realism, its theoretical scope and the definition criteria of this criminal policy movement, within a context of (re-)democratisation in Brazil.

## 6 Final Considerations: The Importance of the Study of Penal Reforms in Limiting Mass Incarceration

In light of this scenario of very substantial law-making, which leads, in some way, to an increase in the exercise of punitive power, one of the following two are ways out. The first is to devise a criminological critique of the illegitimacy of the penal system, including its symbolic nature, as part of which one questions the paradox of Zero Tolerance to the detriment of the minimal state in the social arena (Social Security and Labour Law), "which is precisely the most vital arena, the noblest arena for building up civic consciousness, such that the caricature of the minimal state is equivalent to a zero tolerance system vs. minimal civic consciousness, for some".[79]

[74]Zedner (2018).

[75]Matthews (2005).

[76]Matthews (2005).

[77]Faleiros Júnior (2013).

[78]Lima (2014).

[79]Andrade (2003), p. 27.

The second is to move towards a realistic dimension, aware of the "epistemological range of perception of criminology" according to which "any improvement in the penal system would be nothing other than the reaffirmation of control and thus a legitimising, reactionary attempt that would ultimately require heading toward to the only possible alternative",[80] but that leaving punitive power without any limits also ends up legitimising arbitrary and irrational exercise, in which a share of pain is imposed. Thus, it is indispensable to think about the instrumental alternatives to change this reality, which should seek the satisfaction of the most elementary human needs: "respect for the right to life, rights to integrity ...".[81] In summary:

> For criminal law understood as a filter reducing the irrationality and violence of punitive power, the floodgates of the penal dam holding back the waters of this power must do so intelligently. [...] they cannot allow any water to pass in any way: its quantity, quality and manner of passage must be carefully predetermined. If punitive power is an irrational force and criminal law must give way only to the part of it that least compromises the rationality of the rule of law, penal selection must be rational in order to offset - as far as it can - the irrational selective violence of the punitive torrent.[82]

It may be that the first option of only criticising the correctionalist paradigm does not work, because it ends up being reduced to individual-State monism, without paying attention to possible pluralisms,[83] which may even result in openness to neo-retributionists;[84] or that all criminalisation necessarily corresponds to penal populism and confounds the legitimate aspirations of social groups demanding protection.

In fact, this first option may lead to a kind of criminological irresponsibility, which in turn may come close to the anxiety of "taking crime seriously,"[85] the wave that has spawned the Critical Criminology crisis since the 1980s, seeing as it had not achieved the criminal policy impact that it proposed.[86]

The second option therefore involves the practical effects of the exercise of punitive power; and it is precisely why there is the proposal to lead the fight against the process of mass incarceration starting from the operation - "against and through the State"[87] in favour of human rights and social justice. Of course, this is without ever forgetting that a marginal response to the deaths caused by the penal system is an ethical imperative, after all, the only reality is a matter of the dead.[88]

---

[80]Zaffaroni (2003), p. 9.

[81]Zaffaroni (2003), p. 23.

[82]Zaffaroni et al. (2003).

[83]Melossi (1996).

[84]Garland, David. The sociology of punishment.

[85]Matthews (2014).

[86]Larrauri (2001).

[87]Matthews (2016).

[88]The actual operability of the penal system is the starting point of criminological knowledge, which means assuming pessimism with regards to the penal system and admitting its genocidal projection. In other words, ineffectiveness in the face of unavoidable deaths and deaths from armed clashes, deaths at the hands of vigilante groups, deaths of torture victims, "exemplary" deaths,

In this regard, based on the models presented and taking into account the basic theory, it was realised that not all expansion of criminal law is irrational, useless or populist; thereby differentiating between the categories of "penal populism" and "left realism", the latter having much greater potential for efficacy[89] and effectiveness,[90]— including of a symbolic nature,— than "penal populism" measures; and this does not necessarily mean prison intensification, as the law can create a criminal definition and attribute to it alternative sentences to prison, for example.

Lastly, a discourse has been constructed here that accepts the de-legitimisation of punitive power, and "limits itself to guiding the judicial decisions with the same policy objective of reducing crime, taking into account criminological information on the actual operability of penal systems."[91]

The theory under discussion is that post-1988 Constitution Brazilian criminal policies are a reflection of all the ambiguous elements, permeated by experiences of urban crime, reflected in increasing numbers of crimes against property and homicides in which the right to equality and life is not prioritised. Moreover, they reflect the options of "fighting crime" and demands for new civil rights that face social policy inefficiencies and punitive experiences built on a cultural and historical structure that uses force as an ordinary resource. In other words, legislative policies are not necessarily responsible (solely or mostly) for mass incarceration and do not signify a reflection of penal populism, if identified based on new criminalisation and punishment.

According to Masiero, there will be legitimacy in penal action ("left realism") when the following variables are met: (1) criminal law derives from an actual social problem; (2) it describes a crime involving harm to a relevant legal interest; and (3) it absorbs the discussions produced by the social movements involved in the conflict. If these variables are met, it is understood that even if consisting of an expansion of criminal law, the criminal policy does not fall under "penal populism". In these cases, it is argued that we have a "left realism" criminal policy, which, in addition to being legitimate, tends to present acceptable effectiveness rates.

In light of the foregoing, it can be concluded that, in fact, there is significant ambiguity in Brazilian criminal policy, which even in this specific field of action combines penal populism and left realism criminal policies. It is therefore concluded that Criminal Law can help in social struggles, due to the symbolic power that the word "crime" holds.

---

deaths from error and negligence, deaths of people in the system, deaths from gun use, deaths in prison riots, deaths from violence against prisoners and deaths from untreated diseases in prisons (Zaffaroni 2012).

[89]"The effectiveness of the law, encompassing the most varied situations - observance, enforcement, application and use of law - can be understood generically as statutory implementation of the legal text" (Neves, 2011, p. 46).

[90]Effectiveness refers to the achievement of the purpose of the law and the fulfilment of the "aim" that guided the law-making, that is, the implementation of the means and end deriving abstractly from the legal text (Neves 2011).

[91]Zaffaroni (1991), p. 172.

This condemnatory role is not just a symbolic or subjective role in constructing a common imaginary that censures crime. The point is that public disapproval has a concrete effect on increasing security and it provides possibilities and rights. This goes beyond a subjective feeling, achieving a real redistribution of power. There is a criminal policy tangle that needs to be studied to be unravelled.

Arguing for the legitimacy of criminalisation does not diminish the problems surrounding the issue. One cannot lose sight of the critical analysis on the legal instruments to be used for this purpose and their legal and penal effects (from excessive criminalisation to punitivist reasoning or to victimisation). After all, when it comes to the use of criminal law, one should be aware that "the boundaries between the virtue of the law and its evil side are easy to bridge" (Pires 1999, p. 93)—; the remedy can be as bad as the evil one wants to fight, or even worse. Ultimately, it can be concluded that the categories presented in this paper converge with Díez Ripollés' analysis that they do not fall under penal populism, being inclusive and moderate.

## References


Andrade VRP (2003) Sistema Penal Máximo x Cidadania Mínima: códigos da violência na era da globalização. Livraria do Advogado, Porto Alegre

Baratta A (2000) La política criminal y el derecho penal de la Constitución: nuevas reflexiones sobre el modelo integrado de las ciencias penales. Revista Brasileira de Ciências Criminais 29:27–52

Batista N (2007). Introdução crítica ao direito penal brasileiro. 11. ed. Rio de Janeiro: Revan.

Brasil (2016) Departamento Penitenciário Nacional. Levantamento Nacional de Informações Penitenciárias. Ministério da Justiça, Brasília. http://depen.gov.br/DEPEN/depen/sisdepen/infopen/relatorio_2016_22-11.pdf. Accessed 25 Apr 2018

Campos, M da S (2010) Crime e Congresso Nacional: uma análise da política criminal aprovada de 1989 a 2006. São Paulo: IBCCRIM

Cano I (2006) Mensurando a impunidade no sistema de justiça criminal do Rio de Janeiro. 3o Congresso Latino- Americano de Ciência Política: Democracia e Desigualdades. UNICAMP, Barão Geraldo

Christie N (2016) Limites à dor: o papel da punição na política criminal. D'Plácido, Belo Horizonte

Cifali AC (2015) A Política Criminal brasileira no governo Lula (2003-2010): diretrizes, reformas legais e impacto carcerário. Dissertação de Mestrado. Pontifícia Universidade Católica do Rio Grande do Sul, Porto Alegre

Delmas-Marty M (2004) Os grandes sistemas de política criminal. Manole, São Paulo

Díez Ripollés JL (2015) La política criminal en la encrucijada. Segunda edición actualizada y ampliada. Editorial B de f, Montevideo, Buenos Aires

Faleiros Júnior RG (2013) Direitos Humanos e Tutela Penal: um diálogo marginal. Unesp/Cultura Acadêmica, São Paulo

Ferreira CC (2017) A política criminal no processo legislativo. Belo Horizonte: Editora D'Placido

Fórum Brasileiro De Segurança Pública (2017) 11° Anuário Brasileiro de Segurança Pública. Fórum Brasileiro De Segurança Pública, São Paulo

Freitas R de BAP (2008) O Estatuto Teórico da Política Criminal. In: FÖPPEL, Gamil. Novos desafios do direito penal no terceiro milênio: estudos em homenagem ao Prof. Fernando Santana. Rio de Janeiro: Lumen Juris

Garland D (1999) Castigo y sociedade moderna: un estúdio de teoria social. Sigo XXI editores S.A, Buenos Aires
Garland D (2008) A cultura do controle: crime e ordem social na sociedade contemporânea. Tradução de André Nascimento. Rio de Janeiro: Revan
Gazoto LW (2010) Justificativas do Congresso Nacional brasileiro ao rigor penal legislativo: o estabelecimento do populismo penal no Brasil contemporâneo. Tese de Doutorado. Programa de Pós-Graduação em Sociologia. Universidade de Brasília, Brasília
Larrauri E (2001) La Herencia de la Criminología Crítica. Siglo Veintiuno Editores, Madrid
Lima RS (2011) Contar crimes e criminosos no Brasil. In: Lima RS (ed) Entre palavras e números. Violência, democracia e segurança pública no Brasil. Alameda, São Paulo
Lima RC (2014) O direito penal dos direitos humanos: paradoxos do discurso punivito da Corte Interamericana de Direitos humanos. Tese de Doutorado. Faculdade de Direito da Universidade de São Paulo, São Paulo
Masiero CM (2018) Lutas sociais e política criminal: os movimentos feminista, negro e LGBTQ e a criminalização das violências machista, racista e LGBTQfóbica no Brasil. Tese (doutorado). Universidade do Vale do Rio dos Sinos (UNISINOS). Direito
Matthews R (2005) The myth of punitiveness. Theoret Criminol 9:175–201. SAGE, London
Matthews R (2014) Realismo crítico: un análisis estructural. Política criminal 9(17):182–212
Matthews R (2016) Criminología realista. Edicion punto didot, Madrid
Melossi D (1996) Ideología y derecho penal garantismo jurídico y criminología crítica: ¿nuevas ideologías de la subordinación? Revista "Nueva Doctrina Penal":75–86. Ed. Del Puerto, Buenos Aires
MIR PUIG S, BIDASOLO MC (2007) Política criminal y reforma penal. Buenos Aires: Euros Editores
Neves MA (2011) Constitucionalização simbólica. WMF Martins Fontes, São Paulo
Pires ÁP (1999) Alguns obstáculos a uma mutação 'humanista' do direito penal. Sociologias 1 (1):64–95. PPGS/UFRGS, Porto Alegre
PUCRS. UNB. UFPE (2011) Descarcerização e Sistema Penal — A construção de políticas públicas de racionalização do poder punitivo. CAPES e CNJ Acadêmico
Raupp Rios R (2001) Discriminação por orientação sexual e acesso à justiça: a homossexualidade e a concretização dos princípios processuais. In: Cadernos Themis Gênero e Direito. Porto Alegre 2:46-65
Ribeiro L, Silva K (2010) Fluxo do Sistema de Justiça Criminal Brasileiro: Um balanço da literatura. Cadernos de Segurança Pública 2(1):14–27
Sozzo M (2017) La inflación punitiva: un análisis comparativo de las mutaciones del derecho penal em América Latina (1990-2015). Café de las Ciudades, Ciudad Autónoma de Buenos Aires
Zaffaroni ER (1991) Em busca das penas perdidas. Deslegitimação e dogmática jurídico-penal. Revan, Rio de Janeiro
Zaffaroni ER (2012) A palavra dos mortos: conferências de criminologia cautelar. Saraiva, São Paulo
Zaffaroni ER et al (2003) Direito Penal Brasileiro. Primeiro Volume. Teoria Geral do Direito Penal. Revan, Rio de Janeiro
Zedner L (2018) Los peligros de las distopias en la teoria penal. Una resena de la Cultura del Controle: Crimen y orden social en la sociedade contemporânea. In: Sozzo M (ed) ¿Más Allá De La Cultura Del Control? debates sobre delito, pena y orden social con David Garland. Ad hoc, Buenos Aires
Zipf H (1979) Introducción a la Política Criminal. Editorial revista de Derecho Privado, Madrid

**Carolina Costa Ferreira** PhD (2016) and Master's Degree (2010) in Law, State and Constitution from Brasília University (UnB). Professor for the Master's Programme in Constitutional Law at the Brazilian Institute for Education, Development and Research (IDP). Professor of Criminology, Criminal Law and Criminal Procedural Law for the Brasília University Centre (UniCEUB). Leader of the "Criminology of Conflict" Research Group (UniCEUB/CNPq).

**Clara Moura Masiero** PhD from Rio do Sinos University (UNISINOS-2018), with a sandwich period at the Andalusian Inter-University Institute of Criminology of Malaga University. Master's Degree in Criminal Sciences from the Pontifical Catholic University of Rio Grande do Sul (PUCRS-2014). Professor of Criminal Law and Criminal Procedural Law at Saint Jude University (SP). Member of the "Public Security Policies and Criminal Justice Administration" Research Group (GPESC/PUCRS) and of the Spanish Criminal Legislative Policy Group (GEPLP). Criminal lawyer.

**Érica Babini Lapa do Amaral Machado** PhD from the Federal University of Pernambuco (2014) and Master's Degree from the same institution. Professor for the Catholic University of Pernambuco (UNICAP), as part of the Undergraduate and Graduate programmes.

The manufacturer's authorised representative in the EU is Springer Nature Customer Service Centre GmbH, Europaplatz 3, 69115 Heidelberg, Germany. If you have any concerns regarding our products, please contact ProductSafety@springernature.com

Printed and bound by CPI Group (UK) Ltd, Croydon, CR0 4YY
28/09/2026
02224090-0006